DATE			

SHIELDED

SHIELDED

How the Police
Became Untouchable

JOANNA SCHWARTZ

VIKING

VIKING
An imprint of Penguin Random House LLC
penguinrandomhouse.com

ISBN 9780593299364 (hardcover)
ISBN 9780593299371 (ebook)

Printed in the United States of America
1   3   5   7   9   10   8   6   4   2

Book design by Daniel Lagin

Ignorance, allied with power, is the most ferocious enemy justice can have.

—JAMES BALDWIN

CONTENTS

On the afternoon of February 8, 2018, more than two dozen law enforcement officers crowded into a conference room in the Henry County Sheriff's Office, on the outskirts of Atlanta. They were preparing to execute a no-knock warrant at 305 English Road, the home of a drug dealer who had been under investigation for almost two years, and had gathered for a briefing about the operation. The special agent leading the briefing told the team that 305 English Road was a small house with off-white siding and several broken-down cars out front, showed them an aerial photograph of the house, and gave them turn-by-turn directions to get there.

All of the members of the task force had the opportunity to review a copy of the warrant, which described the target house and its surroundings. But only one—Captain David Cody, who was leading the operation—took the time to read it. And even Captain Cody didn't read it all the way through. The officers piled into their SUVs to head to 305 English Road but ignored the directions they received during the briefing; instead, an officer plugged the address into the GPS on his cell phone, and the convoy got lost.

When the officers finally arrived at their destination, the house described in the warrant was right in front of them—run-down, off-white, with cars strewn across the yard. But the entry team walked swiftly past 305 English Road and toward 303 English Road, forty yards away. The house at 303 English Road looked nothing like the house described in the briefing and in the warrant; it was tidy and yellow, with a carefully maintained grass yard. The mailbox at the end of the driveway made abundantly clear that it was not the house the task force was looking for. Yet, less than a minute after getting out of their cars, officers deployed flash grenades outside 303 English Road and used battering rams to smash open all three doors of the home.

Inside, they found Onree Norris, a seventy-eight-year-old Black man wearing a baseball cap, jeans, and a windbreaker. For more than fifty years, until February 8, 2018, Norris had lived peacefully at 303 English Road. He and his wife had raised their three children there. He had spent decades traveling back and forth from that home to his job at a nearby rock quarry. Now Norris was retired and lived alone; although he was still married to his wife, they got along better living separately and saw each other on Sundays at church. His children had grown up, moved away, and had children of their own. Norris was no drug dealer. He had never been in any trouble with the law; he'd never even received a traffic ticket.

Onree Norris was watching the evening news in an armchair in his bedroom when he heard a thunderous sound, as if a bomb had gone off in his house. He got up to see what the commotion was and found a crowd of men in military gear in his hallway. Norris was more than twice as old as the target of the search warrant, but the officers pointed assault rifles at him anyway and yelled at him to raise his hands and get on the ground. When Norris told the officers that his knees were in bad shape, an officer grabbed Norris, pushed him down, and twisted his arm behind his back. Norris's chest began to hurt, and he had trouble breathing. He told the officers that he had heart trouble—he'd had bypass surgery and used a pacemaker—but they kept him on the ground for several minutes and never sought medical care. Norris was eventually picked up and led outside in handcuffs. When the officers realized they had blasted their way into the wrong house, they turned their cameras off one by one.

—

WHATEVER ONE BELIEVES ABOUT THE JOB OF POLICING—WHETHER it's that well-intentioned officers often must make split-second decisions that are easy to criticize in hindsight or that the profession is corrupt by its very nature—videos that have filled our screens in recent years offer concrete evidence that the police sometimes egregiously abuse their authority. And these videos only scratch the surface of injustices that occur.

Before Minneapolis police officer Derek Chauvin knelt on George Floyd's neck, on May 25, 2020, many others died beneath the knees of police officers. Before Louisville police officer Myles Cosgrove fired sixteen times into Breonna Taylor's apartment, on March 13, 2020, many others were shot during no-knock police raids. Countless people—disproportionately Black and brown—whose names you've never heard, have been unjustifiably killed, assaulted, arrested, searched, and surveilled by police.

Of course, many people have been saved and protected and comforted by police as well. While there may be disagreement about how often police officers abuse their power, hopefully we can agree that police sometimes *do* abuse their power in ways that leave people dead, hurt, or humiliated and that, when they do, there should be meaningful accountability for law enforcement officers and officials, and justice for their victims.

People who've lost loved ones or have themselves been harmed by the police often say they want the officers involved to be punished and assurance that something similar won't happen in the future. That's what Onree Norris and his children and grandchildren wanted as well. In our current system, there are really only three paths toward this type of justice, and none is easy to travel.

One option is criminal prosecution: police officers can be arrested, charged with crimes, and sent to prison. If you believe that our prisons are already too full, you may not have much appetite for a solution that puts more people behind bars. But even if some manner of justice could come from the criminal prosecution of a police officer, it rarely does. Prosecutors have historically been disinclined to bring charges against the officers they rely on to get convictions in other cases, and juries have proven reluctant to indict officers or find them guilty of crimes that will send them to prison. As a result, police officers are criminally charged in less than 2 percent of fatal shootings and convicted in less than one-third of those cases. Officers are even less likely to be prosecuted for using force that does not kill or for violating people's rights in other ways.

Police officers also can be investigated, disciplined, and fired by their departments. But police departments' internal affairs divisions rarely sustain allegations of misconduct. Internal affairs divisions in departments across the country have been criticized for conducting shoddy investigations—failing to interview witnesses, collect and preserve evidence, reconcile inconsistent statements, or question when officers submit essentially verbatim statements that suggest collusion. In the rare event that charges are sustained, officers often have elaborate processes they can use to challenge departments' decisions to discipline or fire them, and those challenges are often successful. As a result, local police departments can't be relied upon to render justice to their own.

Deputies from the sheriff's office repaired Onree Norris's doors a few days after they broke them down. But nothing ever came of the civilian complaint Norris filed against Captain Cody and members of the task force. And no criminal charges were ever brought against the officers who blasted through the doors of Norris's home, pushed him to the floor, handcuffed him, and scared him to death.

For Onree Norris, the only path toward some manner of justice was to sue Captain Cody and the officers who busted into his home. In many ways, a lawsuit was more likely to achieve Norris's goals than a criminal prosecution or internal investigation ever could. Norris could file a lawsuit himself; he did not have to wait for a prosecutor or a police department's internal affairs division to act. During litigation, Norris could demand documents from the law enforcement agencies that participated in the task force and could question officers and supervisors under oath about what happened—information that a prosecutor or internal affairs investigator would be under no obligation to unearth or make public. If Norris could prove that the officers violated his constitutional rights, he could be awarded money to compensate him for the pain, fear, and humiliation he felt—a remedy not available from criminal prosecutions or internal affairs investigations. And that money might not only compensate Norris but also encourage Captain Cody and the rest of the task force to be more careful in the future. As the U.S. Supreme Court has explained, the threat of being sued should cause government officers "who may harbor doubts about the lawfulness of their intended actions to err on the side of protecting citizens' constitutional rights" and judgments against cities should lead them to "discharge . . . offending officials" and "institute internal rules and programs designed to minimize the likelihood of unintentional infringements on constitutional rights." For Onree Norris, and for many people, filing a lawsuit is the best available way to punish police when they violate the law and give police reason not to violate the law again.

But Norris soon discovered—as have so many others—that justice through a civil rights lawsuit is profoundly elusive. Courts, legislatures, and officials at every level of government have created so many protections for police officers and other government officials, at every stage of litigation, that a person who has had their life shaken to the very core by government misconduct can have the courthouse doors shut in their face.

The best known of these protections is qualified immunity. Qualified immunity is a defense created by the Supreme Court that protects officers from being sued for money damages, even if they have violated the Constitution, unless they have violated "clearly established law." According to the Supreme Court, the law is only clearly established if a court has previously found nearly identical conduct to be unconstitutional. In other words, an officer can engage in appalling and unconstitutional conduct but still get qualified immunity if there wasn't a prior court case in which an officer violated the Constitution in precisely that same way.

It was qualified immunity that dashed Onree Norris's hopes of getting justice. The judges who heard Norris's case agreed that the officers searched his home without a warrant and that searching a house without a warrant is "presumptively unreasonable." The judges also recognized that officers who execute a search warrant on the wrong home violate the Fourth Amendment to the U.S. Constitution unless they have made "a reasonable effort to ascertain and identify the place intended to be searched." In fact, the very same court that decided Norris's case in 2021 had ruled five years earlier that it was unconstitutional for an officer who executed a warrant on the wrong house to detain its residents at gunpoint—almost exactly what had happened to Onree Norris. But that prior court decision was not enough to defeat qualified immunity in Norris's case because it was "unpublished"—meaning that it was available online but not in the books of decisions that are issued each year—and so was not technically binding on the court. The court declined to publish its decision in Norris's case as well; so if, in the future, officers hold the wrong person at gunpoint after executing a search warrant at the wrong house, the law still won't be "clearly established" and those officers can receive qualified immunity too.

Just as George Floyd's murder has come to represent all that is wrong with police violence and overreach, qualified immunity has come to represent all that is wrong with our system of police accountability. But the Supreme Court has created multiple other barriers that undermine the power and potential of civil rights lawsuits as well: they have limited, for example, the scope of constitutional protections, the ability to sue local governments for the conduct of their officers, the power to get court orders requiring departments to change their behavior, and the entitlement to attorneys' fees. And the Supreme Court hasn't acted alone. Even when people are able to get past the legal obstacles put in place by the Court and win a settlement or verdict, laws, policies, and practices put in place by state and local governments make it difficult for those victories to influence police behavior or achieve what victims of misconduct seek: some assurance that no one else will suffer the same pain.

Any one of these shields, in isolation, would limit the deterrent and compensatory power of civil rights suits against law enforcement. In combination, they have made the police all but untouchable.

————

THE MANY PROTECTIONS AFFORDED THE POLICE HAVE BEEN JUSTI-fied by concerns about the havoc civil rights lawsuits would cause if they were too easy to bring. Courthouses would be overwhelmed. Lawyers would file frivolous cases and win money that their clients didn't deserve. Well-intentioned officers would be bankrupted for split-second mistakes. Faced with these threats, no one in their right mind would agree to become a police officer. And, without a dedicated police force, the very fabric of our society would come unwound. Court opinions, legislative testimony, scholarly articles, and editorial pages have been filled for decades with these types of catastrophic predictions.

If frivolous civil rights lawsuits actually did threaten to overwhelm courts and bankrupt police officers, the many limitations on the power to sue might make some sense. But those offering passionate and forceful assertions about the threats posed by civil rights lawsuits have few facts to support their claims. I should know; I've spent my career testing them.

I first came to question rhetoric about the impact of lawsuits on police officers more than twenty years ago, when I began working at a small civil rights law firm in New York City. I knew from my law school classes that the Supreme Court had made it difficult to succeed in suits against police and other government officials. But I expected that once we won in court, the cases would have an impact. After all, the Supreme Court's opinions have repeatedly and decisively asserted that the legal barriers it created were necessary: if civil rights lawsuits were too easy to bring, they would discourage officers from vigorously enforcing the law. It logically followed that if the lawsuits we brought overcame the Supreme Court's legal barriers, those successful cases would surely deter officers and officials from doing something similar again.

I quickly learned that the Supreme Court's confident claims about the deterrent power of civil rights lawsuits bore scant resemblance to reality. When we won cases against New York City Police Department officers, it was city taxpayers—not the officers or the department—who paid victims' compensation. How could lawsuit payouts cause government officials to "err on the side of protecting citizens' constitutional rights," as the Supreme Court put it, if they didn't pay a penny of those settlements and judgments?

Perhaps, I thought, officers and officials learned from these cases, even if they didn't have to pay for them. Perhaps officers were disciplined or fired when large settlements or judgments were entered against them. But when I questioned officers under oath, they testified that they didn't know even the most basic information about prior lawsuits brought against them: they didn't know how many times they had been sued, what the cases alleged, or whether anything had been paid to resolve them. Higher-ups reported that they had no information about the lawsuits brought against their supervisees. Officials at the highest levels testified that they had never reviewed lawsuits to identify problem officers or patterns of misconduct. How could the cases we worked so hard to bring possibly cause police departments to "discharge . . . offending officials" and make policy changes, as the Supreme Court assumed they would, if no one paid any attention to them?

When I became a law professor, I dedicated myself to studying the realities of civil rights litigation against law enforcement to better understand the gap between descriptions of civil rights lawsuits' mighty power and what I experienced suing the police. I read thousands of civil rights complaints, motions, judicial opinions, and trial transcripts to understand how civil rights lawsuits fare in court. But I also knew from my time in practice that the realities of civil rights litigation are shaped by multiple influences outside the courtroom. So I started digging.

I filed public records requests with hundreds of local governments to try to understand how often officers are held financially responsible when they violate the law. I waded through hundreds of cities' and counties' budgets to understand where the money actually comes from to satisfy settlements and judgments in civil rights cases. I interviewed scores of plaintiffs' lawyers to understand their case selection decisions and their views about the challenges and rewards of bringing civil rights cases. I spoke with city attorneys who defend these cases; risk managers and city officials charged with managing government budgets; court monitors and police auditors brought in to review police department practices; municipal liability insurers who pay litigation bills on behalf of small cities and towns; and people whose rights were violated by the police and sought justice in the courts.

That research, which forms the cornerstone of this book, has cemented my belief that the legal protections law enforcement officers and agencies enjoy are buttressed by claims about the power of civil rights lawsuits that are exaggerated and, sometimes, simply false. I wrote *Shielded* to set the record straight.

———

THE CHAPTERS THAT FOLLOW DESCRIBE THE PHALANX OF SHIELDS that have been erected to protect the police, the groundless justifications that have ushered those shields into existence, and the ways in which they have gutted our system of justice. You will learn the stories of people whose children were killed even though they posed no threat, people who themselves were shot and nearly lost their lives without justification, who were searched and humiliated without cause, who were raped by officers sworn to protect and serve—each of whom has been told by our courts and elected officials that they must shoulder the costs of the violence they suffered themselves, with no recourse from the officers or from the governments that signed their paychecks and gave them their badges and guns. You will also learn the stories of people who managed to eke a measure of justice out of the system. But even though some succeed, the shields erected to protect police by courts and officials at every level of government make those victories fewer and further between, and harder to achieve, than they should be.

You are unlikely to have heard of most of these people or their stories. When instances of police abuse capture the public's attention—often prompted by a compelling video that goes viral—the shields that protect police from accountability in civil rights lawsuits seem to lose much of their power. The families of many of the people killed by police whose names most people know reached multimillion-dollar settlements without having to overcome any of the barriers to relief described in this book. Qualified immunity and the other protections you will learn about prey on people for whom there is less public attention and fewer calls for justice, even when the wrongdoing they suffered is equally reprehensible.

Many of the people killed by police whose stories make the news are Black men, and several people whose stories I tell in this book are Black men. People of color—particularly Black, Latinx, and Indigenous people—are and historically have been disproportionate targets of police violence and abuse. In the Southeast, modern police forces emerged in the 1830s as an outgrowth of slave patrols and so were inextricably linked to the subjugation of Black people from the start. In the almost two centuries since, racist policing has been a constant. Police turned the other way when mobs assaulted and lynched Black people in the late nineteenth and early twentieth centuries. Police let white people assault and kill Black people without consequence during race riots that erupted across the country after World War I. During these same decades, the Texas Rangers killed thousands of Mexican, Mexican American, and Indigenous people; they were, a historian noted, "as feared on the border as the Ku Klux Klan in the Deep South." Police used tear gas, batons, dogs, and fire hoses against those peacefully protesting segregated schools and lunch counters in the 1950s and 1960s. Beginning in the 1970s, "war on drugs," "broken windows," and "tough on crime" policies gave police license to surveil and overpolice communities of color. Decade after decade, police killings and assaults of Black men—and, less frequently, Black women—have captured public attention, and then those gathered to protest those killings and assaults have sometimes themselves been killed or assaulted by police.

Today, this ignoble legacy lives on. Studies have consistently found that Black people are far more likely to be killed by the police than are white people in America. Among those killed by police, Black people are more likely than white people to be unarmed. Black people are also more likely to be stopped by the police and searched and assaulted once they are stopped. Latinx and Indigenous people also suffer disproportionately at the hands of police, even as their stories less often make the news.

Members of other marginalized and politically divisive groups—including labor organizers, protestors, LGBTQ+ people, people with mental illness, and those who are poor, houseless, or ensnared in the criminal justice system—have also long borne the brunt of police misconduct, violence, and overreach. Of course, people mistreated by the police may identify with several of these overlapping identities. Some—though not all—are also people of color, compounding the likelihood of abuse. And although white people are statistically less likely to be harmed by police, hundreds are killed by police each year, and many more are victims of other types of wrongdoing.

The truth is, police violence and misconduct—and the legal barriers that have been created to protect police from accountability in the courts—can devastate anyone. Although some are far less vulnerable to these dangers because of the color of their skin, gender identity, profession, tax bracket, or zip code, no one is immune. The people whose stories I tell in this book reflect this diversity across multiple dimensions: they are Black, brown, and white; men and women; the young and the old; the wealthy and the unhoused; people with long criminal records and people who have never received a speeding ticket; residents of big cities and small towns; people from the South, Northeast, Midwest, and West.

———

SHIELDED NOT ONLY DESCRIBES THE MANY BARRIERS THAT KEEP PEOPLE from getting justice through the courts; it also offers a path forward. Since George Floyd's murder in May 2020, debates about police reform have focused so intently on qualified immunity that it might seem as if the future of police accountability hinges on whether we keep or abolish this one legal defense. But no reform is a silver bullet. There is no single switch to flip that will create a working system of government accountability. If we want civil rights litigation to compensate people whose rights have been violated and deter future misconduct, we will need to do much more.

In the last chapter of this book, I offer several suggestions for rethinking and reform, including promising steps that state and local governments around the country have already taken. Together, they constitute a set of proposals that you can ask your elected officials to enact to begin to restore the promise of civil rights suits as a tool for justice.

Focusing this book on the power of lawsuits and the ways in which that power has been thwarted is not meant to suggest that making it easier to sue the police and prevail in court is a magic cure-all. Fundamental questions remain about what we should empower the police to do, and how to restore trust between law enforcement and the communities they serve. But no matter how cities and counties across the country ultimately answer these questions, there will almost certainly continue to be people authorized by the government to protect public safety. There will almost certainly be instances in which those people abuse their authority. We will continue to need systems to hold those people accountable when they do wrong and deter them from doing wrong again. We need to get our system of government accountability working better than it does, no matter what our system of public safety looks like.

And we need to get started without delay. We have been engaged in a national conversation about police violence and paths to reform for far too long. Reports of people beaten, blinded, paralyzed, and killed by police have periodically put the failures of our criminal justice system on the front pages of newspapers. In response, legislative committees have held hearings. Blue-ribbon commissions have been convened. Exhaustive reports have been issued, documenting racist policing, unlawful arrests, and excessive force in cities large and small across the country. Reforms have been put into place. Then, invariably, the country's attention has been drawn elsewhere and the conversation has gone quiet.

When the world watched Minneapolis police officer Derek Chauvin murder George Floyd, the conversation began anew. In some ways, it felt different that time around. Police chiefs around the country immediately, publicly, and unequivocally condemned Floyd's killing. Protests were larger and more racially diverse than ever before. Politicians and advocacy groups from across the political and ideological spectrums agreed something needed to change. Important reforms got traction at the federal, state, and local levels. But then the nation's unity and sense of urgency began to slip. Protests died down. Proposed reforms were voted down or abandoned. The Black Lives Matter murals painted in bright colors on city streets began to fade.

We cannot wait for another viral video to restart our national conversation about police violence and reform. And we must foreground the realities of civil rights litigation when we do. Myths about the dangers of making it too easy to sue police have made a mess of our system. A shared understanding of how officers are shielded from the consequences of their actions, and how those shields leave many victims without a meaningful remedy, must fuel a reimagining of what it means to hold government accountable and what it means to protect and serve.

SHIELDED

CHAPTER 1

How We Got Here

In the early hours of October 29, 1958—sixty years before Captain Cody and his team invaded Onree Norris's home—James Monroe, his wife, Flossie, and their six children woke to the sounds of men breaking into their basement apartment on the West Side of Chicago. The intruders were twelve police officers and Frank Pape—the department's chief of detectives, who was known for taking pictures of himself with the corpses of men he killed and whom local newspapers referred to, with reverence, as "Chicago's Toughest Cop." A few hours earlier, a white woman, who claimed her husband had been killed by two Black men, picked James Monroe's photo out of a pile of mug shots. As it happened, James had nothing to do with the crime: the woman had persuaded her lover to murder her husband, hoping to cash in on his $25,000 life insurance policy. But even if the officers had had the right man, their actions on the morning of October 29 were unconscionable.

The officers entered the Monroes' home—without a warrant—and ordered Flossie and James out of bed at gunpoint, threatening to shoot if they didn't move quickly. Both were forced to stand in the center of their living room, naked, while the officers ransacked their home, dumping the

Monroes' possessions out of their closets and drawers and slitting their mattresses top to bottom with razor blades. Frank Pape repeatedly struck James in the stomach with a flashlight, yelling accusations about the murder interspersed with odious racial slurs. When the children screamed and cried, they were assaulted as well. An officer tripped the Monroes' four-year-old boy as he tried to run to his parents. Detective Pape hit two of James's teenage stepchildren, knocking them to the floor.

That horrific morning marked the seventeenth birthday of Flossie Monroe's eldest son, Houston. More than sixty years later, Houston recalled that he and his brothers and sisters yelled at the tops of their lungs to alert the neighbors that officers had broken into their home. He believes that noise might have saved his stepfather's life. "Those were killer cops that raided us," Houston remembered. "If it wasn't for the kids, they probably would have killed him."

James was taken from the apartment and held at the station house for ten hours without being allowed to see a judge or call a lawyer. He was released when the white woman who accused him of murder couldn't pick him out of a lineup. The woman's lover later confessed to the murder and testified against her; he received a life sentence and she was sentenced to sixty years in prison. James was never charged with any crime.

The Monroes decided to sue. An attorney at the Illinois branch of the ACLU agreed to represent them. The Monroes could have filed a lawsuit alleging assault and battery against the officers in Illinois state court— the same type of case that James could have brought against a neighbor who punched him during a backyard birthday party. But such a case brought by a poor Black family against white law enforcement officers, heard by a state court judge in Chicago—or by a state court judge anywhere else, for that matter—was considered at that time destined to fail. As the Monroes' attorney, Donald Page Moore, later explained, "I suspect that any realistic trial lawyer with experience in this kind of litigation anywhere in the country would tend to agree with me that when a penniless Negro family attempts to sue a politically potent high ranking police officer who is white, he is more likely to obtain a fair and impartial trial of his case from a federal judge."

So, Moore and the Monroes pursued a novel legal strategy. They filed the lawsuit in federal court and argued that a rarely used statute enacted by Congress almost a century earlier, in the wake of the Civil War, allowed the Monroes to sue Frank Pape and the other Chicago police officers for violating their constitutional rights. The Supreme Court agreed, and its decision in *Monroe v. Pape*, issued in 1961, breathed new life into that statute—42 U.S.C. § 1983, now commonly referred to as Section 1983. *Monroe v. Pape* also resurrected a long-standing debate about how much power Section 1983 should have.

Periodically over the past 150 years, courts and legislatures have made it easier to bring lawsuits against police and other government officials, in recognition that such suits are critically important tools for accountability and justice. But each time the judicial and legislative scaffolding behind the right to sue has been strengthened, it has thereafter been whittled away by powerful (if unsupported) claims that the federal courts are overreaching, that police can manage themselves, and that public safety will be imperiled by too much oversight. Only by understanding how this debate has been waged in the Supreme Court, in federal and state legislatures, and within public discourse over the past century and a half will it become clear why the power to sue government has waxed and waned, why there are so many limits on the right to sue today, and how, almost exactly sixty years after the Supreme Court recognized the right to sue police for violating the Constitution in *Monroe v. Pape*, a case like Onree Norris's could be kicked out of court.

———

CONGRESS FIRST ENACTED THE LAW THAT BECAME SECTION 1983 DURing the bloody years of Reconstruction. In the five years after the Civil War ended, between 1865 and 1870, Congress passed and the states ratified three constitutional amendments intended to guarantee the freedoms and civil rights of formerly enslaved people: the Thirteenth, ending slavery; the Fourteenth, prohibiting states from denying people due process and equal protection of the laws; and the Fifteenth, prohibiting states from denying people the right to vote on the basis of race, color, or previous condition of servitude. Between 1866 and 1875, Congress also enacted a slew of statutes that created civil and criminal penalties for violations of these Reconstruction Amendments. One of those statutes was the Civil Rights Act of 1871, also known as the Ku Klux Klan Act. At the time, Black people across the South were being tortured and killed by the newly formed Ku Klux Klan and other white supremacist groups, and local law enforcement officials were either participating in the violence or standing idly by. Section 1 of the Ku Klux Klan Act—what would become Section 1983—permitted people to sue in federal court if their constitutional rights were violated by people acting "under color" of state law.

Congressmen who spoke in favor of the Ku Klux Klan Act recounted stories that sound eerily familiar to the Monroes', of Black men and their wives and children being pulled from their beds in the dead of night and brutally assaulted, if not raped or killed. These families could theoretically file lawsuits against Klan members in state court, alleging assault, battery, and false arrest. But the congressmen knew that state courts were hostile places for Black people; in many state court cases, they were not even allowed to testify. Vitally important then—just as it was almost a century later, when the Monroes filed their lawsuit—the Ku Klux Klan Act would allow Black people to bring their cases in federal court and have them heard by federal judges and juries, who supporters of the Act considered more independent and "able to rise above prejudices or bad passions or terror more easily."

The Ku Klux Klan Act also had critics. Congressmen opposed to the Act did not frame their objections as an endorsement of racial violence or resistance to civil rights. Instead, they said they opposed the Act because it gave too much power to the federal courts to resolve disputes that should be left to states. Indiana representative Michael Kerr described the Act as a "covert attempt to transfer a large portion of jurisdiction from the ⌄⌄ tribunals, to which of right it belongs, to those of the United States." Congressmen predicted that lawyers would abuse that expansive federal jurisdiction to weasel their way into federal court with exaggerated claims that their clients' constitutional rights had been violated. Senator Allen G. Thurman of Ohio, speaking against the Act, warned that a constitutional violation "may be of the slightest conceivable character, the damages in the estimation of any sensible man may not be five dollars or even five cents . . . and yet by this section jurisdiction of that civil action is given to the Federal courts instead of its being prosecuted as now in the courts of the States."

After heated debate, Congress passed the Ku Klux Klan Act and President Ulysses S. Grant signed it into law. But almost a century passed before the Supreme Court acknowledged, in the Monroes' case, that Section 1983 could be used to sue police officers for violating the rights enshrined in the U.S. Constitution. It was the Supreme Court's decisions that rendered Section 1983 largely powerless for its first ninety years of existence.

In 1873, just two years after the Ku Klux Klan Act became law, the Supreme Court interpreted the Fourteenth Amendment narrowly to protect only rights related to federal citizenship—such as the right to vote for federal office, or to assemble and petition the federal government for redress of grievances. By this view, the Fourteenth Amendment could not be used to contest the very torture and killing of Black people that had inspired its creation. Then, in a handful of decisions in the 1870s and 1880s, the Supreme Court held that the Fourteenth and Fifteenth Amendments granted Congress authority only to address civil rights abuses by state actors—which meant that the laws passed by Congress to give teeth to the Reconstruction Amendments could not be used to combat private actors' violence and discrimination. In 1896, in *Plessy v. Ferguson*, the Supreme Court ruled that the Fourteenth Amendment did not prohibit racial segregation so long as the available facilities were "separate but equal."

Congress didn't push back against any of these decisions—instead, in 1894, southern Democrats who had regained control of the House and Senate, and the presidency, repealed most of the Reconstruction-era statutes that remained. With this decisive retreat from the federal enforcement of civil rights, Jim Crow laws pervaded the South, Black people were disenfranchised, Klan violence resurged, and the federal government did little to intervene.

In the early twentieth century, in the wake of the courts' and Congress's abandonment of the goals of Reconstruction, civil rights groups including the NAACP began to form, and they protested, lobbied, and litigated against discriminatory laws and practices. This same period marked the beginning of the Great Migration as millions of Black Americans made their way north to escape the Klan and police violence. In fact, sixteen years before Flossie and James Monroe were pulled out of their bed at gunpoint in Chicago, Flossie—along with her first husband and their infant son, Houston—was run out of Opelika, Alabama, by the town's sheriff. Flossie's then husband was accused of throwing popcorn at a white man from the balcony of a segregated movie theater, and he punched the usher who ejected him from the theater. The sheriff and his posse arrested Flossie's husband and took him back behind the jailhouse. Flossie's sister, who had also been at the theater, ran to get Flossie's husband's father, who was, in Houston's words, a "well-respected" and "important person around town." Flossie's father-in-law raced to the jailhouse to beg the sheriff for his son's life, and the sheriff told him that Flossie's husband had to leave town by sundown. So Flossie's husband boarded the Illinois Central that day and headed to Chicago. Flossie and Houston soon followed. As Houston later described it, his family "escaped from behind the Cotton Curtain. That was fascism living in the South."

When Black people arrived in places like Chicago, New York City, and Detroit, they quickly came to learn that the South did not have a monopoly on discrimination, mob violence, and police abuse. In the summer of 1919, after a seventeen-year-old Black boy's raft veered into the "whites only" part of Lake Michigan, a white beachgoer pelted him with rocks until he fell off his raft and drowned. Chicago erupted into violence, with Black people suffering the lion's share of injuries and death. When the Chicago Commission on Race Relations investigated the Chicago riot, they found Black people's distrust of the police was widespread and well earned; as Maclay Hoyne, Cook County state's attorney, testified before the commission, police had "shut their eyes to offenses committed by white men while they were very vigorous in getting all the colored men they could get."

The first federal government report documenting widespread police misconduct was published in 1931. In 1929, President Herbert Hoover had convened the National Commission on Law Observance and Enforcement, known as the Wickersham Commission, to examine the impact of Prohibition on police tactics. Two years later, the commission issued a report called *Lawlessness in Law Enforcement* that concluded, based on evidence from more than a dozen cities across the country, that "the third degree— that is, the use of physical brutality, or other forms of cruelty, to obtain involuntary confessions or admissions—is widespread." Following uprisings in Harlem and Detroit in the 1930s and 1940s, investigations found that police were regularly and egregiously violating Black people's rights. During this same period, and particularly as Black men were returning home after serving in World War II, there were growing calls to end segregation, discrimination in employment, and police abuse.

As the civil rights movement began to pick up steam, the Supreme Court came to revisit its narrow interpretation of the Fourteenth Amendment and the Civil Rights Acts. A key decision marking that shift and setting the stage for the revitalization of Section 1983 was *Screws v. United States*, issued in 1945, which forced the Supreme Court to confront the gravity of police violence and the need for federal intervention.

Sheriff M. Claude Screws of Baker County, Georgia, along with a policeman and deputy, arrested thirty-year-old Robert Hall at his home late one night for allegedly stealing a tire. After driving Hall to the courthouse, Sheriff Screws and the officer and deputy beat Hall with their fists and a two-pound blackjack until he was unconscious, then dragged him through the courthouse yard to the jail floor. Hall was taken by ambulance to the hospital, where he died. The sheriff and officers on the scene offered an excuse that sounds all too familiar today: they claimed that they had beaten Hall only after he had reached for a gun. But this explanation hardly made sense given that Hall was handcuffed the whole time.

Although Georgia prosecutors declined to bring charges against Sheriff Screws or the officers, federal prosecutors—part of the newly formed Civil Rights Section of the Department of Justice—pursued a case under a criminal law also enacted during Reconstruction. The federal indictment charged that the men, "acting under color of the laws of Georgia, 'willfully' caused Hall to be deprived of 'rights, privileges, or immunities secured or protected' to him by the Fourteenth Amendment." A jury found them guilty.

On appeal to the Supreme Court, Sheriff Screws and the officers argued that they were not acting "under color of state law" because Georgia law would have prohibited them from killing Hall without justification. Justice William O. Douglas, writing for the majority, rejected this argument, ruling that it was enough that the men were acting in their official capacity as law enforcement officers when they assaulted and killed Hall. In reaching this conclusion, *Screws* defined "under color of law" to include conduct that was not expressly authorized by law but was nevertheless taken "under 'pretense' of law."

Although *Screws* was a criminal case, courts began applying its definition of "color of state law" to Section 1983 cases, allowing people to sue for police brutality and other government abuses. But thirteen years later, in 1958, when the Monroes were pulled from their beds and beaten in Chicago, the Supreme Court had yet to decide whether *Screws*'s interpretation of "under color of state law" applied to Section 1983 cases.

—

AS DONALD PAGE MOORE BEGAN REPRESENTING THE MONROES, HE was also investigating thousands of illegal detentions by the Chicago Police Department—similar to James Monroe's—for a report published in 1959 by the ACLU. That report set out the ACLU's multipronged advocacy strategy against illegal police detentions, which included bringing the department's conduct to the attention of the public, pushing for legislation that would clarify officers' obligations, and calling for more vigorous discipline against officers who violated people's rights. But, the ACLU report emphasized, lawsuits against the police, and the resulting damages awards, "are one of the most effective sanctions available to the victims of police lawlessness, and for this reason serve an important public interest."

Although lawsuits were, in theory, among the most powerful tools to combat police abuse at the ACLU's disposal, these suits rarely succeeded when brought in state court under state law, decided by state court judges and juries. Dissatisfied with the limitations of state law, Moore and other civil rights attorneys began filing police abuse cases in federal court under Section 1983, with limited success. When Moore filed the Monroes' Section 1983 case, the Illinois federal district court dismissed the case and the court of appeals affirmed that decision. Both courts ruled that the Monroes should pursue any relief for the officers' conduct under state law in an Illinois court. But the Supreme Court reversed.

In 1961, six years after the Montgomery bus boycott began, four years before police beat John Lewis on the Edmund Pettus Bridge in Selma, Alabama, and amid growing reports of police violence around the country, the Supreme Court ruled for the first time that people could use Section 1983 in federal court to sue law enforcement officers who violated their constitutional rights. Justice Douglas, writing for the majority in *Monroe*, extended the logic of *Screws* to cases seeking civil remedies against government officials, explaining that Section 1983 was meant to "enforce provisions of the Fourteenth Amendment against those who carry a badge of authority of a State and represent it in some capacity, whether they act in accordance with their authority or misuse it."

When the Supreme Court issued its decision in *Monroe v. Pape* in February 1961, it sent the case back for trial. On December 4, 1962, a federal jury of nine men and three women, all white, found that Frank Pape and the other Chicago officers had violated the Monroes' constitutional rights. The jury awarded the Monroes $13,000—$8,000 against "Chicago's Toughest Cop" and the remainder against four other officers who had participated in the assaults and arrest. But the impact of the Supreme Court's decision was felt far beyond the dollars awarded to the Monroes.

Monroe v. Pape paved a way for people to sue government officials in federal court when they violated the Constitution. In the years after *Monroe v. Pape* was decided, there was what commentators referred to as an "explosion" of Section 1983 lawsuits. Annual civil rights filings invoking Section 1983 jumped from the hundreds in the 1960s to more than twenty thousand in the late 1970s, alleging a wide array of unconstitutional conduct, including mistreatment by police and prison guards, school segregation, First Amendment violations, and government policies that discriminated against women.

———

WITH THE SUPREME COURT'S REINVIGORATION OF SECTION 1983 CAME renewed debate—in the pages of newspapers, law review articles, court opinions, and legislative hearing testimony—about how strong the power to sue government was and should be. Back in 1871, congressmen who supported the Ku Klux Klan Act argued that it was necessary to "protect and defend and give remedies for [constitutional] wrongs to all the people." Supreme Court opinions interpreting Section 1983 in the years after *Monroe v. Pape* embraced this same view. To hear the Supreme Court tell it, victims of government misconduct and overreach like James Monroe should be made whole through damages awards, and the payment of those awards should discourage officers like Frank Pape and his comrades from conducting future warrantless searches, arresting people without sufficient cause, or liberally using their flashlights and fists. The Supreme Court imagined that these awards would also encourage police department officials to "discharge . . . offending officials" and modify policies and practices "so that if there is any doubt about the constitutionality of their actions, officials will 'err on the side of protecting citizens' rights.'" In these ways, Justice William J. Brennan Jr. explained in a 1980 decision, a damages remedy under Section 1983 "is a vital component of any scheme for vindicating cherished constitutional guarantees."

But some feared that *Monroe v. Pape* had opened the federal courthouse doors too wide. Arguments against *Monroe* echoed the view held by congressmen opposing the Ku Klux Klan Act almost a century earlier—that civil rights protections should simply be left to the states. In the estimation of one federal judge, Ruggero J. Aldisert, whose writings epitomize these concerns, criticisms of state courts might have been warranted in the years after the Civil War, when Section 1983 became law, but by 1973 the conditions in state courts were "radically different and the wisdom of distrusting state courts [was] questionable, if not entirely inappropriate."

Judge Aldisert and others also resuscitated the century-old concern that attorneys would abuse their power to bring Section 1983 suits in federal courts. Just as Senator Thurman had predicted, in 1871, that people would use the Civil Rights Act to bring minor claims into federal court, Judge Aldisert wrote a century later that Section 1983 "made the federal court a nickel and dime court. A litigant now has a passport to federal court if he has a 5-dollar property claim and can find some state action."

Critics expressed concern not just that these types of cases were more properly brought in state court but that most civil rights claims had no merit at all. Marvin Aspen, an attorney who defended the City of Chicago and its employees against civil rights suits, warned a classroom of Northwestern law students in the summer of 1966 that people were using

Section 1983 to bring frivolous cases against the Chicago police with the hope of "making a quick buck." Like Judge Aldisert, Aspen believed that the laudable goals of Section 1983 were being warped. As Aspen told the students, "Federal civil rights action cases seem to have passed thru the phase of alleviating deprivations, which was the intent of the civil rights act, and are reaching a stage where actions are being filed for the prime hope of reaping financial gain."

Although the Supreme Court had decided *Monroe* and applauded civil rights suits as a tool of compensation and deterrence, a majority of justices on the Court came to share the view that the blade of the tool it had created was too sharp. The Supreme Court decided *Monroe* while Earl Warren was Chief Justice—a period in which the Court expanded constitutional protections in multiple dimensions. But after the leadership of the Court transferred to Warren E. Burger and then to William Rehnquist and to John Roberts, and as the liberal justices who made up the majority of the Warren Court were replaced with more conservative justices, the Supreme Court's decisions about the right to sue government for constitutional violations tended in the opposite direction.

In its opinions the Supreme Court continued to acknowledge that civil rights suits served an important role: they were, in many instances, what one of its opinions described as "the only realistic avenue for vindication of constitutional guarantees." Yet the Court became increasingly concerned that the right to sue government might be abused and that those abuses carried with them serious consequences.

Some Supreme Court opinions raised the same concerns opponents to Section 1983 voiced in 1871: that federal courts should be cautious about interfering with state and local governments, and that frivolous cases threatened to flood the courts. Other opinions railed against the harms "insubstantial" civil rights suits imposed on defendants and society as a whole. As Justice Lewis F. Powell Jr. wrote in 1982, those harms included "the expenses of litigation, the diversion of official energy from pressing public issues, and the deterrence of able citizens from acceptance of public office," as well as "the danger that fear of being sued will 'dampen the ardor of all but the most resolute, or the most irresponsible [public officials], in the unflinching discharge of their duties.'"

The Supreme Court never overturned *Monroe*. But, just as its decisions after Reconstruction limited the power of the Civil Rights Act, the weight of many Supreme Court decisions after *Monroe* pulled against its spirit, and did so with express concern about the dangers of an expansive interpretation of Section 1983 on local governments and officers. Qualified immunity is the best-known shield that the Supreme Court created in response to these perceived dangers. But the Court has also used these same concerns to justify a host of other limitations—on, for example, the scope of constitutional rights, the power to sue local governments, the ability to get court-ordered reforms, and the entitlement to attorneys' fees.

In the six decades between the Supreme Court's decision in *Monroe v. Pape* in 1961, and the dismissal of Onree Norris's lawsuit in 2021, the Supreme Court also limited the power of tools that victims of police overreach could use in criminal courts. Four months after the Court decided *Monroe*, it decided *Mapp v. Ohio*, allowing evidence unconstitutionally seized by police to be excluded from criminal trials in state court. Five years after deciding *Monroe* and *Mapp*, in 1966, the Supreme Court decided *Miranda v. Arizona*, requiring police to notify people of their right to an attorney and their right to remain silent before being questioned. But in the decades that followed, as the Supreme Court became more conservative, it riddled the exclusionary rule and the protections afforded by *Miranda* with exceptions and qualifications. The Court has justified limitations on *Mapp* and *Miranda* in the same way it has justified limitations on *Monroe*—with concerns that police cannot effectively do their jobs and keep people safe if they must meticulously respect people's rights.

During this same time, forces outside the courts also worked to shield police officers from accountability. Police unions rose in power, fueled by the familiar claims that police need maximum discretion to do their jobs, and used that power to negotiate with cities for decreased public transparency and accountability. In addition, during this period, state and local laws were enacted across the country obligating local governments to pay the entirety of damages awards in lawsuits against police officers. When state legislatures and city councils passed these laws, they often echoed the Supreme Court's fears—that without these protections, no one would agree to become a law enforcement officer. In other words, as Supreme Court rulings made it more difficult to seek justice and accountability through the courts, local governments made it more difficult for people to seek justice and accountability through police complaints, discipline, financial sanctions, and other forms of oversight.

There has also been progress alongside these backward steps. Commissions investigated the underlying causes of the Watts Rebellion in 1965, the rebellions in Detroit and Newark in 1967, and police corruption in New York City in 1994 and in Los Angeles in 2000. In 1994, Congress gave the Department of Justice authority to investigate police departments for patterns and practices of unconstitutional policing, and the Department of Justice used that power to unearth evidence of systemic misconduct in cities across the country and oversee important changes in those cities' police departments. In the 2010s, killings of Black people prompted the birth of the Black Lives Matter movement, refocused national attention on the problem of police violence, and inspired the convening of President Barack Obama's Task Force on 21st Century Policing. In 2020, the killings of George Floyd and Breonna Taylor prompted ambitious police reform proposals in Congress and statehouses across the country.

During these six decades, some proposals for reform have been adopted by police departments, local governments, and states. Departments as a whole have become more professional and have improved their policies and trainings—to a degree. Some departments work more collaboratively with the communities they police. But there are approximately eighteen thousand law enforcement agencies across the country with few limits on their power and little in the way of external oversight. Departments' and governments' tentative steps toward reform have not been enough to address the fundamental failures revealed by countless commissions and task forces. Despite its limitations, the ability of people wronged by the police to sue remains one of the most important available tools to seek accountability and reform.

———

FRANK PAPE LEFT THE CHICAGO POLICE DEPARTMENT IN 1961, ONE month after the Supreme Court's decision in *Monroe v. Pape*, to head security at a local racetrack. Four years later, when he decided to return to the department, residents of the Monroes' neighborhood protested. Reverend John Porter, president of the Chicago chapter of the Southern Christian Leadership Conference, who led the protests, declared that Pape "should not be allowed to wear a badge and carry a gun and a stick."

Pape did return to the department but retired for good in 1972. He remained a hero to many: fifteen hundred people attended his retirement dinner, including Chicago's mayor, Richard J. Daley, and the toasts lauding Pape reportedly lasted more than three hours. Yet, in Pape's view, the department had changed for the worse after *Monroe v. Pape* was decided. A 1994 article in the *Chicago Tribune* admiringly described Pape as coming from the era "before you read an offender his rights. Before police captains got management training." Pape was quoted in that *Tribune* article as discouraging a young relative from joining the police force because "every move a policeman makes is scrutinized by the public, more so than the criminal. Hell, they are investigated within the department, from without the department and by anyone else who wants to take a crack at them." Given Pape's brutal reputation, it might not be such a bad thing that he found the Chicago Police Department so inhospitable. According to the *Chicago Defender*, which reported on Pape's return in April 1965, police sources had told reporters that "Pape did no more than have many Chicago officers, but they didn't get caught. The difference is that they are not committing such offenses now."

We can't know how Pape would view the Chicago Police Department today; he died of a heart attack in 2000, at the age of ninety-one. But when the U.S. Department of Justice opened an investigation into the Chicago Police Department in 2015, fifteen years after Pape's death, it found widespread patterns of unconstitutional conduct: officers repeatedly used unjustifiable force against adults and juveniles; the department failed to investigate most of the misconduct allegations it was required to by law; when the department did investigate, the DOJ found, "the questioning of officers is often cursory and aimed at eliciting favorable statements justifying the officer's actions rather than seeking truth"; and "discipline is haphazard and unpredictable, and is meted out in a way that does little to deter misconduct." In other words, Chicago police officers were still using excessive force against residents of the city, and internal affairs was still not up to the task of reining in misconduct.

For many—in Chicago and elsewhere—Section 1983 lawsuits remain the best available path toward justice. Yet the many restrictions placed on the right to sue by courts and government officials have left that path woefully narrow.

CHAPTER 2

LAWYERS

Alonzo Grant worked seven days a week. Monday through Friday he was a delivery driver for St. Joseph's hospital in Syracuse, New York, and on Saturdays and Sundays he worked at a sawmill. He kept up this schedule for two decades to provide for his family, and he spent what downtime he had with his wife and his four children and ten grandchildren, who lived in their neighborhood.

When Alonzo got off work from the sawmill a few hours early on the afternoon of Saturday, June 28, 2014, he pulled a chair out to the front yard to catch some sun, ready to relax. His daughter Alyssa brought him a beer. He and his wife, Stephanie, decided to barbecue for the family. Alyssa went to the store to get supplies, and Alyssa and Alonzo's fifteen-year-old son, Alonzo Jr., brought the meat out for Alonzo to grill.

At around six thirty the meat was ready, and Alonzo Jr. and Alyssa brought it inside. Alonzo came in a few minutes later, after the grill had cooled down, and was annoyed to see his grandchildren's toys on the floor and dishes in the sink. When Alonzo asked Stephanie to straighten up the house, Alyssa got upset. A neighbor, Sharon, could hear the conversation through the Grants' open window and yelled at Alyssa to treat her father more respectfully. Alyssa went outside and started arguing with Sharon on the Grants' front lawn. As their confrontation grew heated, Alonzo called the police to ask them to come and break it up.

By the time Syracuse officers Damon Lockett and Paul Montalto arrived at the Grants' home, Alyssa had already walked back to her own house down the street and Sharon had gone inside. Stephanie, looking out the front window, told the officers that they no longer needed assistance. But Officer Lockett walked into the Grants' home, uninvited. Lockett saw Alonzo at the top of the stairs, in his socks, and ordered him outside. Alonzo followed the officer's instruction.

The shock on the Grants' metal screen door was broken, and when Alonzo exited his home, the screen door hit the metal railing on his front steps and made a loud bang. That was, apparently, enough justification for Officer Lockett to grab Alonzo from behind and for Officer Montalto to take hold of his feet, throw him over the railing of the stairs, and slam him to the ground. Alonzo Jr. watched from a neighbor's yard as Officer Lockett put his father in a chokehold. Both officers punched Alonzo until blood was coming out of his nose and mouth. One of Alonzo's daughters took out her cell phone and recorded the assault as a growing crowd of family and neighbors yelled at the officers to stop. "He called you! Why are you beating him?" screamed Stephanie. Officer Lockett yelled back, telling Stephanie to get in her house or he would shock her with his Taser.

The officers handcuffed Alonzo—his first time in handcuffs in his fifty-three years—and took him away in an ambulance. Alonzo's family did not see him until the next day, when he appeared in court with shackles on his wrists and ankles. He was charged with resisting arrest, disorderly conduct, and harassing a police officer and was released from custody. When Alonzo got home, he sat down on his front steps and Stephanie brought him a cup of coffee. Alonzo drank his coffee, smoked a cigarette, and cried. It was the first time Alonzo Jr. remembers seeing his father in tears. Alonzo Jr. has seen his father cry many times since.

The officers had broken Alonzo's nose, given him a concussion, split his lip, injured his shoulder, permanently injured his left arm, and herniated a disc in his neck. Other injuries were harder to see. Before his arrest, Alonzo Grant was sharp as a tack. He would play with his grandchildren, shoot hoops with his son, mow lawns around the block, shovel his neighbors' snow, go out on dates with his wife. Afterward, he had constant headaches and body aches. He suffered from anxiety and depression. He couldn't remember things that had happened ten minutes before or tolerate loud noises. He didn't play with his grandchildren. He was afraid to go out in public for fear the police would stop him. His injuries kept him out of work for two weeks. When Alonzo returned to work at St. Joseph's, unloading his truck made him dizzy, and his injured arm was no longer strong enough to pick up boxes. A few years later, St. Joseph's eliminated Alonzo's position.

The morning after Alonzo was assaulted and arrested, Jesse Ryder, an attorney in the area, got a phone call from the owner of the sawmill where Alonzo worked. The sawmill owner told Ryder what had happened to Alonzo. Ryder and Alonzo, who had been friends for years, met the next day. When he heard Alonzo's story and saw his swollen face, Ryder concluded that Alonzo needed not only to fight the criminal charges but also to sue the officers. Ryder was a seasoned criminal defense attorney and knew that Alonzo was far from the first person whom Syracuse police had mistreated. But Ryder had no experience bringing civil suits against the police, and he knew of no lawyer in Syracuse, or anywhere in upstate New York, who regularly filed these types of cases. There were lawyers bringing civil rights cases in New York City, but they didn't typically accept cases in Syracuse; it takes eight hours, round trip, by car to get there, and they had more than enough work to keep them busy downstate. The only experienced civil rights lawyer Ryder could think of who might agree to take the Grants' case lived in the Bay Area—three thousand miles away.

———

WHEN A PERSON IS ACCUSED OF A SERIOUS CRIME THAT COULD SEND them to prison, the Sixth Amendment to the U.S. Constitution requires that the government appoint a lawyer if they cannot afford to hire one. But if a person believes that his or her constitutional rights have been violated by a police officer and wants to file a lawsuit seeking money or court-ordered reforms, they have no comparable right to a lawyer. And they are unlikely to want to go it alone. Even lawyers who regularly litigate civil rights suits will tell you that the law is complicated, gathering evidence to prove a case is time-consuming and expensive, and persuading a judge and jury to rule in your favor is challenging. Winning is hard even when you have a lawyer; losing is almost certain if you don't.

In the popular imagination, finding a lawyer to bring a civil rights case should be no problem. Those who view civil rights attorneys in the most positive light might imagine armies of lawyers like Thurgood Marshall, who founded the NAACP Legal Defense Fund and worked to develop the legal strategy that ultimately led to *Brown v. Board of Education* before he became a justice on the U.S. Supreme Court. For those who believe the most disparaging descriptions of civil rights attorneys, an entirely different type of lawyer army may spring to mind—one brimming with ambulance chasers, festooned with tacky jewelry, bright-white smiles, and slicked-back hair, eager to make a buck from other people's misery. But when it comes to finding experienced civil rights attorneys who know how to navigate the law's complexities, the search is far harder than conventional wisdom suggests.

There are small, tight-knit communities of civil rights lawyers with expertise and passion in the cities of the Great Migration—places like New York, Los Angeles, Oakland, Chicago, and Philadelphia. But fewer civil rights attorneys practice outside those urban areas, and in the southern states whose violence inspired the enactment of Section 1983, civil rights attorneys are in particularly short supply. You can count on one hand the attorneys who regularly bring cases against the Houston Police Department and its officers—the fifth-largest law enforcement agency in the country.

Finding a lawyer who takes civil rights cases is only the first challenge; you then have to persuade that attorney to represent you. Many civil rights lawyers only accept cases with horrific facts, irrefutable evidence, and sympathetic victims. Attorneys' selectivity means that a person with a weak case is going to have a hard time finding a lawyer. But a person whose constitutional rights have been violated may not be able to find a lawyer either if they live in a part of the country with few or no experienced civil rights attorneys to speak of; if there isn't a video or witness supporting their side of the story; if something about them might rub a judge or jury the wrong way; or if they cannot prove substantial medical costs or other damages.

Less than 1 percent of people who believe that their rights have been violated by the police ever file a lawsuit. Finding a lawyer is, and has always been, one of the most challenging first steps.

———

IN 1959, WHEN ACLU ATTORNEY DONALD PAGE MOORE FILED THE Monroes' case against Frank Pape and the other Chicago police officers who barged into their home, the ACLU, NAACP Legal Defense Fund, and National Lawyers Guild had been engaged in campaigns against police brutality for a decade or more, but were largely alone in their efforts. After the Supreme Court's 1961 decision in *Monroe v. Pape*, and as the civil rights movement gathered steam, civil rights organizations recruited lawyers to go to the South to represent people who had been abused by the police. During that same period, a handful of attorneys associated with the National Lawyers Guild began bringing Section 1983 civil rights suits against the police in Philadelphia, New Haven, Chicago, and other cities in the North. But *Monroe* did not inspire a dramatic or immediate expansion of the civil rights bar. The reason was primarily financial: even if a lawyer believed in the principles of civil rights enforcement, it was hard to earn enough money through civil rights litigation to keep the lights on.

People assaulted by the police rarely had the money to pay for a lawyer themselves. Attorneys at nonprofits like the ACLU and the Legal Defense Fund had their modest salaries paid by their organizations' donors. The lawyers called to the South in the 1960s to take on civil rights clients did so pro bono—meaning without pay. Private attorneys hoping to support themselves with civil rights work entered into contingency-fee relationships with their clients, meaning that the client would pay their lawyer a portion of any money that they recovered in a settlement or jury verdict. If the client lost, then the lawyer received nothing for their time.

Contingency-fee arrangements are common in cases where the plaintiff does not have the money to pay a lawyer. But these types of arrangements limit the kinds of cases that it makes financial sense for lawyers to take. Lawyers deciding whether to accept a contingency-fee case must weigh the costs of bringing the case against the likelihood that their client will win and the amount of money that their client will receive—from which the lawyer will take their cut. So even if a case is strong on the merits, it may not make financial sense for a lawyer to accept that case on contingency if it is going to cost a lot to bring, or if the lawyer does not expect to recover much in the way of damages.

In the late 1960s and early 1970s, concerns that the contingency-fee arrangement gave plaintiffs' attorneys insufficient financial incentives to bring civil rights cases led some courts to require defendants, when they lost, to pay plaintiffs' attorneys' fees. This kind of fee shifting had already been built into some civil rights statutes, including the Civil Rights Act of 1964, which allowed people to sue for discrimination in public accommodations and employment. The Supreme Court explained in a unanimous 1968 opinion that these discretionary attorneys' fee awards should usually be granted because plaintiffs in these cases were acting in the public interest as a "'private attorney general,' vindicating a policy that Congress considered of the highest priority." Judges began using the "private attorney general" rationale as the basis to award attorneys' fees to plaintiffs in other types of civil rights cases where attorneys' fees weren't explicitly authorized by statute—including Section 1983 cases. Judges reasoned that the same rationale for attorneys' fees applied in these types of cases: people should not have to bear the financial burdens of bringing suits that advance important public interests.

In 1975, the Supreme Court stepped in, ruling that attorneys' fee awards were appropriate for "private attorneys general" only when Congress expressly authorized them. Congress responded the next year, enacting a statute—Section 1988—allowing people who win Section 1983 suits and other types of civil rights cases to have their lawyers' fees and costs paid by the defendants who violated their rights. As the legislative statement read, "If private citizens are to be able to assert their civil rights, and if those who violate the Nation's fundamental laws are not to proceed with impunity, then citizens must have the opportunity to recover what it costs them to vindicate these rights in court."

Section 1988 also had its detractors. One, Alabama senator James Allen, asked during debate over the legislation, "Is the concern for protecting civil rights, or is it for protecting the fees of attorneys, who have grown fat on litigation of this sort?" Senator Allen was no friend of civil rights protections; he had led an antibusing filibuster two years prior and participated in a weeklong filibuster of the bill that became Section 1988. But the way in which he framed his opposition to the bill—that fee shifting was helping lawyers get rich off civil rights cases instead of helping people whose rights had been violated—became a common theme after Section 1988's passage. As a contributor to *The Wall Street Journal*'s op-ed page argued, Section 1988 amounted to a "massive, nationwide giveaway" to "moral ambulance chasers."

This disagreement about the benefits and dangers of fee shifting was aired in two opinions issued by the Supreme Court in 1986, the same year that *Wall Street Journal* opinion piece was published. In the first, *City of Riverside v. Rivera*, Riverside police officers broke up a gathering at the home of a Mexican American couple, using tear gas and excessive force against the hosts and six guests. A jury awarded the plaintiffs $33,350 for their injuries. The lawyers then sought more than $245,000 in attorneys' fees under Section 1988, for more than two thousand hours of work on the case. The trial court judge granted the request, finding the attorneys' hourly rates and time spent to be reasonable, and the court of appeals affirmed. The city sought review by the Supreme Court, arguing that the lawyers' fee award should be "modeled upon the contingent-fee arrangements commonly used in personal injury litigation"—which would be $11,000, based on a standard one-third contingency.

The Supreme Court upheld the more than $245,000 in attorneys' fees awarded by the trial court. Four justices signed on to an opinion rejecting the city's suggestion that attorneys' fee awards under Section 1988 should be limited to what a contingency-fee lawyer would receive. That opinion, authored by Justice William J. Brennan—a leader of the Court's liberal wing during the thirty-four years he was on the bench—explained that the value of the *Rivera* case was far greater than the $33,350 awarded by the jury. As the trial judge in *Rivera* had found, the Riverside officers' conduct was "motivated by a general hostility to the Chicano community. . . . The institutional behavior involved here . . . had to be stopped and . . . nothing short of having a lawsuit like this would have stopped it." To limit the attorneys' fee award to one-third of the plaintiffs' recovery would "seriously undermine Congress' purpose in enacting Section 1988," which included remedying the fact that "the private market for legal services failed to provide many victims of civil rights violations with effective access to the judicial process." Indeed, no lawyer in the private market would presumably agree to work more than two thousand hours on a case for a fee of $11,000.

But four dissenting justices ignored the public benefits conferred by *Rivera* and saw the bill for almost one-quarter of a million dollars in attorneys' fees as patently unreasonable because no private client would ever have agreed to pay their lawyer more than seven times their recovery. As Justice Rehnquist, writing for himself and three others, scoffed, one may "agree with all of the glowing rhetoric . . . about Congress' noble purpose in authorizing attorney's fees under §1988 without concluding that Congress intended to turn attorneys loose to spend as many hours as possible to prepare and try a case that could reasonably be expected to result only in a relatively minor award of monetary damages."

Justice Lewis F. Powell Jr., the ninth justice, aligned himself with parts of Justice Brennan's and Justice Rehnquist's opinions. Justice Powell agreed with Justice Brennan's bottom line—that the attorneys' fee award should stand—but did so out of deference to the lower courts' detailed findings in *Rivera*, not because he agreed with Justice Brennan's broader statements about the purposes of Section 1988. Instead, Justice Powell's decision was more sympathetic to the substance of Justice Rehnquist's dissent: Justice Powell expressed "serious doubts as to the fairness of the fees awarded in the case" and made clear that "it probably will be the rare case in which an award of *private damages* can be said to benefit the public interest to an extent that would justify the disproportionality between damages and fees reflected in this case." Although Justice Powell's decision offered a fifth vote in favor of affirming the award to the lawyers in Rivera's case, it was also a fifth vote of skepticism about attorneys' fee awards that dwarf plaintiffs' verdicts.

Although the Supreme Court's decision in *Rivera* was a modest win for plaintiffs and their attorneys, another opinion issued by the Supreme Court that same year, *Evans v. Jeff D.*, made *Rivera* irrelevant in most cases. In *Evans*, Idaho Legal Aid represented a group of institutionalized children challenging the education and health care provided by the state. Idaho fought the case almost until the bitter end but offered to settle days before trial began, giving the plaintiffs all of the policy changes that they requested on one condition—that they agree not to seek their attorney's fees under Section 1988. This meant that the attorney, who had dedicated years to the case, would be paid nothing for his time; he could not even get a portion of the plaintiffs' award, because the plaintiffs sought policy changes instead of money damages.

A six-justice majority in *Evans* ruled that defendants could make this type of settlement offer with a fee waiver because it was consistent with the purpose of Section 1988—defendants, eager to avoid paying attorneys' fees, may give civil rights plaintiffs attractive settlement offers that advance civil rights. Justices Brennan, Thurgood Marshall, and Harry Blackmun—who had supported a broad entitlement to attorneys' fees in *City of Riverside v. Rivera*—dissented, arguing that fee waivers would undermine the goals of Section 1988. Perhaps the plaintiffs in *Evans* would be pleased with the result, they explained, but the lawyer representing them would be reluctant to take civil rights cases in the future, knowing that he might not get paid. Other lawyers would take heed as well, resulting in less access to the courts for people whose rights have been violated. Justice John Paul Stevens, writing for the majority in *Evans*—and who, notably, joined Brennan's decision in *Rivera*—waved away that possibility because there was no "reason or documentation to support such a concern at the present time." But, in the dissenting justices' view, "it does not require a sociological study to see that permitting fee waivers will make it more difficult for civil rights plaintiffs to obtain legal assistance."

———

IN PRACTICE, *EVANS* HAS DONE JUST WHAT JUSTICES BRENNAN, MAR-shall, and Blackmun feared. When plaintiffs recover money in Section 1983 cases against the police, it is almost always through settlements, and those settlement agreements almost always waive lawyers' ability to recover attorneys' fees. Defendants, particularly as trial nears, may offer larger settlements that take into account the likelihood that the plaintiff could win at trial and be awarded attorneys' fees. But the contingency-fee system that Congress intended to avoid by enacting Section 1988 is basically back in place.

On the rare occasion that a plaintiff goes to trial and wins, they can recover their reasonable attorneys' fees, and that amount can exceed what the plaintiffs won at trial. But lawyers are rarely paid for all the time and money they spent. The Supreme Court has instructed lower courts assessing the reasonableness of a fee award to exclude unreasonable hours, and reduce unreasonable rates, cautioning that "cases may be overstaffed, and the skill and experience of lawyers vary widely." Whether a successful plaintiff's attorneys have exercised proper billing judgment often turns into its own satellite litigation about how much the lawyers should be paid for each hour of work, and how many hours they reasonably spent litigating the case, and it can take months or years to resolve. During those months and years, the attorneys will not get paid. And, in the end, judges seem almost always to give plaintiffs' attorneys' fee applications a haircut, because they conclude either that the lawyers could have done the work in less time or that they have billed their time at too generous a rate, or both.

When I interviewed dozens of civil rights lawyers across the country, most viewed the financial risks and benefits of taking Section 1983 cases the way they would any other contingency-fee case. Most lawyers I interviewed were disinclined to take a case on behalf of a person whose rights had clearly been violated unless the potential damages were significant enough that one-third of the plaintiff's award would adequately compensate them for their time. For many lawyers, if a case did not involve death or a serious physical injury, it was not worth the risk. One attorney used particularly colorful language to describe a sentiment many shared: "It sounds crass but we say, 'Well, is there blood on the street?' Because if there isn't, why are we doing it?"

Even when a person suffered serious injuries, attorneys I interviewed were reluctant to take their case if a judge or jury might not find them sympathetic. As a result, attorneys reported looking for cases with "likable," "credible," and "articulate" victims—criteria that may make attorneys less likely to represent people of color, LGBTQ+ people, and people with mental illness, even as they are disproportionately the victims of unconstitutional policing. Some of the attorneys I interviewed will not represent a person who was convicted of a crime in connection with the incident that is the basis for the civil rights case. Some attorneys will not represent a person who has *ever* been convicted of a crime, for fear that a jury would rule against them or award minimal damages.

The limits on attorneys' fees in Section 1983 cases not only discourage lawyers from taking risky or low-damages cases; they also may lead lawyers to stop bringing civil rights cases altogether. Most lawyers who bring civil rights cases are jacks of many trades whose case dockets include personal injury, medical malpractice, or criminal defense cases. In fact, many lawyers I interviewed brought their first Section 1983 case without appreciating its financial risks. Someone came into their office with an infuriating story of unjust treatment at the hands of government officials, and they accepted that first case despite not really knowing how to litigate civil rights cases at all. These lawyers often reported expecting that bringing a civil rights case would be like any other personal injury case—comparable to a suit brought by a person who had been hit by a car. But they came to realize, quite quickly, that the risks are greater and the rewards are smaller in civil rights cases: it is more difficult to get information from the government, more difficult to prove a legal violation and overcome qualified immunity, more difficult to get to a jury, and more difficult to win.

Lawyers often learn this lesson the hard way, by having a case dismissed after investing thousands of dollars' worth of their time pursuing it. In the wake of that almost inevitable disappointment, lawyers tend to go one of two ways: Some dig in and commit themselves to understanding the intricacies of civil rights law and practice. Others decide to stop bringing civil rights cases altogether and focus instead on other types of cases where they can more easily and reliably make a living.

Even among those lawyers who choose to commit themselves to civil rights litigation, most would agree that there are many better ways for them to earn money. One lawyer I spoke with said that she was only fully able to dedicate herself to her civil rights practice once she had paid off her mortgage with income from other types of legal work. Another joked that he would probably have a more stable income if he sold candy bars door to door.

Some lawyers who have spent years litigating civil rights lawsuits have reduced the number of Section 1983 cases they accept in recent years because, they told me, these cases have become increasingly difficult to win. An attorney from Florida who used to bring only police misconduct cases now takes on dental malpractice cases with the hopes that "the dental stuff perhaps will pay some bills." An attorney from Pennsylvania who used to focus primarily on Section 1983 cases now spends most of his time on personal injury and medical malpractice cases, which he considers "easier work that pays a lot more money."

Section 1988 was intended to encourage lawyers to bring cases vindicating constitutional rights that are important, even if they are worth relatively little in the way of compensable damages. But the current scheme means that a lawyer will likely only take this kind of case for the principle. And principles don't pay the bills.

———

WHEN JESSE RYDER WENT LOOKING FOR A LAWYER TO REPRESENT Alonzo Grant in a lawsuit against the police officers who threw him over his front stairs and beat him, no skilled civil rights attorney in the Syracuse area came to mind. Instead, he called Charles Bonner. Bonner grew up in Selma, Alabama, and, while still a teenager, walked the Edmund Pettus Bridge with John Lewis. A member of the Student Nonviolent Coordinating Committee, Bonner was repeatedly arrested for civil disobedience. During court appearances for those arrests, Alabama judges used the n-word to refer to his and his fellow defendants' mothers, but paid relative respect to the Black attorneys who appeared before them. Those courtroom experiences inspired Bonner to become a civil rights attorney.

He practices in the Bay Area, just outside San Francisco, with his son, Cabral. But he has taken on civil rights cases around the country: in Mobile, Alabama; in North Carolina; and throughout California. He had taken a case in Syracuse, New York, a few years back, which was when he had met Ryder. So, Ryder knew, Bonner was willing to travel across the country for a case he believed in.

The day after Charles Bonner took Jesse Ryder's call, he was on a plane to Syracuse. From 2014 to 2018, Charles and Cabral Bonner and Jesse Ryder spent more than twenty-five hundred hours on the Grants' case. They got all criminal charges against Alonzo dismissed and then gathered evidence of systemic problems in the Syracuse Police Department. They learned that the officers had lied during the internal affairs investigation of Alonzo Grant's arrest and assault and that the department almost always rejected recommendations by the local oversight board to punish its officers. They defeated defendants' efforts to get the Grants' case dismissed before trial. After a nine-day trial, with twenty-eight witnesses, they convinced the jury that the officers had falsely arrested Alonzo and used excessive force against him. The jury awarded $1.13 million to Alonzo and $450,000 to his wife, Stephanie.

After their decisive victory, the Bonners and Ryder submitted a fee application to the trial judge under Section 1988, seeking $1.56 million for their work. The fee application included sworn statements from several lawyers affirming that there were no experienced civil rights attorneys in the Syracuse area who could have brought the Grants' case; a description of previous police misconduct trials in and around Syracuse that had ended in defense verdicts or small plaintiffs' verdicts, showing that the results achieved in the Grants' case were remarkable; and dozens of pages of exhibits detailing, in six-minute increments, how the three attorneys spent their time during the four years that the Grants' case was pending. But the judge ruled that only 75 percent of their hours were "reasonable" because they had not been successful on all of the claims they had brought and had, in the judge's view, spent too much time on some of their filings—

including their attorneys' fees application. The judge also ruled that the Bonners should be paid the going rate for lawyers in Syracuse—less than half their hourly rate in the Bay Area.

Ultimately, the judge awarded the Bonners and Ryder just over one-third of the attorneys' fees that they had requested. Syracuse appealed the jury verdict for the Grants, and the Bonners and Ryder cross-appealed the trial court's decision to reduce their fees so drastically. Seven years after Alonzo Grant was beaten by Officers Lockett and Montalto, the court of appeals affirmed the jury verdict and attorneys' fee award—a victory for the Grants but a disappointment for their lawyers. The Bonners and Ryder have continued to bring cases against the Syracuse Police Department and its officers. But no one would have blamed the Bonners if they had decided against continuing to fly across the country to represent people in lawsuits for which they might never get paid their due.

———

CONGRESS IMAGINED THAT THROUGH THE FEE-SHIFTING PROVISION in Section 1988, attorneys would be encouraged to bring Section 1983 cases on behalf of plaintiffs acting as "private attorneys general" to vindicate constitutional rights. But, as a result of the Supreme Court's decisions interpreting Section 1988, attorneys who represent successful plaintiffs are often paid for only a fraction of their time. And if they lose—which happens more often in civil rights cases than in other types of cases—they will be paid nothing at all.

These limitations on attorneys' fees hurt lawyers most directly. But they also unquestionably hurt people whose rights have been violated—by reducing the number of lawyers willing to take civil rights cases, limiting the types of cases these lawyers are willing to take, and leaving some whose rights have been violated to fend for themselves in court.

Alonzo and Stephanie Grant were lucky that Jesse Ryder knew to call Charles Bonner. As a local criminal defense and personal injury attorney wrote in support of the Bonners' and Jesse Ryder's fee application after trial, many had "complained of similar treatment" by the Syracuse Police Department, but there was no experienced civil rights attorney in the area willing to take on these cases. And the Bonners and Ryder not only accepted the Grants' case; they also "redefined the parameters for representation in cases where the civil rights of the citizens of this community are violated," in that defense attorney's words, and won one of the top three verdicts in an excessive-force case in that district. But how many lawyers in the Bonners' and Ryder's shoes would have agreed to take the Grants' case? How many lawyers would agree to keep bringing these types of cases in Syracuse—or anywhere else, for that matter—after being paid just over one-third of what they believed they were owed for four years of work? And, as a result, how many people whose rights have been violated in Syracuse and elsewhere must go without a lawyer and so, likely, without relief?

CHAPTER 3

THE COMPLAINT

On a Wednesday evening in August 2016, Vicki Timpa's phone rang. It was her ex-husband. A sergeant from the Dallas Police Department had called him with unimaginable news: their thirty-two-year-old son, Tony, was dead.

Although Tony had struggled with drugs and alcohol, anxiety, and schizophrenia, in many ways he led an enviable life. He was a white college-educated executive who made more than a quarter-million dollars a year working at a trucking logistics firm. He had an eight-year-old son and was engaged to be married. He had been arrested and sentenced to probation for driving while intoxicated a few years prior but had never been in more serious trouble with the law. In fact, Vicki remembers that Tony grew up trusting, even idolizing, the police.

Vicki was desperate to learn what happened to her son. She called the Dallas Police Department multiple times after receiving the news, and each time she got a different story. One officer told her that Tony had had a heart attack while sitting in a bar. Another told her that he had been found dead, lying next to his car. A third told her he had called 911 and had been put in an ambulance without incident—even waving to the officers through the ambulance window as he left the scene. None of these conflicting accounts explained why, when Vicki visited her son in the morgue, he had bruises on his arms and grass and dirt in his nose.

A woman who worked at the morgue suggested that Vicki call the paramedics who had attended to Tony. When she did, the person who answered told her to call the police and hung up. Two weeks after Tony's death, with no information from the City of Dallas, Vicki filed a public records request that contained a simple plea: "I want to know what happened."

A reporter at *The Dallas Morning News* who had received an anonymous tip about Timpa's death tracked down the Dallas police incident report. It said only, "Sudden Death. Complainant died by unknown means." But then the reporter uncovered a mandated report by the police department to the Texas attorney general's office that revealed a startling piece of information: Tony had been in handcuffs when he died. That report divulged another crucial fact: three of the Dallas police officers on the scene at the time of Tony's death had been wearing body cameras.

Vicki called a lawyer, Geoff Henley, who agreed to take her case. Henley—who makes his living on personal injury cases—usually declines lawsuits against the police unless there is video in hand or other compelling evidence supporting the plaintiff's side of the story. In his experience, Texas judges and juries are likely to believe police officers unless there is incontrovertible proof that they are lying. But the possibility that Henley could track down the officers' body camera videos, and the report that Tony had been in handcuffs when he died, were enough for him to make an exception to this rule—particularly given how compelling Vicki's sorrow was, and how sympathetic a jury might be to the untimely end of this wealthy white executive's otherwise fortunate life.

The Dallas Police Department refused to give Henley the body camera videos or any other evidence they had about the circumstances of Tony's death. They would not even disclose the names of the Dallas police officers who had been on the scene, citing an ongoing investigation. None of this came as a surprise to Henley. Texas law allows law enforcement agencies to withhold records if "release of the information would interfere with the detection, investigation, or prosecution of a crime." Henley had come up against this same brick wall with Texas law enforcement agencies before. And he knew their refusals were going to make bringing Vicki's lawsuit much harder.

Once a person decides to sue and finds a lawyer, the next step is to file a complaint with the court. A complaint—also known as a pleading—is a document that translates the story of what happened into legal language. In a Section 1983 case, the complaint must describe the facts of the case and how those facts amount to a violation of constitutional rights. Henley knew that Timpa had died in the custody of Dallas police officers and that he was in handcuffs when he died. But Henley knew that might not be enough: a judge could dismiss Vicki's case because her complaint did not allege *how* Tony died, even though the Dallas police officials she was aiming to sue were withholding that information from her. In our legal system, it is exceedingly difficult to seek justice when you don't know what exact injustice occurred.

———

HOW MUCH DETAIL IS NECESSARY TO INCLUDE IN A COMPLAINT HAS been the subject of centuries of debate. Until the mid-nineteenth century, a person seeking to sue had to file a complaint with all sorts of stylized and technical language about the legal claim—language that revealed very little about the underlying facts of the case. In 1848, the Field Code—a series of rules named after the lawyer who drafted them—was adopted in New York and then many other states, requiring that complaints focus on the facts instead of the law. Although the Field Code was intended to better enable courts to distinguish between strong and weak cases at their outset, it inadvertently created its own brand of confusion as judges and lawyers began fighting about what "facts" were and how they differed from legal "conclusions." In 1935, a committee of lawyers and academics was convened by the Supreme Court to create a uniform set of rules for federal litigation practice. Those rules, issued in 1938—and rather unimaginatively called the Federal Rules of Civil Procedure—offered a new vision for what a legal complaint should do and how it should fit into the life cycle of a lawsuit.

The Federal Rules abandoned the Field Code's effort to sort strong from weak cases at the pleading stage, requiring only that a complaint include a "short and plain statement of the claim showing that the pleader is entitled to relief." And, after the plaintiff offered that short and plain statement, the Federal Rules expanded the parties' ability to engage in discovery, a period during which each side could demand documents and information from the other and question witnesses and parties under oath. In the discovery stage, the strengths and weaknesses of the plaintiff's claims would become apparent. If, after discovery, the parties saw eye to eye about those strengths and weaknesses, they might settle. If one side believed the other had no evidence supporting their version of the story, they could ask the judge to enter summary judgment in their favor, ending the case. If instead, during discovery, both sides unearthed evidence supporting their version of what happened, the case could go to trial and a judge or jury could decide whom to believe. No matter how a case might conclude, the Federal Rules expected that discovery—not pleadings—would reveal its merits.

In 1957, in a case called *Conley v. Gibson*, the Supreme Court made clear that the "short and plain" requirement for the initial complaint was a low bar. Like *Monroe*, *Conley* is a case with facts that speak volumes about the era in which it arose. Black railway workers had sued their union, arguing that their employer, the Texas and New Orleans Railroad, had abolished forty-five jobs held by Black workers, only to hire white workers to fill their places. The men alleged that the union did nothing to protect them, discriminating against them in favor of white union members. The union moved to dismiss the complaint, arguing that it did not "set forth specific facts to support its general allegations of discrimination."

The Supreme Court rejected the union's argument, explaining that the plaintiffs' complaint fulfilled their obligations under the Federal Rules. According to the Court's unanimous decision in *Conley*, a complaint should only be dismissed if "it appears beyond doubt that the plaintiff can prove no set of facts in support of his claim which would entitle him to relief." This easily met standard at the complaint stage, *Conley* made clear, "is made possible by the liberal opportunity for discovery and the other pretrial procedures established by the Rules to disclose more completely the basis of both claim and defense and to define more narrowly the disputed facts and issues."

Conley's interpretation of the Federal Rules offered a clear litigation road map: write a basic complaint that gives defendants notice of what they are accused of doing, then sort out the strengths and weaknesses of the case during discovery, then have a judge or jury decide whose version of the truth should prevail. But four years after *Conley*, *Monroe v. Pape* was decided, allowing people to sue government officials for constitutional violations under Section 1983. And soon thereafter, against the Supreme Court's clear instructions in *Conley v. Gibson*, trial judges began ruling that plaintiffs in Section 1983 cases should be singled out for more restrictive pleading standards.

In a commonly cited decision, issued in 1968, T. Emmet Clarie, a federal judge in Connecticut, dismissed a Section 1983 suit brought against two City of Bristol police officers because the complaint did not, in his mind, set out in sufficient detail precisely what the officers were alleged to have done. The plaintiffs argued that they had followed the Federal Rules—offering enough information to put the officers on notice of the nature of the claim and pave the way for discovery. But Judge Clarie was unmoved. As he explained,

In recent years there has been an increasingly large volume of cases brought under the Civil Rights Acts. A substantial number of these cases are frivolous or should be litigated in the State courts; they all cause defendants—public officials, policemen, and citizens alike—considerable expense, vexation and perhaps unfounded notoriety. It is an important public policy to weed out the frivolous and insubstantial cases at an early stage in the litigation, and still keep the doors of the federal courts open to legitimate claims.

Judge Clarie cited no evidence in support of his concerns about a "substantial number" of "frivolous and insubstantial" civil rights cases flooding federal courts. And not all judges agreed with him. Court of appeals judge John Gibbons observed a few years later, in 1973, that civil rights cases "are not overwhelming the federal courts to the exclusion of other worthwhile business, and have not been, in my experience at least, any more likely to be frivolous than other classes of litigation."

Evidence backed up Judge Gibbons's point of view. When two Cornell law professors, Theodore Eisenberg and Stewart Schwab, reviewed lawsuit filings around the country between 1975 and 1984, they found that there were fewer Section 1983 cases than critics claimed and that the increase in civil rights suits was comparable to increases in federal filings of all kinds. When Eisenberg and Schwab dug into court files in the Los Angeles area in 1975 and 1976 and again from 1980 to 1981, they found that Section 1983 cases made up only about 4 percent of the civil cases filed, and "result[ed] in the transfer of relatively small amounts of money." Eisenberg and Schwab urged that "decision makers demand evidence to support assertions about constitutional tort cases, and that they not act in the empirical void that has dominated discussion to date." But many judges around the country did exactly the opposite, latching on to the types of unsupported assertions made by Judge Clarie and requiring civil rights plaintiffs to include additional detail in their complaints or risk having their cases dismissed.

Over the next three decades, the Supreme Court would twice reject a more stringent pleading requirement for civil rights cases—first in

1993 and then in 2002. In both unanimous decisions, the Court emphasized that complaints in all kinds of cases—including police misconduct cases and those alleging discrimination in employment—need not include detailed facts. And, in both opinions, the Supreme Court reiterated its long-standing view that discovery and summary judgment—not complaints—were the right tools to weed out weak cases. But, less than a decade later, the Court did an about-face.

The facts and ruling of the Supreme Court decision that changed pleading standards, *Ashcroft v. Iqbal*, say as much about its moment in time as *Conley v. Gibson* and *Monroe v. Pape* said about theirs. Javaid Iqbal, a Pakistani citizen, was arrested in New York City a few months after the September 11 attacks on the World Trade Center and taken to a federal detention facility in Brooklyn. Iqbal was charged with identity fraud: he had used another person's Social Security card to secure employment. But the government also decided, for reasons that were never made apparent to Iqbal, that he was a person of interest in their investigation related to the attack on the World Trade Center. During his detention, Iqbal and other prisoners were assaulted, kept in their cells for twenty-three hours a day with the lights on, regularly strip-searched and body cavity searched, prevented from praying, deprived of food, and denied requests to see their lawyers.

Iqbal ultimately pleaded guilty to the crime of using false identification documents and was deported to Pakistan. In 2004, he sued the guards who had abused him at the federal detention facility. He also sued Attorney General John Ashcroft and the FBI director, Robert Mueller, arguing that Ashcroft and Mueller had instituted a policy to arrest thousands of Arab and Muslim men and hold them in highly restrictive conditions solely based on their religion and national origin.

In 2007, as *Ashcroft v. Iqbal* was making its way through the courts, the Supreme Court decided another case, *Bell Atlantic v. Twombly*, in which a seven-justice majority led by Justice David Souter stated that *Conley*'s language—that a case should be dismissed only if "it appears beyond doubt that the plaintiff can prove no set of facts in support of his claim which would entitle him to relief"—had "earned its retirement" and was "best forgotten." Instead, the majority opinion explained, the allegations in a complaint must be "plausible." In *Twombly*, which was a case alleging price-fixing by several phone companies, that meant plaintiffs had to include evidence not only that the telephone companies' prices were the same but also that they had intentionally coordinated their pricing. Otherwise, the majority feared, plaintiffs with "a largely groundless claim" could "take up the time" of defendants, and expensive discovery could "push cost-conscious defendants to settle even anemic cases."

In the view of Justice John Paul Stevens and Justice Ruth Bader Ginsburg, who dissented in *Twombly*, requiring the plaintiffs to include detailed evidence in their complaint put the cart before the horse: plaintiffs could only access the phone companies' records and question company officials about their motivations once they got to discovery. They also believed trial judges could protect defendants from the kinds of forced settlements feared by the majority by limiting the amount of discovery exchanged in their cases. Just five years earlier, the Supreme Court had expressed confidence that trial judges could use their case management powers in just this way. But the *Twombly* majority rejected the possibility, citing—without any empirical support—"the common lament that the success of judicial supervision in checking discovery abuse has been on the modest side."

In 2009, the Supreme Court dismissed Javaid Iqbal's case, relying heavily on its 2007 decision in *Twombly* and ruling that Iqbal had not pleaded facts to support "plausible" claims of discrimination. While the Court in *Twombly* had not explained what a "plausible" complaint was, the *Iqbal* majority gave courts a formula to follow. Justice Anthony Kennedy, writing for the five-justice majority, instructed that courts should decide which allegations in a complaint are "facts" and which are "conclusions," disregard the "conclusions," and then assess whether the "facts" state a plausible claim for relief in light of the judge's "judicial experience and common sense." The Field Code—the prior regime that had instructed plaintiffs to allege "facts," not "conclusions"—had been widely criticized as confusing and burdensome. But in *Iqbal*, the Supreme Court embraced the distinction between "facts" and "conclusions" once again.

Applying the "plausibility" test to the complaint in *Iqbal*, Justice Kennedy disregarded as "conclusions" all statements that Ashcroft and Mueller created a discriminatory detention program, leaving only the allegations that Iqbal and other Arab and/or Muslim men were detained and held in harsh conditions. Justice Kennedy acknowledged that Iqbal's allegations were consistent with claims of discrimination, but concluded that those claims were not plausible "given more likely explanations." The most likely explanation, in Justice Kennedy's mind, was that the government's legitimate interest in arresting people with possible connections to the attack "produce[d] a disparate, incidental impact on Arab Muslims, even though the purpose of the policy was to target neither Arabs nor Muslims."

Of course, there was no way for Javaid Iqbal to know at that point of the litigation what the intentions of Ashcroft and Mueller were when they created the post-9/11 detention program; there was no way for Justice Kennedy to know either. That is precisely what discovery is for. But, to the *Iqbal* majority, allowing discovery was too dangerous—particularly in this type of civil rights case against high-ranking government defendants. As Justice Kennedy explained, "Litigation, though necessary to ensure that officials comply with the law, exacts heavy costs in terms of efficiency and expenditure of valuable time and resources that might otherwise be directed to the proper execution of the work of the Government." In other words, it was more important to protect Ashcroft and Mueller's time than it was to investigate Iqbal's allegations that they had violated the Constitution.

———

THE SUPREME COURT MAJORITIES IN *IQBAL* AND *TWOMBLY* proclaimed—without evidence—that a stricter pleading standard was necessary to combat widespread discovery abuse that leads defendants to settle weak cases. Claims that discovery costs too much and that discovery tools are regularly abused have circulated for decades without evidentiary support. In 1998, when Judge Paul Niemeyer repeated one common claim—that more than 80 percent of litigation costs are spent on discovery—he acknowledged that there was no empirical support for that often-cited statistic but embraced it anyway, noting that "the fact that the claim was made and is often repeated by others, many of whom are users of the discovery rules, raises a question of whether the system pays too high a price for the policy of full disclosure in civil litigation."

Yet decades of research—beginning in the 1960s, when Judge Clarie made his unfounded claims about frivolous civil rights cases—make clear that allegations of runaway discovery and blackmail settlements are overblown. Multiple studies have found that the majority of civil cases require little or no discovery; that civil cases rarely involve extensive discovery; and that the costs of discovery are generally proportional to the stakes of the case. The year the Supreme Court decided *Iqbal*, the Federal Judicial Center—the research arm of the federal judiciary—published a survey of twenty-three hundred attorneys revealing that a majority of those attorneys believed discovery costs were "just the right amount" as compared with the stakes in the case and did not force unwarranted settlements.

Even if discovery costs are sometimes excessive and do sometimes pressure defendants to settle weak cases, requiring plaintiffs to know the facts that would prove their claims at the complaint-drafting stage is the wrong cure for the disease. The plausibility pleading standard does not necessarily weed out weak cases; it weeds out cases in which plaintiffs do not have access to the evidence they need to prove their claims before discovery.

Legal scholar and civil rights attorney Alexander Reinert, who represented Javaid Iqbal and argued his case before the U.S. Supreme Court, has examined the *Iqbal* decision's impact in several important studies. In one, Reinert reviewed cases decided over the course of ten years, isolated approximately one hundred that would likely have been dismissed under the *Iqbal* standard, and found that more than half of them resulted in a settlement or plaintiff's verdict. As Reinert wrote, these findings "seem to contradict" the contention that "the vast majority of the cases that will be dismissed under a heightened pleading scheme like that imposed by *Iqbal* and *Twombly* are meritless and frivolous."

Iqbal's heightened pleading standard may be particularly difficult for plaintiffs in civil rights cases to overcome. Civil rights allegations are not always difficult to plead "plausibly"; Alonzo and Stephanie Grant and their family could describe Alonzo's assault by the Syracuse police officers and had cell phone video to back up their claims. But there are some kinds of civil rights cases, like Javaid Iqbal's case, that turn on evidence of government officials' unlawful intent. There are other civil rights cases that challenge local governments' conduct—claims, for example, that a police department does not properly train or supervise its officers. A plaintiff will not likely have any evidence about officials' intentions or local governments' inner workings until they get to discovery.

The heightened pleading requirement puts these civil rights plaintiffs in a bind: they are only allowed discovery if their complaints include evidence supporting their claims, but they need the tools of discovery to access that evidence. How could Javaid Iqbal possibly allege facts that Ashcroft and Mueller created a discriminatory detention policy without access to government records about the detention program or the decision to arrest him? Seventh Circuit judge David Hamilton has imagined that *Brown v. Board of Education* would have been dismissed if the *Iqbal/Twombly* standard had been in effect in 1954. The plaintiffs in *Conley v. Gibson*, who were alleging discrimination by their union, would likely have had their case dismissed as well, because they did not have access to evidence of union leaders' discriminatory intent at the beginning of the case.

———

THE *IQBAL* STANDARD ALMOST KICKED VICKI TIMPA OUT OF COURT. Even though the City of Dallas had information in its possession that would allow Geoff Henley to write a complaint describing in detail the events that led to Tony's death, Texas law allowed Dallas not to disclose that information. So Henley had to write a complaint that was based on the bare-bones information he gathered from the police report and the report the police department made to the Texas attorney general. He could only identify the police officers on the scene when Tony died as "John Does" because the Dallas Police Department would not turn over any information about them.

After receiving Henley's complaint in Tony Timpa's case, the City of Dallas moved to dismiss it, arguing that the complaint did not include the necessary detail that was required by the *Twombly* and *Iqbal* decisions. The city argued that the complaint included the types of "naked assertions devoid of further factual enhancement" that the Supreme Court had said were insufficient. Nowhere in its motion to dismiss did the City of Dallas acknowledge that it did not need to be put on notice of the facts of the case: it already had in its possession the body camera videos and reports that told the story of what happened that night. Nowhere did the City of Dallas acknowledge that the allegations in the complaint were "conclusory" only because it would not reveal the information it had.

Luckily for Geoff Henley and Vicki Timpa, the City of Dallas turned over the officers' names, the video, and the officers' reports before the court ruled on the motion to dismiss. But it was far from inevitable that it would. Henley first had to file public records requests and then sued the city in a separate lawsuit for failing to respond to those requests. Dallas did not appear to defend itself in that lawsuit, so the court entered a default judgment against it. Then Dallas moved for a new trial. The day that trial was scheduled to begin, Henley and the city attorney hashed out an agreement; the Dallas Police Department would release the video and records to Henley, but the evidence would not be released to the public. It was more than six months after Tony Timpa's death, and after countless hours spent fighting for release of the body camera recordings and other evidence, that Vicki Timpa got some clarity about what happened in her son's final hours.

The evidence reluctantly turned over by the City of Dallas revealed that on that hot Wednesday evening in August 2016, Tony Timpa called the police from the parking lot of an adult film store. Tony told the emergency dispatcher that he suffered from anxiety and schizophrenia, that he was off his medication, that he was unarmed, and that he needed help. After hanging up the phone, Tony ran onto a busy stretch of road in his shorts and bare feet—standing in front of cars, trying to climb on top of a bus, yelling that someone was trying to kill him. A security guard who happened to be driving by saw Tony in the street and stopped to help. The guard put Tony in handcuffs and sat him next to a bus stop beside the road. Then a Dallas police sergeant and four officers arrived at the scene. Their body cameras were on. In the recordings, Tony is rolling from his back to his stomach and screaming for help. An officer asks Tony what he is on; he tells them he has taken cocaine. "I know it's illegal," he says, "but I only took a little bit."

The officers replace the security guard's handcuffs with their own and zip-tie Tony's feet. One of the officers, Danny Vasquez, puts both knees on Tony's lower back. Another, Dustin Dillard, puts his knee on Tony's upper back and pins his neck to the ground with one hand. The two officers, with their body armor, weigh more than three hundred pounds. Keeping someone held down like this, in what is called a prone position, has been known for more than a quarter century to increase the risk of death— particularly for someone who has used cocaine. The Dallas police policy manual instructs officers to move people from a prone position "as soon as [they] are brought under control," and every officer at the scene had received at least two trainings regarding this rule. But Officer Dillard keeps his knee pressed on Tony's back for more than fourteen minutes.

During that time, Tony repeatedly cries out, pleading with the officers, yelling, "You're gonna kill me!" The officers tell Tony to relax and that he is going to be okay. As they look through Tony's wallet, they laugh about the fact that he has memberships at a yacht club and a fancy fitness center and that he owns a Mercedes. Tony can be heard saying something, but his words begin to slur. After eleven minutes under Officer Dillard's knee, Tony goes limp, then silent. An officer asks Tony if he is going to be all right, but no one checks to see if Tony is breathing or feels for a pulse. Another officer says he thinks Tony must have fallen asleep and that he heard him snore. Officers start calling out to Tony, joking that he is like a young boy who doesn't want to go to school.

"Tony, we bought you new shoes for the first day of school—come on!"

"We made you waffles. Rooty-tooty-fruity waffles."

There's only silence from Tony. An officer says, "I think he's out cold now."

After more than fourteen minutes of kneeling on Tony's back, and more than three minutes after Tony had lost consciousness, Officer Dillard raises his knee and paramedics who had arrived on the scene lift Tony onto a gurney. Looking down at Tony, his eyes partially open, Officer Dillard says, "I don't think he died, did he? I hope I didn't kill him." More laughter. Soon after Tony is put in the ambulance, a paramedic can be heard announcing that he is dead. The sergeant, who had been speaking to Tony's stepmother, abruptly ends the call, walks over to Officer Vasquez, and says, "What the fuck?" Officer Vasquez then turns off his camera, in violation of department policy. But Officer Dillard leaves his camera on, and video footage from his camera shows him and Officer Rivera in the ambulance, futilely giving Tony CPR. Less than an hour after Tony called the police, asking for help, he was dead.

Only with access to the officers' body camera videos could Geoff Henley name Officers Vasquez and Dillard and others on the scene as defendants, and state with particularity what these officers did to Tony Timpa the night he died. With all of this additional detail, the city and officers could no longer argue that Vicki's complaint wasn't "plausible." A six-month fight for body camera footage and other information finally allowed Geoff Henley and Vicki Timpa to begin formal discovery.

This victory was critically important. A grand jury indicted three of the officers, but the district attorney dropped the charges. There were no meaningful consequences at work either. The Dallas Police Department gave only a written reprimand to the officers who killed Tony Timpa, and sent them back to work. At the end of their disciplinary hearing, the officer in charge said to the men who had killed Tony, "As long as you don't come back before me with the same type of allegations, I believe you guys will have a fruitful career still ahead of you." Dillard and Vasquez remain on the force, and Dillard was promoted to senior corporal in May 2022, making him responsible for training rookie officers. Only through a civil suit did Vicki Timpa have any chance at some form of justice. But the pleading requirements set out in *Iqbal* nearly foreclosed any possibility of relief.

A slight change in circumstances—having nothing to do with the merits of Vicki Timpa's case—could have changed this result. What if Henley had not agreed to represent Vicki? What if Henley had not taken the time to file the public records requests or the separate lawsuit to demand the records? What if the officers had not been wearing body cameras that day? What if the officers had turned their body cameras off before they arrived at the scene? What if the officers had destroyed the body camera recording before Henley could demand it be turned over? Without more information, the initial complaint Henley filed likely would not have survived a motion to dismiss because it did not state a "plausible" entitlement to relief.

Many civil rights attorneys I have spoken with have had what they considered righteous claims dismissed simply because they did not have access to enough information at the complaint-drafting stage to get past *Iqbal*'s plausibility pleading standard. In some cases, judges have rejected requests for limited discovery so that plaintiffs could access information already in defendants' possession to put in their complaint, explaining that to allow discovery under those circumstances would amount to an "end-run around well-established pleading standards."

But requiring a plaintiff to know the facts that would prove their case before they get to discovery goes against the core vision underlying our modern system of litigation. Discovery, not legal complaints, is the tool best suited to get to the truth. In the 1960s, trial judges, skeptical of the merits of civil rights suits, took it upon themselves to require added detail in police misconduct complaints. In 2009, the Supreme Court applied those standards to all cases based on a fear of widespread discovery abuse that looms large in the judicial imagination even as that fear is not supported by the evidence. And, even if it were, the heightened pleading standard the Supreme Court put into place in *Twombly* and *Iqbal* is not well designed to weed out weak cases. Instead, courthouse doors remain closed to people like Vicki Timpa unless they know precisely how their rights were violated before their case has even begun.

CHAPTER 4

THE CONSTITUTION

On July 15, 2012, twenty-six-year-old Andrew Scott came home from his evening shift at Hungry Howie's pizzeria in Leesburg, Florida, and settled in for a quiet night at home—a late dinner and video games in pajamas with his twenty-year-old girlfriend, Miranda Mauck, in the living room of the apartment they shared. At one thirty in the morning, the couple, both of whom were white, heard loud pounding on their front door. They looked at each other, Mauck remembers, wondering, "What the hell's going on?" They both went to the bedroom to throw on some clothes. Scott got his 9-millimeter handgun from his bedroom nightstand—a gun that he legally possessed—and walked through the living room and toward the front door, his gun down at his left side. Two seconds after Scott opened the front door, six shots rang out. Mauck, who was walking into the living room behind Scott, watched him stagger back and fall onto the sofa where they had been relaxing just moments before. Scott said Mauck's name a few times. He said, "They shot me. They fucking shot me." Then he said, "I'm dying."

Andrew Scott was killed by Lake County sheriff's deputy Richard Sylvester. Deputy Sylvester had ended up at Scott's apartment through pure happenstance. Earlier that night, Sylvester had seen a motorcycle speeding down the street. He had tried to pursue the motorcycle, but it quickly pulled out of sight, and his commander ordered him to stop the chase. Deputy Sylvester could not identify the motorcycle or even see what color it was. But the dispatcher told him that a suspect in an armed assault and battery five miles away had escaped on a motorcycle earlier that night. Then another deputy radioed Deputy Sylvester and said that he had found a motorcycle, still warm from having recently been driven, outside the Blueberry Hill Apartments in Leesburg, Florida—about a mile from where Deputy Sylvester had seen the person speeding.

There was no reason to believe that the motorcycle that sped away from Deputy Sylvester was the same one involved in the assault and battery or that it was the same motorcycle parked outside the Blueberry Hill Apartments; Leesburg is a city of twenty thousand people. But Deputy Sylvester operated on the assumption that this remarkable coincidence had occurred. He ran the plates and learned it was registered to a man named Jonathan Brown. Had the deputies called the property manager for the Blueberry Hill Apartments, they would have learned that Brown lived in apartment 124. Instead, the deputies decided to go door to door in the apartment complex, at one thirty in the morning, to try to figure out to whom the motorcycle belonged.

The deputies began with apartment 114—where Scott and Mauck were sitting on their sofa, discussing which television show they should watch—because the lights inside the apartment were on and it was close to where the motorcycle was parked. Although the deputies did not have any reason to suspect that the people in apartment 114 owned the motorcycle, four deputies took tactical positions around the front door with their guns drawn.

Deputy Sylvester pounded on the door so loudly that the neighbor in apartment 115 came out to ask what the commotion was all about. When another deputy explained that they were looking for the owner of the motorcycle, the neighbor said the owner lived in a different building in the apartment complex. A few seconds later, Deputy Sylvester saw the door of apartment 114 opening, glimpsed a gun, and started shooting.

As Scott fell against their sofa, Mauck tried to run to him. A deputy held her back and led her out of the apartment, and another deputy put her into a patrol car. When Mauck asked to go to the bathroom, she was told to wait. When she asked what was going on, she heard a few deputies joking with one another, saying that she should know by now. When a female deputy finally came to take Mauck to the bathroom, she asked Mauck where she got her T-shirt and said she thought it was funny. Mauck looked down and realized she was wearing one of Scott's shirts. It had a stick figure with bulging eyes and waving hands next to a police car. It said, "It's all fun and games until the cops show up."

When Andrew Scott's parents, John Scott and Amy Young, got the news that their son had been killed, they decided to try to find a lawyer. "I don't want this to happen to anyone else," John later said. "I don't want anyone else to have to bury their child." And if they didn't file a lawsuit, it seemed nothing would be done to prevent this type of tragedy from happening again. The Lake County Sheriff's Office brought no disciplinary charges against Deputy Sylvester; when it investigated the shooting, it found that it was "consistent with agency policy and the agency's use-of-force training." No criminal charges were brought either; the state attorney's office found that the shooting was "legally justified."

An Orlando law firm agreed to take a case on behalf of Andrew Scott's parents and Miranda Mauck; what happened was, in the attorneys' view, a clear injustice. But evidence of clear injustice is not enough to win in court.

A person bringing a Section 1983 lawsuit must show that government officials violated their constitutional rights. Although there are several different rights that police can violate, the Section 1983 lawsuit brought by Miranda Mauck and Andrew Scott's parents—like most cases brought against police—alleged violations of the Fourth Amendment to the U.S. Constitution, which reads,

> The right of the people to be secure in their persons, houses, papers, and effects, against unreasonable searches and seizures, shall not be violated, and no Warrants shall issue, but upon probable cause, supported by Oath or affirmation, and particularly describing the place to be searched, and the persons or things to be seized.

Deputy Sylvester did not have a warrant to search Scott and Mauck's home or probable cause to believe that they had done anything wrong. Scott was shot and killed by Deputy Sylvester when he opened his front door with a gun he legally possessed by his side. If that isn't "unreasonable," it is hard to imagine what is. But the Supreme Court has defined "reasonableness" under the Fourth Amendment not in terms of the rights that people like Andrew Scott have but in terms of what is reasonable for law enforcement officers like Deputy Sylvester to do under the totality of the sometimes fast-moving circumstances unfolding before them. And courts have interpreted that standard—"reasonableness" under the "totality of the circumstances"—in a manner so deferential to police that officers have few meaningful limits on their power. As a result, officers can stop, arrest, search, beat, shoot, or kill people who have done nothing wrong without violating their constitutional rights.

———

THE FOURTH AMENDMENT TO THE U.S. CONSTITUTION WAS DRAFTED in response to the British Parliament's practice of using general warrants, which allowed customs officers to enter colonists' homes without any evidence of wrongdoing and without any limits placed on what they could seize. Concern that the U.S. Congress could similarly authorize general warrants led James Madison to add the Fourth Amendment to the Bill of Rights, which was ratified in 1791. But only federal officials were bound by the Fourth Amendment; state laws governed state, county, and city law enforcement officers.

The Fourth Amendment's influence over local police really began in 1961, with a pair of Supreme Court decisions. The first was *Monroe v. Pape*, which held that the Monroe family could sue Frank Pape and his fellow Chicago police officers in federal court under Section 1983 for violating their constitutional rights. Just four months after the Supreme Court decided *Monroe v. Pape*, it decided another watershed case, *Mapp v. Ohio*. Like *Monroe*, *Mapp* involved the warrantless search of a Black person's residence—this time in Cleveland, Ohio, where police entered Dolly Mapp's home and seized books considered obscene that were then used to convict her of a crime. When Mapp appealed her conviction, the Supreme Court reversed, ruling that the officers violated the Fourth Amendment when they entered her home without a warrant. The Court also ruled that the evidence seized as a result of that unconstitutional search should not have been used against Mapp in her criminal prosecution—a remedy referred to as the exclusionary rule that had previously only been used against federal officers but, with the Supreme Court's decision in *Mapp*, became available to people whose property was unlawfully seized by the police and used against them in state prosecutions.

Through the Supreme Court's decisions in *Monroe* and *Mapp*, the Fourth Amendment came to govern a tremendous amount of local law enforcement officers' activity. The Fourth Amendment placed limits on when police could search a person's home, office, car, land, suitcase, or other property, and when police could seize evidence from any of those places. It placed limits on when police could search a person's clothes and body for possible evidence of a crime. And it placed limits on when police could "seize" a person—by stopping them briefly, arresting them, or using force against them. *Monroe* and *Mapp* also created consequences for an officer who violated the Fourth Amendment—a damages award in a Section 1983 case, or the exclusion of unconstitutionally seized evidence from a defendant's criminal prosecution.

Following *Monroe* and *Mapp*, the Fourth Amendment was poised to serve as a critically important check on police—especially because state and local governments imposed few other limits on their power. But as the Supreme Court sorted out what precisely was protected by the Fourth Amendment, it repeatedly erred on the side of giving police officers leeway in the name of public safety.

The Supreme Court's decisions about police power to stop and frisk epitomize this type of constitutional backsliding. After *Monroe* and *Mapp*—and long before—police regularly stopped and searched people on the street, and there was fierce disagreement about whether and how the Fourth Amendment applied to these interactions. The Fourth Amendment requires "probable cause" before a search or seizure—which, the Court has explained, is "not a high bar," requiring "only a probability or substantial chance of criminal activity." But law enforcement groups were of the view—and some courts and legislatures agreed—that an officer should be able to stop someone they suspect is involved in criminal activity, and frisk them for weapons, without probable cause. Civil rights groups maintained, in contrast, that officers should have probable cause before stopping people on the street and running their hands over their clothes and bodies.

When the Court agreed to hear *Terry v. Ohio*, in 1967, which concerned the constitutionality of stops and frisks, briefs to the Court portrayed starkly diverging perspectives about the police practice. Without broad latitude to stop and search people for weapons, the Americans for Effective Law Enforcement argued, "the ability of the police to prevent crime and catch criminals will be sharply constrained. And the consequent physical and social impoverishment of our people will, tragically, increase." The brief submitted by the NAACP Legal Defense Fund challenged this dire prediction, noting that "proponents of stop and frisk are fond of asserting that 'aggressive patrol' keeps the crime rate down" but that there is no "convincing evidence of this proposition." Moreover, the Legal

Defense Fund brief argued, even if stop and frisk might play some positive role in controlling crime, it caused more harm than good:

> The policeman today is the object of widespread and intense hatred in our inner cities. The [1967] National Crime Commission's Task Force on Police points to stop and frisk practices as one (obviously, only one) of the causes of this phenomenon. . . . We are gravely concerned by the dangers of legitimating stop and frisk, and thus encouraging, and increasing the frequency of occasions for, police-citizen aggressions. Speaking bluntly, we believe that what the ghetto does *not* need is more stop and frisk.

In *Terry v. Ohio*, issued in 1968, the Court took note of these "difficult and troublesome issues regarding a sensitive area of police activity" and tried to navigate a middle path. Chief Justice Earl Warren, who wrote the majority opinion, rejected the notion that stops and frisks were wholly outside the protections of the Fourth Amendment. But Chief Justice Warren also rejected the notion that officers needed probable cause. Instead, *Terry* instructed, a stop and frisk need only comply with "the Fourth Amendment's general proscription against unreasonable searches and seizures" and could be based on what has come to be known as "reasonable suspicion." The opinion explained officers must have more than an "inchoate and unparticularized suspicion or 'hunch,'" but shied away from a more robust definition of "reasonable suspicion," explaining that "the limitations which the Fourth Amendment places upon a protective seizure and search for weapons . . . will have to be developed in the concrete factual circumstances of individual cases."

Justice William O. Douglas—whom *Time* magazine described, in 1975, as "the most doctrinaire and committed civil libertarian ever to sit on the Court"—was the lone dissent in *Terry*. In his view, the Fourth Amendment spoke only of probable cause, and allowing police to search and seize when they had reasonable suspicion would take the country "a long step down the totalitarian path." He wrote,

> There have been powerful hydraulic pressures throughout our history that bear heavily on the Court to water down constitutional guarantees and give the police the upper hand. That hydraulic pressure has probably never been greater than it is today. Yet if the individual is no longer to be sovereign, if the police can pick him up whenever they do not like the cut of his jib, if they can "seize" and "search" him in their discretion, we enter a new regime.

Justice Douglas was right to be worried. *Terry* was decided amid the violence and turbulence of the late 1960s—marked by rebellions in Watts, Detroit, and around the country; antiwar protests; and unrest following the assassinations of Martin Luther King Jr. and Robert Kennedy—and those particularly unsettled times may have prompted the Court to give police more latitude. But *Terry*'s reasonable suspicion standard has come to mean, in practice, that police have the power to stop and frisk almost anyone at any time.

State laws criminalize all sorts of run-of-the-mill behavior: loitering, spitting, and sleeping in public; driving too slowly or too fast. *Terry* gives a police officer authority to stop a person if they have reasonable suspicion that the person is breaking these laws or any of the hundreds of other laws on the books. The Supreme Court has ruled that a police officer's reasonable suspicion that a person is breaking the law—justifying a stop—can take into account a person's ethnicity, where they live, and what they are wearing. The Supreme Court has ruled that an officer even complies with the reasonable suspicion standard if their alleged reasonable suspicion is pretext for another unreasonable motivation for the stop. In other words, an officer can pull someone over or stop them as they are walking down the street because of their race, their clothes, their accent, or no reason at all. So long as the officer can come up with any basis for reasonable suspicion that the person was breaking the law, they do not violate the Fourth Amendment.

Once an officer has reasonable suspicion for a stop, they can frisk the person so long as they have reasonable suspicion that the person might be armed or dangerous. As Chief Justice Warren recognized in *Terry*, a frisk is a "serious intrusion upon the sanctity of the person," in which an officer can "feel with sensitive fingers every portion of the . . . body . . . the . . . arms and armpits, waistline and back, the groin and area about the testicles, and entire surface of the legs down to the feet." But, again, the reasonable suspicion standard offers little in the way of guidance or limits about officers' power to subject someone to this type of "annoying, frightening, and perhaps humiliating" experience.

Where does all of this police discretion leave us? Millions of people are stopped and searched while walking and driving each year. Studies of police stops in cities across the country—from New York City to Los Angeles, from Washington State to Washington, D.C.—have found that people of color are stopped and frisked at rates much higher than white people and the vast majority of them have done nothing wrong. The fear and humiliation caused by these stops do not amount to a Fourth Amendment violation so long as an officer can offer some reasonable suspicion, after the fact, to believe that the person was breaking the law.

The leeway that the Supreme Court has given police to stop and search not only leads to more stops and searches; it also leads to more violence. As my UCLA Law colleague Devon Carbado has powerfully observed, "The police killings of Michael Brown, Walter Scott, and Eric Garner began as ordinary police interactions. Officer Wilson engaged Brown because Brown was walking in the street. Officer Slager engaged Scott because Scott was driving with a broken taillight. Officer Pantaleo engaged Garner because Garner was selling loose cigarettes." Each of these interactions began with the police entirely within their constitutional authority to approach, stop, and engage. The easier it is for police to stop and search, the more likely it is that the person being stopped and searched may respond in a way that then authorizes the police to use force and, even, to kill.

———

THE FOURTH AMENDMENT'S PROTECTIONS ARE AT THEIR VERY STRONGEST inside the home. The Fourth Amendment was ratified to ensure that Congress would not send government officials inside people's homes without a warrant or probable cause. In 1886, the Supreme Court made clear that the Fourth Amendment protects against "all invasions on the part of the government and its employees of the sanctity of a man's home and the privacies of life." In 1961, Justice Potter Stewart wrote that "at the very core" of the Fourth Amendment "stands the right of a man to retreat into his own home and there be free from unreasonable government intrusion." And in 2013, Justice Antonin Scalia wrote that "when it comes to the Fourth Amendment, the home is first among equals." But the fact that Andrew Scott was inside his home when he was shot and killed does not necessarily mean that his Fourth Amendment rights were violated. Having a reasonable expectation of privacy protected by the Fourth Amendment is only one part of the equation; the other is knowing what limits that Fourth Amendment protection put on Deputy Sylvester and his fellow deputies. And the same sorts of "hydraulic pressures," in Justice Douglas's words, that led the Court in *Terry* to allow stops and frisks with only reasonable suspicion have expanded police powers around and inside the home.

For example, there are all sorts of things police officers can do *near* a person's home without running afoul of the Fourth Amendment. There's no expectation of privacy in the airspace over a person's home: if police fly a plane one thousand feet above the ground and see evidence of illegal activity from the air, that search does not fall under the Fourth Amendment's protections. If police search through a person's garbage left on the street, the Fourth Amendment also does not apply, because there is no reasonable expectation of privacy in garbage placed on the street "for the express purpose of having strangers take it." And—most relevant to the case brought by Andrew Scott's parents and Miranda Mauck—a police officer can go to a person's front door, knock, and ask to speak to the person inside without implicating the Fourth Amendment. As the Supreme Court has reasoned, most doors have a doorbell or knocker, an "implicit license" for visitors—including Girl Scouts, trick-or-treaters, and the police—to approach and knock, commonly referred to as "knock and talk." Because police officers can fly a plane above your home, or search your garbage, or come to your door and knock without triggering the Fourth Amendment's protections, police can do these things for any reason or no reason at all.

Even when police officers' conduct does implicate the Fourth Amendment, its protections are not particularly robust. In 1967, in *Katz v. United States*, the Supreme Court presumed that police needed a warrant to search most areas protected by the Fourth Amendment, "subject only to a few specifically established and well-delineated exceptions." Requiring an officer to go to a judge or magistrate to get a warrant meant, as the Court explained in *Katz*, that "the deliberate, impartial judgment of a judicial officer . . . [would] be interposed between the citizen and the police."

But that seemingly definitive warrant requirement has become swallowed by exceptions to the rule. The Supreme Court explained in 1978, in a case called *Mincey v. Arizona*, that officers do not need a warrant when "the exigencies of the situation make the needs of law enforcement so compelling that a warrantless search is objectively reasonable under the Fourth Amendment." And when deciding whether there are exigent circumstances, courts consider the "totality of the circumstances." The Supreme Court has ruled that all kinds of warrantless searches are justified by the exigencies of the situation, including when officers are in hot pursuit of a fleeing suspect; trying to protect someone from injury; trying to provide emergency assistance to someone who is injured; trying to protect their own safety; or believe suspects may destroy evidence or escape. As Justice Scalia commented in 1991, the warrant requirement has "become so riddled with exceptions that it [is] basically unrecognizable."

The Supreme Court has also blurred a related Fourth Amendment line: whether and when officers must knock and announce their presence before executing a warrant. In 1995, Justice Clarence Thomas, writing for a unanimous Court, explained that the "knock and announce" requirement was a centuries-old principle of the common law and was mandated by the Fourth Amendment. But in that same opinion, Justice Thomas explained that it was a "flexible requirement" and "should not be read to mandate a rigid rule of announcement that ignores countervailing law enforcement interests." The Court would not lay out what those law enforcement interests might be; instead, it decided to "leave to the lower courts the task of determining the circumstances under which an unannounced entry is reasonable under the Fourth Amendment." Two years later, in another unanimous decision, the Court watered down the knock and announce requirement further, explaining that officers can make a "no-knock" entry anytime they have a "reasonable suspicion" under the circumstances that knocking and announcing would "be dangerous or futile, or . . . inhibit the effective investigation of the crime." The Court explained that the "reasonable suspicion" standard it first announced in *Terry* struck "the appropriate balance between the legitimate law enforcement concerns at issue in the execution of search warrants and the individual privacy interests affected by no-knock entries."

In a 2006 decision, *Hudson v. Michigan*, Justice Scalia, writing for the majority, recognized that requiring an officer to knock and announce protected three important interests: "human life and limb, because an unannounced entry may provoke violence in supposed self-defense by the surprised resident"; property, so that a person can "avoid the destruction of property occasioned by a forcible entry"; and the "elements of privacy and dignity that can be destroyed by a sudden entrance." But the Court's decisions have done little to protect these interests—even as law enforcement agencies around the country have executed warrants without knocking and announcing for decades, repeatedly leading to the type of property destruction, injury, and death that the Court has recognized would likely follow.

———

THE SECTION 1983 COMPLAINT FILED BY MIRANDA MAUCK AND AN-drew Scott's parents alleged that Deputy Sylvester violated Scott's and Mauck's Fourth Amendment rights by pounding on their door in the middle of the night without probable cause to believe they had committed a crime, without exigent circumstances justifying his decision not to get a warrant, and without announcing that he was a law enforcement officer. Scott was shot and Mauck was injured as a result of these Fourth Amendment violations, they argued.

After discovery, both sides moved for summary judgment. Their briefs to the judge went back and forth about whether and how the Fourth Amendment applied to the case. Deputy Sylvester contended that when he and his fellow deputies knocked on Scott and Mauck's door, it was no more than a "knock and talk," and so did not implicate the Fourth Amendment at all.

Miranda Mauck and Andrew Scott's parents responded that pounding on the door in the middle of the night with guns drawn was not a "knock and talk"; it was far more invasive than anything a Girl Scout or trick-or-treater might do. Instead, Deputy Sylvester's actions should be treated as a "constructive entry" into the home, requiring him to have a warrant (or probable cause and exigent circumstances justifying his failure to get a warrant) and also requiring him to announce he was a law enforcement officer—an announcement, Mauck testified, that would almost certainly have caused Scott not to bring his gun to the door.

Florida courts had found a "knock and talk" turns into a "constructive entry" when police use "overbearing tactics that essentially force the individual out of the home." Deputy Sylvester argued that nothing he did was so overbearing that it forced Scott to come outside. Pounding loudly on the door was not, in itself, an "overbearing tactic." And although the deputies had their guns pointed at the door, Scott did not know this, so that fact did not force him outside. Deputy Sylvester argued that he did not violate "knock and announce" requirements because those requirements would only have applied if the deputies had planned to enter Scott and Mauck's home.

The judge sided with Deputy Sylvester. If Deputy Sylvester had actually entered apartment 114, that would have been a search protected by the Fourth Amendment. Deputy Sylvester would have needed probable cause to believe Scott or Mauck was involved in a crime and exigent circumstances that excused him from getting a warrant—neither of which Deputy Sylvester had. If Deputy Sylvester had entered the apartment, he would also have had to announce beforehand that he was a sheriff's deputy, unless he had reasonable suspicion that announcing himself would put him or others in danger or lead to the destruction of evidence, and even this lax standard would be difficult to meet given that there was no reason to believe Scott and Mauck had committed a crime. But the Lake County sheriff's deputies did not actually set foot into Scott and Mauck's apartment—until after they killed Scott. The judge concluded that what Deputy Sylvester did was just a "knock and talk," and nothing more. So Deputy Sylvester's conduct was not a "search" or "seizure" that triggered any of the protections of the Fourth Amendment.

———

ANDREW SCOTT'S PARENTS AND MIRANDA MAUCK ALSO ALLEGED ANother type of Fourth Amendment violation in their complaint: that Deputy Sylvester used excessive force when he shot Andrew Scott. This claim implicated the Fourth Amendment's protection against unreasonable seizures. But the Supreme Court has given police even more power and discretion in this realm.

In the years after *Monroe* was decided, courts were uncertain whether uses of force by police were protected by the Fourth Amendment's prohibition of unreasonable seizures, or the Fourteenth Amendment's due process protections. In 1985, in a case called *Tennessee v. Garner*, the Supreme Court clarified that the Fourth Amendment—not the Fourteenth—applies when a police officer uses deadly force in the course of an arrest. The Fourth Amendment standard—which prevents "unreasonable" seizures—was better for plaintiffs than the Fourteenth Amendment's due process standard, which courts had interpreted to be violated only by force imposed with the intention of causing harm.

Garner also created a bright-line rule about the scope of police power to use force. Edward Garner, a fifteen-year-old Black boy, was shot in the back of the head as he was running away from a house that had been burgled. The officer saw Garner had no weapon, but shot him because he would have escaped otherwise. The officer's decision to kill Garner was consistent with Tennessee law, which allowed officers to use deadly force to stop a person fleeing arrest. But the Supreme Court ruled that the Tennessee statute "did not adequately limit the use of deadly force" and that officers violate the Fourth Amendment when they use deadly force unless they "have probable cause . . . to believe that the suspect [has committed a felony and] poses a threat to the safety of the officers or a danger to the community if left at large."

Four years later, in a case called *Graham v. Connor*, the Supreme Court confirmed that the Fourth Amendment applied to force used by police during an arrest, but smudged *Garner*'s bright line. Justice Rehnquist, writing for the Court in *Graham*, instructed courts to consider the totality of the circumstances when deciding whether force violated the Fourth Amendment, including "the severity of the crime at issue, whether the suspect poses an immediate threat to the safety of the officers or others, and whether he is actively resisting arrest . . . or attempting to evade arrest by flight."

The *Graham* opinion also told courts, in multiple ways, to give officers the benefit of the doubt when making this assessment. *Graham* instructs courts to take account of the "tense, uncertain, and rapidly evolving" circumstances in which officers used force when deciding whether the force was unreasonable. *Graham* instructs courts to assess the reasonableness of force that was used based on what the officers perceived at the time "rather than with the 20/20 vision of hindsight." And the Court emphasized that a use of force can be constitutional, even if it was unnecessary: "Not every push or shove, even if it may later seem unnecessary in the peace of a judge's chambers, violates the Fourth Amendment."

Graham has become the constitutional touchstone for Fourth Amendment excessive-force claims. *Graham*'s balancing test is cited in virtually every Section 1983 case concerning the use of force, and in the vast majority of police training manuals as the key guidance about officers' powers to use force. But *Graham* has been criticized for the same reasons as *Terry*: it does not give courts or police officers enough guidance. The decision does not clarify how much force is reasonable under any given situation, how immediate the threat must be to justify force, or whether an officer's decisions leading up to the use of force should be considered in the assessment of reasonableness. The Supreme Court has decided only a few Fourth Amendment excessive-force cases since *Graham*. Those decisions have not made the standard any clearer.

Unfortunately, bright-line rules are what police experts believe officers need, particularly regarding the use of force. And available evidence shows that they can work. Some large police departments, including those in New York City, Oakland, and Philadelphia, implemented more restrictive use-of-force policies in the late 1960s and early 1970s, and studies found that those departments significantly reduced injuries and killings by police. Similar studies in Atlanta, Georgia, and Kansas City, Missouri, in the 1980s found police shootings decreased after implementation of more restrictive deadly force guidelines. After the Supreme Court's 1985 decision in *Garner*, departments adopted its rule prohibiting deadly force against a person fleeing arrest who was not a threat, and studies found a 16 percent reduction nationwide in fatal police shootings. More recently, Seattle and San Francisco have adopted standards less flexible than *Graham* and have reported a significant reduction in the number of force incidents without a decrease in officer or community safety.

In recent years, police accountability and law enforcement groups—including the Police Executive Research Forum, Law Enforcement Action Partnership, Campaign Zero, Communities United Against Police Brutality, and the NAACP Legal Defense Fund—have argued that police should have use-of-force policies more restrictive than *Graham*. Since June 2020, a handful of states and hundreds of law enforcement agencies across the country have constrained police power in various ways that go beyond the requirements in *Graham*: they have banned or restricted chokeholds and other neck restraints; prohibited or limited shooting into cars; required officers to issue a warning before using deadly force; and limited force to only those circumstances where it was necessary. But these bright-line rules have not been adopted by the Supreme Court. That means that when officers cross these bright lines, they do not necessarily violate the Constitution. And that means people on the other end of an unnecessary but "reasonable" shooting, chokehold, or tasing are without a remedy under Section 1983.

———

RELYING ON *GRAHAM*, THE JUDGE HEARING THE CASE BROUGHT BY Andrew Scott's parents and Miranda Mauck dismissed their excessive-force claim. According to the judge, the events were "tragic," "sad," and "unfortunate," but did not violate the Fourth Amendment, because Deputy Sylvester reasonably feared for his life when he shot Scott. Although the judge took Deputy Sylvester at his word that he only intended to "knock and talk" with the people in apartment 114 when he pounded on the door at one thirty in the morning, she also accepted that he feared the person who opened the door of apartment 114 might be the dangerous motorcycle owner. So when Deputy Sylvester saw a gun in that person's hand, it was reasonable for Deputy Sylvester to believe he was in harm's way. According to the judge, Deputy Sylvester's decision to shoot Scott was reasonable even if—as Mauck had testified—Scott was pointing his gun to the ground when he opened the door. As the judge explained,

> In light of the information Sylvester had at the time the door opened, as well as the tense, uncertain, and rapidly evolving situation Sylvester confronted when Scott opened the door wielding a gun, the Court concludes that in the totality of the circumstances—even if Scott's gun was pointed down—Sylvester's use of deadly force was reasonable and it declines to second-guess his split-second judgment.

The court of appeals affirmed, "echo[ing] the district court's expression of sympathy for the plaintiffs' loss," but concluding that "while the facts of this case are tragic, we can find no reversible error in the district court's ultimate . . . rulings."

Andrew Scott's parents and Miranda Mauck sought a rehearing by all eleven court of appeals judges on the Eleventh Circuit, and although four judges issued two passionate dissents arguing that the case should be reheard, seven of the judges denied the request. The Supreme Court declined to hear the case. Miranda Mauck and the Scotts recovered nothing from Lake County or Deputy Sylvester in recompense for killing their boyfriend and son—not even a "sorry for your loss."

———

DEPUTY SYLVESTER'S DECISION TO SHOOT ANDREW SCOTT WAS DEEMED reasonable under the Fourth Amendment because Scott had a gun, even if it was pointing to the ground. But what if Scott had been holding a video game controller instead of a gun when Deputy Sylvester shot him? To read *Graham*, and courts' application of *Graham*, the judges would have come out the same way so long as Deputy Sylvester's mistaken belief that Scott was holding a gun was reasonable.

Consider, for example, David Collie, who was shot in the back by an officer while he had his hands in the air but whose constitutional rights were not violated, according to the judges who heard his case. In 2016, on a warm July night in Fort Worth, Texas, a 911 call came into the police department: Two Black men had robbed someone at a gas station. Both men were in their late teens or early twenties. One was six feet one with a short Afro and the other was six feet four. Both were shirtless. When Fort Worth police officer Hugo Barron and Tarrant County Sheriff's Department deputy Vanessa Flores heard the police alert, they were off duty, working security at an apartment complex a half-mile from the gas station. As they were driving around, looking for the men, they saw David Collie.

Collie was at least ten years older, six inches shorter, and thirty pounds lighter than the smaller of the two robbery suspects. He was almost bald. But he was Black and happened to not be wearing a shirt when Officer Barron and Deputy Flores saw Collie walking through the apartment complex on his way to visit a friend. Officer Barron jumped out of their car and called for Collie to raise his hands. Collie did. Just seven seconds after getting out of his car, and while he was standing more than thirty feet away from Collie, Officer Barron shot Collie in the back while he had his hands in the air. Officer Barron's hollow-point bullet entered Collie's lung, punctured his spine, and left him paralyzed from the waist down.

Police found a box cutter ten feet from where Collie fell, and Officer Barron later claimed Collie had that box cutter in his hand when Barron shot him. According to Collie, he did have a box cutter in his pocket for work, but his hands were empty when he was shot. Collie was nevertheless charged with aggravated assault on a public servant, for allegedly threatening Barron and Flores with the box cutter from more than thirty feet away, and was kept shackled to his bed and under armed guard for almost the entirety of his two-month hospital stay. A grand jury refused to indict Collie for aggravated assault, and he was never implicated or charged in the robbery at the gas station.

When David Collie sued Officer Barron and Deputy Flores for violating his Fourth Amendment rights, the court granted the officers summary judgment, dismissing his case, and the court of appeals affirmed. The court of appeals called the case "tragic," and a prime example of "an individual's being in the wrong place at the wrong time," but concluded that the officer's conduct was reasonable because Officer Barron allegedly—and mistakenly—thought he saw a gun in David Collie's raised hand.

———

IN 2006, JUSTICE STEPHEN BREYER WROTE A CONCURRENCE SEEMING to endorse the lack of bright-line rules in the Supreme Court's Fourth Amendment cases. He wrote,

> The Fourth Amendment does not insist upon bright-line rules. Rather, it recognizes that no single set of legal rules can capture the ever-changing complexity of human life. It consequently uses the general terms "unreasonable searches and seizures." And this Court has continuously emphasized that "reasonableness . . . is measured . . . by examining the totality of the circumstances."

The lack of bright-line rules in Fourth Amendment cases may well capture "the ever-changing complexity of human life," but it has also left police with few limits on their power. Even when courts find the consequences of that tremendous leeway to be tragic, sad, or unfortunate, the victims of those misfortunes can have no remedy under the Constitution.

In August 2020, Reuters reporters interviewed David Collie, who had been living in a nursing home in the years since he was shot in 2016, battling infections and depression. Officer Barron faced no discipline or criminal consequences for shooting Collie. And Collie never received a penny from the City of Fort Worth or Officer Barron for this devastating error, because the officer's conduct was found to be objectively reasonable under the Fourth Amendment standard created by the Supreme Court. "You shoot me, paralyze me, put me in a nursing home, ruin everything, and I can't get no type of compensation?" Leaning back in bed, David Collie said, "This ain't justice."

CHAPTER 5

QUALIFIED IMMUNITY

In the late evening of August 23, 2006, Jayzel Mattos asked her fourteen-year-old daughter, Cheynice, to call the police. As Cheynice told the officer on the line, Jayzel and her husband, Troy, were arguing and things were being thrown around. When four police officers in Wailuku, a town on the Hawaiian island of Maui, responded to the scene, Troy was sitting outside. An officer asked Troy to bring Jayzel outside so the officers could confirm she was safe. Troy went into the house to get Jayzel, and another officer, Darren Agarano, followed him inside. When Troy returned with Jayzel, he yelled at Officer Agarano for being in his home.

Jayzel asked the officers and her husband to calm down and go outside so that they would not disturb her sleeping children. Instead, a third officer, Ryan Aikala, entered the hallway to arrest Troy. Jayzel was cornered between the officers: Officer Agarano was in front of her, Officer Aikala was at her right, and her back was against Troy's chest. Officer Aikala moved to grab Troy and bumped against Jayzel. She raised her hands, palms forward, to keep the officer's body from smashing against her breasts. Officer Aikala stepped back, said, "Are you touching an officer?" and then, without warning, tased Jayzel in her hand and breast. She felt what she later described as "an incredible burning and painful feeling locking all of my joints and muscles." She fell hard to the floor and must have lost consciousness for a moment; when she came to, she saw her four-year-old son crouched next to her, looking into her eyes, and her husband in handcuffs.

Jayzel Mattos was arrested for harassment and obstructing government operations and was taken to the police station. When she was released later that night, she first made sure that her children were asleep and then went to the hospital to seek treatment for her bruises and burns.

The next day, after getting her kids to school, Jayzel began researching the Maui Police Department's Taser policies. She worked for Maui County as a building permit clerk and knew generally whom to call. The Hawaii State Office of the Ombudsman and the ACLU recommended that she file a complaint with the police department's internal affairs division. When she did, she was interviewed by someone in the division who took photos of her bruised arm, singed hand, and the bright red burned area at the base of her areola. Nothing ever came of the investigation. After five months, the criminal charges against her were dismissed.

Jayzel Mattos was referred to Eric Seitz, one of the only lawyers in all of Hawaii who was regularly bringing civil rights cases at the time. Seitz took the case. He drafted and filed a complaint describing what happened and alleging, among other things, that Officer Aikala violated the Fourth Amendment's prohibition against unreasonable force when he tased Jayzel.

At the end of discovery, Officer Aikala moved for summary judgment, arguing that the Section 1983 excessive-force claim against him should be dismissed. The district court denied the request, concluding that Aikala had used excessive force if a jury believed the evidence supporting Jayzel's version of the story.

When Aikala appealed, the court of appeals reversed. But the court of appeals granted Jayzel's request for a rehearing before eleven appeals judges, all but two of them agreed with the trial court that Officer Aikala had violated the Constitution. Although the appeals court recognized that the Supreme Court's Fourth Amendment cases allow officers leeway because they "are often forced to make split-second judgments . . . about the amount of force that is necessary in a particular situation," and that domestic violence calls can be volatile, they could not "identify any reasonableness in the conclusion—whether made in a split-second or after careful deliberation—that tasing the innocent wife of a large, drunk, angry man when there is no threat that either spouse has a weapon, is a prudent way to defuse a potentially, but not yet, dangerous situation." This was especially so, they explained, given that children were present. And the fact that Officer Aikala did not warn Jayzel before tasing her "pushe[d] this use of force far beyond the pale" in the appeals judges' view.

But proving that Officer Aikala had violated the Constitution was not enough. Jayzel Mattos could only defeat his efforts to get her Section 1983 excessive-force claim dismissed if her lawyer could find a Supreme Court or appellate court decision holding that tasing a person under similar circumstances was unconstitutional. The court of appeals observed that no prior decision from that court of appeals or the Supreme Court had ever addressed the use of a Taser in "dart mode"—where the Taser shoots out darts with electrical currents that attach to a person—the setting Officer Aikala used against Jayzel. And, at the time, that court of appeals had never issued an opinion finding that an officer's decision to use a Taser violated the Fourth Amendment.

Because no prior court opinion had similar facts, the judges dismissed Jayzel's excessive-force claim, even though they believed Officer Aikala's decision to tase a potential domestic violence victim went "far beyond the pale" and violated the Fourth Amendment. Welcome to the upside-down world of qualified immunity.

——

THE SUPREME COURT CREATED QUALIFIED IMMUNITY OUT OF THIN air six years after it recognized the right to sue under Section 1983. The incident that led to that first qualified immunity decision occurred just seven months after the Supreme Court decided *Monroe v. Pape*. In the late summer of 1961, fifteen Black and white Episcopal clergymen traveled to the South as part of the Freedom Rides. On the morning of September 13, 1961, the ministers were headed from Jackson, Mississippi, to Chattanooga, Tennessee. About a half hour before their bus was scheduled to depart, the clergymen entered the Jackson bus terminal's racially segregated coffee shop. Two police officers told them to leave. When they refused, the ministers were arrested for breaching the peace. Although the clergymen were found guilty and sentenced to four months in jail, the law they were convicted of violating was subsequently found to be unconstitutional and their cases were dismissed on appeal.

The clergymen sued under Section 1983 for the violation of their rights. A jury found for the defendants, and the ministers appealed. When the case, called *Pierson v. Ray*, got to the Supreme Court in 1967, Chief Justice Earl Warren, writing for the Court, held that the officers had good-faith immunity under Mississippi law because they thought the arrests were proper, and that that immunity should apply to the Section 1983 claim as well. Chief Justice Warren explained that this qualified immunity from suit was necessary because, otherwise, officers could be held liable when they mistakenly believed the law authorized an arrest. As Chief Justice Warren explained, "A policeman's lot is not so unhappy that he must choose between being charged with dereliction of duty if he does not arrest when he has probable cause and being mulcted in damages if he does."

Although a good-faith defense was the impetus for qualified immunity, today officers are entitled to qualified immunity even if they act in *bad faith*, so long as there is no prior court decision with nearly identical facts. How did a protection for officers' good faith turn into a protection for officers with the good fortune to have done something unlawful that no prior court has ruled unconstitutional? For more than five decades,

the Supreme Court has repeatedly strengthened qualified immunity's protections, describing each additional layer of defense in increasingly terri-
fied tones as necessary to protect officers from the unyielding power of
civil rights lawsuits.

The first—and arguably most seismic—shift to qualified immunity
came in 1982 in a case called *Harlow v. Fitzgerald*. In *Harlow*, the Court
concluded that officers' entitlement to qualified immunity should not depend on whether they acted in good faith. In order to prove good faith,
officers would have to be deposed—questioned under oath—about their
state of mind at the time they violated the Constitution, and a case would
go to a jury if an officer's good faith was in dispute. Justice Powell, who
wrote the majority opinion in *Harlow*, reasoned that requiring officers to
participate in discovery and trial in an "insubstantial case" was a burden
to the officer, who would need to spend time defending himself instead of
doing his job. And the Court feared that this type of distraction would
harm not only the officer but also "society as a whole" by discouraging
"able citizens from acceptance of public office" and "dampen[ing] the ardor
of all but the most resolute, or the most irresponsible [public officials], in
the unflinching discharge of their duties." So, to protect officers from having to participate in discovery and trial in "insubstantial cases," the Court
held in *Harlow* that an officer's intentions do not matter to the qualified
immunity analysis. Instead, officers are entitled to qualified immunity so
long as they do not violate what the Court called "clearly established law."

The Supreme Court's decision in *Harlow* did not explain what it meant
by "clearly established law." But the Court's decisions over the next forty
years have created a standard that seems virtually impossible to meet. The
Court has repeatedly instructed that except in extraordinary circumstances the law can only be "clearly established" by a prior court decision.
And the Court has emphasized that the prior court decision cannot simply set out a constitutional principle in general terms. It is not enough, for
example, to find a case that says it is unconstitutional to use force against

a person who is not resisting arrest. Instead, the prior court decision must include facts that are so similar to the facts in the present case that *every* reasonable officer would know that what he was doing was wrong. In recent years, the Supreme Court has repeatedly reversed lower courts that have denied officers qualified immunity, chastising those courts for not appreciating the importance of qualified immunity to "society as a whole" and arguing that they "misunderstood the 'clearly established' analysis" because they "failed to identify a case where an officer acting under similar circumstances as [the defendant] was held to have violated the Fourth Amendment."

Lower courts appear to have gotten the message, repeatedly citing the Supreme Court's instruction that clearly established law should not be defined "at a high level of generality" when assessing whether officers are entitled to qualified immunity. Courts have granted officers qualified immunity even when they have engaged in egregious behavior—not because what the officers did was acceptable, but because there wasn't a prior case in which that precise conduct had been held unconstitutional.

The hairsplitting can be extreme. In *Baxter v. Bracey*, an appeals court granted qualified immunity to officers who released their police dog on a burglary suspect who had surrendered and was sitting down with his hands up. Although a prior court decision had held that it was unconstitutional to release a police dog on a suspect who had surrendered and was lying down, the court in Alexander Baxter's case granted qualified immunity to the officers because, it held, the prior decision did not clearly establish the unconstitutionality of the officers' decision to release a police dog on a person who was seated with his hands in the air.

In *Kelsay v. Ernst*, an appeals court held that an officer who slammed a nonviolent, nonthreatening woman to the ground—breaking her collarbone and knocking her unconscious—was entitled to qualified immunity. Prior cases had held that "where a nonviolent misdemeanant poses no threat to officers and is not actively resisting arrest or attempting to flee, an officer may not employ force just because the suspect is interfering with police or behaving disrespectfully." But, the court held, the officer was entitled to qualified immunity because this precedent did not clearly establish that "a deputy was forbidden to use a takedown maneuver to arrest a suspect who ignored the deputy's instruction to 'get back here' and continued to walk away from the officer."

In *Jessop v. City of Fresno*, police officers stole more than $225,000 in cash and rare coins when executing a warrant. Prior cases had held that it was unconstitutional for officers to steal, but those cases were factually distinct—involving the theft of different types of property under different circumstances. According to the appeals court, the officers "ought to have recognized" that it was wrong to steal the coins and cash, but "they did not have clear notice that it violated the Fourth Amendment" because prior court decisions "did not put the constitutional question beyond debate."

This could also have been the fate of a lawsuit brought on behalf of George Floyd's family. Qualified immunity never threatened Floyd's family's ability to recover money for his murder at the hands of Minneapolis police in May 2020. They settled their case with the City of Minneapolis for $27 million before a lawsuit was ever filed in which qualified immunity could be raised. This is likely because the city anticipated the blowback that would come from arguing that a Section 1983 case against Derek Chauvin should be dismissed because Floyd's family could not point to a prior case with nearly identical facts. But if George Floyd's case had not received the press scrutiny it did and had not inspired the same degree of public attention and rage, a lawyer for the City of Minneapolis could well have argued that qualified immunity shielded Chauvin from liability. Officers have killed people in Alabama, Florida, Georgia, Illinois, Missouri, New Hampshire, Oklahoma, and Texas in just the way Chauvin killed Floyd—with a knee on their back or neck—but have had their civil rights lawsuits dismissed on qualified immunity grounds.

In a 2009 decision, the Supreme Court made it even more difficult for plaintiffs to find "clearly established law." Eight years earlier, the Court had made clear that lower courts, when granting qualified immunity, should also decide whether the officer had violated the Constitution to allow "the law's elaboration from case to case." But in 2009, in a case called *Pearson v. Callahan*, the Court reversed itself and held that lower courts could grant qualified immunity without first ruling on the constitutionality of a defendant's behavior. In other words, the Supreme Court has instructed lower courts to grant defendants qualified immunity unless the plaintiff can find a prior case in which an officer violated the Constitution under nearly identical circumstances, and has also instructed lower courts that they do not need to issue these types of constitutional rulings.

For a plaintiff's civil rights attorney trying to defeat a qualified immunity motion, the challenges of finding "clearly established law" are almost too many to count. Think about all the stars that would have had to align for Jayzel Mattos to be able to defeat Officer Aikala's qualified immunity motion.

First, another officer would previously have had to tase someone in "dart mode" under circumstances similar to Jayzel Mattos's case. Then the person who was tased would have had to file a lawsuit—which is hardly certain, given that it can be difficult in many parts of the country to find a lawyer, and lawyers are unlikely to agree to represent people who judges and juries might find unsympathetic, or who have limited claims for damages. Next, that prior lawsuit would have had to result in a court opinion explaining that the officer's use of the Taser in dart mode was unconstitutional. Importantly, it would not be enough if the plaintiff in the prior case won some money in a settlement; if the case was settled before the judge issued an opinion ruling that the officer's use of the Taser in dart mode was unconstitutional, then that case could not clearly establish the law for Mattos's case.

Even if there was a prior court opinion finding that the use of a Taser in dart mode under similar circumstances was constitutional, then Mattos's lawyer would have had to find it. Scott Michelman—the legal director of the Washington, D.C., branch of the ACLU and a lecturer at Harvard Law School, who has argued before the Supreme Court and seven courts of appeals and has authored a legal casebook dedicated to civil rights litigation—has spent upward of a week researching court decisions in order to find "clearly established law" to defeat a single qualified immunity motion. Many lawyers who bring civil rights cases do not have Michelman's expertise. And many lawyers, even those experienced in civil rights litigation, may not be able to dedicate dozens of hours to hunting down prior cases with similar facts—especially if they are working on contingency, and so will be paid nothing if their client loses.

———

THE SUPREME COURT HAS CREATED ONE ADDITIONAL QUALIFIED IMMunity hurdle for plaintiffs: defendants' right to immediately appeal any qualified immunity denial. Federal courts usually operate under what is called a final judgment rule—meaning that a decision by a trial court cannot be appealed until the case is over. So, if one side gets a ruling it does not like—requiring discovery of information they would prefer to keep secret, or denying a motion to dismiss—the parties usually have to wait to appeal that decision until one side or the other wins. The rule is based on notions of efficiency: if each side could appeal every time they were unhappy with their judge's decision, and each appeal could take a year or more, cases would never end. The final judgment rule also expects that a judge's decision that seems outrageous on the day it is issued might not seem worth challenging by the end of the case.

But qualified immunity is different. Because, as the Supreme Court has said, qualified immunity is meant to protect officers from the burdens of discovery and trial, an officer who is denied qualified immunity can immediately appeal that decision. What this means in practice is that officers can call time-out in the middle of a case, adding months or years to the case and dramatically increasing the costs of litigation.

The right to an immediate appeal meant that it took the family of Ryan Cole more than eight years to defeat qualified immunity, even though every court that considered the case concluded that the young man's constitutional rights had been violated. On the morning of October 25, 2010, in a suburb of Dallas, the Sachse Police Department called available units to the neighboring town of Garland. Cole, a seventeen-year-old white high school senior, was reportedly walking around the neighborhood with a handgun. When three police officers—Michael Hunter, Carl Carson, and Martin Cassidy—found Cole, he was holding the gun to his right temple. Cole was facing away from the officers and unaware of their presence when, without warning, Officer Hunter shot multiple rounds. A bullet entered Cole's body, going through his left arm, into his back, breaking a rib, and bruising his lung. As an involuntary reflex to being shot, Cole pulled the trigger of his own gun, shooting himself in the temple. Officer Cassidy, standing more than one hundred feet away, opened fire on Ryan Cole as he fell to the ground.

As Cole lay facedown, unconscious and bleeding, the officers did nothing to help. Several minutes later, when paramedics arrived, the young man was moments from going into cardiac arrest. At the hospital, doctors told Cole's parents, Randy and Karen, that their son would not likely survive the night. Although Ryan Cole managed to live, much of the right side of his brain was destroyed and the left side of his body was paralyzed. He has no use of his left arm and limited use of his left leg. He has regular seizures. His face, head, arm, and back are permanently disfigured. Randy and Karen will need to provide their son with twenty-four-hour medical care for the rest of his life.

Officers Cassidy, Carson, and Hunter told police investigators that Officer Hunter shot Cole only after he had pointed his gun at Officer Hunter and Officer Hunter had told Cole to drop the weapon. Based on this testimony, a Dallas grand jury charged Cole with felony aggravated assault. But forensic evidence established that the officers had lied. The trajectory of Officer Hunter's bullet showed Cole had his back to Officer

Hunter when he was shot. Stippling on Cole's temple showed he had not pointed his gun at the officers; instead, he had been pointing his gun at his own head when Officer Hunter shot him. Officer Hunter's body microphone revealed that he gave no warning before shooting Cole. Based on this evidence, the Dallas County prosecutor dropped the aggravated-assault charge against Cole. But the officers were never charged with a crime or disciplined by their department for shooting Cole or lying to investigators.

In 2012, Ryan Cole's parents sued, alleging that the officers used excessive force and fabricated evidence against their son. The officers twice asked the court to dismiss the case against them on qualified immunity grounds—once before and once after discovery. The trial court denied both requests in 2014. Then, over the next six years, the officers—represented by lawyers hired by the city's insurance company—filed multiple appeals to the court of appeals and the U.S. Supreme Court in an effort to get the denials of qualified immunity reversed.

First, the defendants appealed both trial court decisions. On September 25, 2015, the court of appeals affirmed that the officers were not entitled to qualified immunity on the excessive-force and fabrication-of-evidence claims against them. The officers then requested a rehearing before all the judges on the court of appeals, which the court of appeals denied. The officers again invoked their right to appeal the denial of qualified immunity—this time to the U.S. Supreme Court. The Supreme Court did not issue an opinion in the case, but issued an order on November 28, 2016, instructing the court of appeals to rehear the case.

The court of appeals asked for a new round of legal briefs and another oral argument. It took the court of appeals almost two years to issue its second decision in the case, but when it did, on September 25, 2018, it reached the same conclusion—the officers were not entitled to qualified immunity. The officers again sought a rehearing before all eighteen judges on the court of appeals. This time their motion was granted, but the majority opinion issued on August 20, 2019, was consistent with those that came before: qualified immunity was inappropriate. Then the officers filed a second petition for review of the qualified immunity denials to the Supreme Court. On June 15, 2020, the Court declined to hear the case and sent it back to the trial court. The officers asked the trial court, once again, to dismiss the case on qualified immunity grounds. Their request was denied on October 29, 2020. In January 2021, as trial was approaching, the case settled for $2 million.

More than eight years elapsed between the time Ryan Cole's parents filed their case and the case reached its conclusion. Attorneys provided by the City of Sachse's insurer spent thousands of hours trying to dodge responsibility for a shooting that every court considering the case found was unconstitutional. Scores of briefs were filed by Ryan Cole's parents, the officers, and advocacy groups. Judges on the district court and court of appeals likely spent hundreds of hours hearing arguments, reviewing briefs, and drafting decisions. Every single court that ruled on the case decided that qualified immunity was inappropriate. The right to an immediate appeal—intended to reduce the expenses of litigation and the burdens and distractions of being sued—added exponentially to the time it took to resolve Ryan Cole's case. And, of course, fee shifting did not apply to the case, because it settled; the Coles' attorneys were paid for just a fraction of the time they spent fighting the officers' qualified immunity motions from a portion of the settlement.

———

DEFENDERS OF QUALIFIED IMMUNITY HAVE NOT BEEN ABLE TO SUM-mon a reason why officers who violate the Constitution should be protected from liability simply because a court has not previously ruled nearly identical conduct to be unconstitutional. Instead, the strongest defenses of qualified immunity have been various predictions that the world would be worse off without it. But claims about the need for qualified immunity are unsupported by the facts on the ground.

Although the Supreme Court and defenders of qualified immunity are quick to say that the doctrine protects officers from bankruptcy, settlements and judgments against officers are almost always paid by their employers. I studied police misconduct settlements and judgments in eighty-one jurisdictions across the country, over a six-year period, and found that officers paid just 0.02 percent of the more than $735 million that plaintiffs received. Officers in only two of the jurisdictions were required to contribute anything to settlements and judgments entered against them; their average payment was $4,194, their median payment was $2,250, and no officer paid more than $25,000. Officers do not need qualified immunity to protect them from bankruptcy when they are sued; local governments almost always pick up the tab.

Defenders of qualified immunity also argue that the doctrine is necessary to protect officers from liability when they make good-faith mistakes. The Supreme Court has said that qualified immunity "gives government officials breathing room to make reasonable but mistaken judgments about open legal questions." The International Association of Chiefs of Police has argued that qualified immunity "allows police officers to respond to incidents without pause" and "make split-second decisions" and that, without qualified immunity, officers would not be shielded from liability when taking "good-faith actions." But qualified immunity is not necessary to shield officers from liability when they make reasonable mistakes; the Fourth Amendment, as interpreted by the Supreme Court, already shields officers from responsibility in these types of cases. Courts have held that officers can mistakenly search or arrest someone without adequate cause, or use force against someone who was not posing a threat; so long as their mistakes were reasonable, they have not violated the Constitution.

The Supreme Court has also repeatedly described qualified immunity as necessary to protect officers from the burdens and distractions of defending themselves in "insubstantial" cases. But there are plenty of other ways that weak cases are weeded out of court. People without strong evidence to support their claims will have a harder time finding a lawyer to represent them, a harder time filing a lawsuit with enough facts to get past the barriers of *Iqbal*, and a harder time proving a constitutional violation. I reviewed almost twelve hundred police misconduct suits filed in five federal districts across the country over a two-year period and found that for every case dismissed on qualified immunity, twelve were dismissed for these and other reasons. When the Supreme Court passionately describes the importance of qualified immunity doctrine to officers and "society as a whole," it ignores all of the other shields it has already put in place—including limits on attorneys' fees, pleading requirements, and constitutional protections pared down out of deference to law enforcement.

The Supreme Court has asserted that "the driving force" behind qualified immunity is to spare government officials the burdens of participating in litigation. But qualified immunity may actually increase litigation costs and delays. Defendants raised qualified immunity in more than 37 percent of the almost twelve hundred cases I studied—sometimes multiple times during the case and on appeal, as it was in *Cole v. Carson*. Each time qualified immunity is raised, it must be researched, briefed, and argued by the parties and decided by the judge. And litigating qualified immunity is no small feat. As law professor John Jeffries has remarked, qualified immunity is "a mare's nest of complexity and confusion." One court of appeals judge remarked that "wading through the doctrine of qualified immunity is one of the most morally and conceptually challenging tasks federal appellate court judges routinely face."

The time and effort necessary to resolve qualified immunity motions could still advance the goals of the doctrine if it effectively protected officers from discovery and trial. But in my study, just 8.6 percent of defendants' qualified immunity motions led to the dismissal of the plaintiffs' cases. In the remaining 91.4 percent of motions, parties and courts dedicated time and money to research, brief, argue, and decide defendants' entitlement to qualified immunity without avoiding the costs of discovery and trial.

The Supreme Court has also explained that the protections of qualified immunity are necessary so that officers are not held liable unless they have notice of the unconstitutionality of their conduct. The Court has written that factually similar cases are necessary to "clearly establish" the law because "it is sometimes difficult for an officer to determine how the relevant legal doctrine . . . will apply to the factual situation the officer confronts," and that "precedent involving similar facts can . . . provide an officer notice that a specific use of force is unlawful." But upon studying hundreds of policies, trainings, and other materials used by California law enforcement officers, I found that they are not actually being educated about the facts and holdings of the court decisions that could clearly establish the law for qualified immunity purposes. Instead, officers are taught general legal principles—like the holding in *Graham v. Connor* that officers can use force if it is "objectively reasonable under the circumstances." Then officers are trained to apply that general standard in the innumerable situations that might come their way.

Even if officers learned about the cases that clearly establish the law for qualified immunity purposes, there is no reason to believe that they could remember the facts and holdings of those cases and then recall those facts and holdings during high-speed, high-stress interactions. As one federal judge wrote, "It strains credulity to believe that a reasonable officer, as he is approaching a suspect to arrest, is thinking to himself: 'Are the facts here anything like the facts in *York v. City of Las Cruces*?'"

Less than 4 percent of the almost twelve hundred police misconduct cases I examined were dismissed because of qualified immunity. This finding makes it seem as if qualified immunity is not so bad after all. But because there are so many other ways for weaker cases to get dismissed, qualified immunity ends up leading to the dismissal of the cases with compelling claims of unconstitutional policing that have managed to overcome all these other barriers. Although the Supreme Court has described qualified immunity as a tool to weed out "insubstantial" cases, it actually does its work on the most substantial cases that cannot be kicked out of court any other way.

And even when a case is not dismissed on qualified immunity grounds, the doctrine can make winning harder. Although the officers who tased Jayzel Mattos were granted qualified immunity, this did not actually end Mattos's case. Her attorney, Eric Seitz, had included state law claims for battery and assault against Officer Aikala in Mattos's complaint, for which qualified immunity did not apply.

Five and a half years after Mattos filed her case, her state law claims settled for $40,000. Seitz split the award with Mattos. He estimated that he spent at least $40,000 out of his own pocket, including trips from Hawaii to the mainland for the court of appeals arguments, and about $200,000 of his time. Seitz told *The Maui News* that the case had been worth bringing, even though it resulted in a significant financial loss to him, because the court of appeals issued a ruling that the officer's Taser use was unconstitutional—a ruling that has been used in later cases to defeat qualified immunity. "We do [these cases] because they're important to do," Seitz said. But the members of Congress who enacted Section 1983 in 1871—and enacted Section 1988 a century later to ensure lawyers who brought successful civil rights cases were paid—surely did not expect that plaintiffs' attorneys would have to bankroll years-long efforts just to clarify the scope of constitutional rights.

———

DESPITE THE STRENGTH OF QUALIFIED IMMUNITY, ITS ARMOR MAY BE beginning to crack. If one had to pick a moment the ground began to shift, it would likely be June 19, 2017, when Supreme Court Justice Clarence Thomas wrote that the Court should "in an appropriate case . . . reconsider qualified immunity." It's not that Supreme Court justices hadn't criticized the defense before; in fact, just two years earlier, Justice Sonia

Sotomayor had complained that qualified immunity protects officers even when they violate the law and promotes a "'shoot first, think later' approach to policing." But Justice Sotomayor is one of the most liberal justices on the Court, outspoken on criminal justice issues. Justice Thomas, in contrast, is part of the Court's most conservative wing. His criticism of qualified immunity focused not on its impact on policing but, rather, on the Court's role: Justice Thomas argued that the Supreme Court's qualified immunity doctrine bore no resemblance to any immunity that existed in 1871, when Section 1983 became law, and instead reflected "precisely the sort of 'freewheeling policy choice[s]' that we have previously disclaimed the power to make."

Lower court judges appointed by every president elected since Jimmy Carter, Republican and Democrat, have offered scathing critiques of qualified immunity. Judge Don Willett, a Donald Trump appointee, has written that "qualified immunity smacks of unqualified impunity, letting public officials duck consequences for bad behavior—no matter how palpably unreasonable—as long as they were the *first* to behave badly." The doctrine is, Judge Willett writes, "an Escherian Stairwell. Heads government wins, tails plaintiff loses."

Legal scholars and advocacy groups across the ideological spectrum—including the ACLU, the NAACP Legal Defense Fund, the Cato Institute, and the Institute for Justice—have repeatedly petitioned the Supreme Court to abolish or reform qualified immunity doctrine. In its 2019–20 term, the Court took months to decide whether to agree to hear any of the more than one dozen qualified immunity petitions that were pending before it. Some took the Court's hesitation as a sign that it might finally revisit its qualified immunity decisions. But, in June 2020, the Supreme Court declined to hear all the pending qualified immunity cases on its docket.

It seemed that the Supreme Court might take no action on qualified immunity at all. But, on November 2, 2020, the Court issued a short, unsigned opinion in a case called *Taylor v. Riojas*, brought by a Texas prisoner who was kept in a pair of "shockingly unsanitary cells"—one of which was "covered, nearly floor to ceiling in massive amounts of feces"—for six days. The court of appeals granted the officers qualified immunity, but the Supreme Court reversed, explaining that "any reasonable officer should have realized that Taylor's conditions of confinement offended the Constitution."

Only once before had the Supreme Court ruled that qualified immunity could be denied in the absence of a prior court opinion on point. In that 2002 case, *Hope v. Pelzer*, the Court ruled that officers did not need to consult a court decision to know that it was wrong to leave a prisoner shackled to a hitching post all day beneath the Alabama sun: such conduct was obviously unconstitutional. Since 2002, the Court had only paid lip service to the notion that qualified immunity could be defeated without a prior case on point. The Court's unsigned opinion in *Taylor* revived the notion in *Hope* that qualified immunity could be denied if a constitutional violation is obvious, even if the precise fact pattern is novel. But the opinion did not indicate what impact *Taylor* should have—whether it was an extraordinary decision responsive to extraordinary facts that would be quickly ignored by the Court (as *Hope* had been), or whether it reflected a shift in the Court's thinking about qualified immunity.

In March 2021, the Supreme Court offered one more clue. The case before it was *McCoy v. Alamu*, in which a Texas prisoner, Prince McCoy, alleged that a corrections officer sprayed him in the face with a chemical agent "for no reason at all." When the court of appeals granted the officer qualified immunity in February 2020, it relied heavily on Supreme Court precedent, writing that "the pages of the *United States Reports* teem with warnings about the difficulty of showing that the law was clearly established" for qualified immunity purposes. But the Supreme Court vacated the circuit court's judgment and sent it back, instructing the circuit court to reconsider its decision in light of *Taylor*.

The Supreme Court did not write an opinion in *McCoy*; it merely issued a three-sentence summary disposition. But the Court's reliance on *Taylor* in its order in *McCoy* suggested that it does not see *Taylor* as an aberration. Instead, the Court appeared to be sending a message that lower courts could deny qualified immunity for clear misconduct, even without a case with identical facts.

———

THE SUPREME COURT'S DECISIONS IN *TAYLOR* AND *MCCOY* MIGHT ULtimately have been what saved Vicki Timpa's case against the Dallas police officers who knelt on the neck and back of her son, Tony, for more than fourteen minutes until he died. Vicki and her attorney, Geoff Henley, fought for more than six months for the body camera videos and other evidence documenting the night of Tony's death—evidence that allowed Henley to include facts in Vicki's complaint detailed enough to overcome *Iqbal*'s plausibility pleading standard and get to discovery. But in July 2020, six weeks after Derek Chauvin murdered George Floyd, the trial court dismissed Vicki's case.

The judge assumed that the officers who killed Tony violated the Constitution, but granted them qualified immunity because there was no prior court case holding that it was unconstitutional to restrain an unarmed person in a prone position for more than fourteen minutes or to stand by without stopping another officer from doing so. The court of appeals had previously found that officers used excessive force when they hog-tied a person—restraining his hands and feet together, behind his back—and placed him facedown, killing him. But the judge hearing Timpa's case concluded that that prior case did not "clearly establish" that what the officers did to Tony was unconstitutional. Although the officers handcuffed Tony's wrists, zip-tied his ankles, and placed him facedown in a prone position, the officers did not attach his ankle and wrist restraints. So, Tony was not hog-tied. Based in significant part on that minor factual distinction, the judge concluded the law was not clearly established and dismissed Vicki's case.

In December 2021, more than five years after Tony was killed, the court of appeals reversed the trial court's grant of qualified immunity and sent the case back for trial. Judge Don Willett, the Trump appointee who called qualified immunity an "Escherian Stairwell" and has been an outspoken and eloquent critic of the doctrine, was on the panel, although he did not write the opinion.

The court of appeals' decision in *Timpa v. Dillard* was a "shocker" to civil rights attorneys, given other qualified immunity decisions that have been issued by this conservative court. Perhaps the judges were compelled by a June 2021 Supreme Court decision that made clear that keeping someone in a prone position can violate the Constitution, or by evidence that the Dallas officers who killed Tony were trained about the dangers of this very maneuver. Perhaps the judges were moved by the similarities to George Floyd's murder, or by the sympathetic facts of Tony Timpa's case. Perhaps the judges were responding to widespread and growing criticisms of qualified immunity doctrine and the Supreme Court's decisions in *Taylor* and *McCoy*—both of which reversed qualified immunity decisions by the same court of appeals hearing Vicki Timpa's case. Whatever the reason, *Timpa v. Dillard* is an important decision that offers a glimmer of hope for people whose rights have been violated in this court of appeals' jurisdiction—Texas, Mississippi, and Louisiana.

This decision is of course also an enormous victory for Vicki Timpa. With the court of appeals' decision, Vicki did not win her lawsuit; she only won the right to go to trial. And Texas juries are notoriously hostile to plaintiffs in civil rights cases. But a trial promises some measure of justice, no matter the verdict. As Vicki told reporters after learning of the court of appeals win, "I look forward to having the trial. I've never had closure. I've just had lies."

The Supreme Court's decision in *Taylor* may mark a shift in qualified immunity doctrine, if it is understood by lower courts as an indication that the Court is stepping back from its most robust depictions of the doctrine's power. But so long as qualified immunity remains a defense officers can repeatedly raise, so long as there is no clear guidance about its limits, and so long as officers can immediately appeal any denial of its protections, this nonsensical and indefensible doctrine is going to continue to sabotage efforts by people like Jayzel Mattos, Ryan Cole, and Vicki Timpa to seek justice when their rights have been violated.

CHAPTER 6

SUING THE CITY

Those who study law enforcement have repeatedly and unequivocally concluded that individual acts of police violence and misconduct are the product of deeper, structural forces. Some believe that those structural forces are part and parcel of having a law enforcement system that grew out of slave patrols, and that it is impossible to have a police apparatus that is disentangled from that racist and violent history. Others view police misconduct less through a historical lens than through an institutional one, bred in the bureaucratic crevices of individual agencies. Either way, it is common wisdom that individual acts of police misconduct can't be wholly separated from the culture of a department or from leaders who encourage that misconduct or look the other way when it occurs. There may be bad apples, but they often come from rotten trees.

Local governments can be sued under Section 1983 if their policies or customs cause their officers to violate the Constitution. But the way in which the Supreme Court has interpreted local government liability—also called municipal liability—under Section 1983 makes it tremendously difficult to succeed in constitutional challenges to these types of institutional failures. Deeply and obviously dysfunctional police forces regularly escape liability for abuses by their officers. Case in point: Vallejo, California.

———

VALLEJO, A CITY OF ABOUT 120,000 PEOPLE THIRTY MILES NORTH OF Oakland, is one of the most racially diverse places in the entire country. As *The New York Times* put it in 2017, Vallejo "can seem like a respite from the divided nation . . . where black, white, Asian and Hispanic people not only coexist in nearly equal numbers, but actually connect." Vallejo is exceptional in another way as well: its mostly white police force is one of the deadliest in the United States.

Vallejo police officers killed nineteen people between 2010 and 2020. That's more than thirteen people per hundred thousand Vallejo residents. More people are shot by Vallejo police officers, per capita, than officers in any other city in Northern California. More people are killed by Vallejo police officers, per capita, than by officers in all but one of the hundred largest law enforcement agencies in the United States. A Pew Research Center survey of almost eight thousand police officers nationwide found that 27 percent had ever fired their weapons while on duty, and that number dropped to 23 percent for officers working in cities with fewer than 400,000 people. By contrast, as of August 2019, nearly 40 percent of the approximately one hundred officers on the Vallejo police force had been involved in at least one shooting, and more than one-third had been involved in two or more.

By my count, eighty-five Section 1983 lawsuits were filed against the City of Vallejo and its officers between 2010 and 2020. Although several of these lawsuits tell of shootings by Vallejo police officers, many more reveal gratuitous force used during routine stops and arrests—of officers beating people with batons; punching and kicking people in the head; slamming people into the concrete and against patrol car doors; and repeatedly tasing people when they posed little or no threat. Here are the allegations in ten of these lawsuits, filed over the course of just eight months in 2012:

On February 27, 2012, Joshua Deleon filed a lawsuit alleging that, while being arrested, a Vallejo police officer put him in a carotid restraint for so long that the blood vessels in both eyes popped and he passed out. The officer also allegedly slammed Deleon's head into the concrete, and tased him while he was in handcuffs.

On February 29, 2012, Toby Wilson filed a lawsuit alleging that Vallejo police forced entry into his home, tased him while he was asleep in his bed, ordered their police dog to attack him, and struck him in the face.

On March 6, 2012, Frederick Marc Cooley filed a lawsuit alleging that he was arrested and placed in handcuffs and then, while lying facedown, Vallejo officers beat him with a flashlight and slammed him, chin first, into the rear of a patrol car.

On May 14, 2012, Rahim Muhammad filed a lawsuit alleging that he was arrested and placed in handcuffs and then, while lying facedown, Vallejo police officers beat him with batons, and punched and kicked him in his head, back, and legs.

On May 29, 2012, Leroy Black filed a lawsuit alleging that he was standing by an ATM when a Vallejo police officer approached him. When he started running, the officer tased him from behind. When he fell, he broke his jaw and his teeth were knocked out. The officer allegedly said, "You better be glad I didn't shoot you."

On June 18, 2012, the daughter of Michael White filed a lawsuit alleging that her father had locked himself in the bathroom of a friend's house when four Vallejo officers broke into the bathroom, punched him, put him in a carotid hold, and repeatedly tased him. White died at the scene.

On July 30, 2012, Roosevelt Robinson filed a lawsuit alleging that a Vallejo officer struck him in the head and upper torso and stomped on the back of his head during the course of an arrest, chipping his tooth and breaking his chin.

Also on July 30, 2012, Dennis Gardner filed a lawsuit alleging that a Vallejo officer stopped him while he was walking down the street and told him to sit on the ground. When Gardner asked why, the officer tased him in the arm.

On September 24, 2012, Edwin Tayag filed a lawsuit alleging that a Vallejo officer, along with officers from neighboring departments, stepped on his head and face while he was having a psychotic episode, dislocating his jaw.

On October 12, 2012, Eric Nichols and Sara Foley filed a lawsuit alleging that they were in a crowd, watching Vallejo officers arrest two men, when one of the officers pushed Foley. An officer shot Nichols in the groin with his 37mm riot gun at close range, and then a second officer tased Nichols and a third officer beat him with his baton while he was on the ground.

During this same eight-month stretch of 2012, as people were filing Section 1983 lawsuits every month or so alleging excessive force, Vallejo officers shot and killed six people—accounting for nearly one-third of all people killed in Vallejo that year. Franklin Zimring, a criminologist and law professor at the University of California, Berkeley, who studies police killings, was appalled by that statistic. "If you were to ask me, have I ever heard in an American city of a situation in which the police force is responsible for 25 or 30 percent of total homicides in the community," Zimring said, "the answer is I haven't heard of that before, ever, and I would hope not to hear of it again."

Mario Romero was one of the six people killed by Vallejo police officers that deadly year. In the early morning hours of September 2, 2012, twenty-three-year-old Romero, who identified as Black, Indigenous, and Latino, pulled up to his family's Vallejo home with his sister's boyfriend, Joseph Johnson. At around the same time, Vallejo officers Sean Kenney and Dustin Joseph drove by. Kenney reportedly thought Romero's white Thunderbird looked similar to a car that had recently been involved in a drive-by shooting. Romero and Johnson had nothing to do with the shooting. But the officers stopped near their car, shined a spotlight on the men, and yelled at them to put their hands up. The officers claimed that Romero got out of the car and reached into his waistband for a gun. But Romero's family, watching from their living room window, saw the officers open fire into the Thunderbird as the men sat in the car, hands raised. Officer Kenney discharged his weapon so many times that he needed to reload; at one point he climbed onto the hood of the Thunderbird and shot repeatedly at the men through its front windshield. Johnson was shot but survived. Romero died at the scene, with thirty gunshot wounds to his head, neck, and torso. After killing Romero, Officer Kenney claimed that he found a pellet gun wedged between the rear part of the Thunderbird's driver's-side seat and the center console. But neither Romero's nor Johnson's fingerprints were found on that pellet gun.

One of Romero's friends, Jared Huey, a white seventeen-year-old, had been shot and killed by Vallejo police just a few months before. The officers said that Huey was pointing a gun at them when they shot him; witnesses said Huey had no gun and his hands were in the air. Romero's sister, Kris, remembers her brother grieving his friend and brooding on the circumstances of his death. "He put up his hands and they still shot him," Kris remembers Romero saying. "What if you put up your hands and they still shoot you?"

Mario Romero was one of three men Officer Kenney killed over a five-month period in 2012, and all three apparently had their hands up in surrender when they were shot. Three months before killing Romero, Kenney fatally shot Anton Barrett Sr., a forty-one-year-old Black man, when he had his hands in the air; Kenney later said that he thought the wallet Barrett had in his hand was a gun. Seven weeks after killing Romero, Kenney fatally shot Jeremiah Moore, a twenty-nine-year-old autistic white man who was, according to a next-door neighbor, naked and standing on the porch of his home with his hands raised when he was killed.

Between 2010 and 2018—when Officer Kenney left the Vallejo Police Department to open a law enforcement consulting and training company—Kenney shot five people and was named as a defendant in eight Section 1983 lawsuits. The City of Vallejo paid more than $2.5 million to settle five of these suits. But the district attorney never brought criminal charges against Officer Kenney, and the Vallejo Police Department never disciplined him. Instead, just months after killing Barrett, Romero, and Moore, Kenney was promoted.

Officer Kenney may sound like a particularly bad apple, but in the Vallejo Police Department he fit right in. Officer Kenney was part of a group known locally as the Fatal 14—fourteen Vallejo officers (out of the approximately one hundred officers on the force) who had been involved in more than one fatal shooting. The names of these fourteen officers can be found in virtually every use-of-force report, lawsuit, or misconduct allegation against Vallejo police between 2010 and 2020. Yet, during that decade, none of the Fatal 14 were criminally charged, disciplined, or fired by the Vallejo Police Department, and, like Kenney, several were promoted.

The Fatal 14 reportedly celebrated shootings at bars and backyard barbecues by bending the tips of their badges and called their modified star a "Badge of Honor." Although Vallejo officials initially denied that officers bent their badges after shootings, several former Vallejo officers have now confirmed the existence of that ritual, and at least seven Vallejo officers' badges have been seen with bent tips—including Kenney's. One officer, Steve Darden, has been involved in the killings of four people while on duty, two as primary shooter. The blunted edges of two of the prongs of Darden's star-shaped badge can be seen in the photograph taken for his promotion from officer to lieutenant. In 2019, Captain John Whitney, a twenty-year veteran of the department, raised concerns about the badge bending with Vallejo's city manager, mayor, and city attorney and pushed for an investigation. Instead, Captain Whitney was fired.

One member of the Vallejo Police Department told a reporter, "Some days I feel like I work with a bunch of thugs who take pleasure out of hurting people." But, as of yet, the City of Vallejo has escaped legal responsibility for the violence inflicted by its officers. The Supreme Court's decisions limiting municipal liability are a key reason why.

———

DONALD PAGE MOORE, THE CHICAGO ACLU ATTORNEY WHO REPRE-sented James and Flossie Monroe, was driven to understand and address the structural forces that led police abuses to occur. At the Chicago ACLU, Moore had been researching the Chicago Police Department's widespread practice of secret and unlawful detentions for two years when James Monroe was assaulted and arrested. Moore's research revealed that in 1956 alone approximately twenty thousand Chicago arrestees had been held incommunicado for at least seventeen hours, and two thousand had been held for forty-eight hours or more. Moore surely saw what happened to the Monroes as part of this larger trend. For Moore and other lawyers at the Chicago ACLU, Section 1983 suits, dormant for nearly a century, held the promise of creating financial and political pressures for the Chicago Police Department to change its detention practices.

The Monroes' case alleged not only that Frank Pape and the other officers who broke into James and Flossie Monroe's home should be sued under Section 1983 but that the City of Chicago could also be named as a defendant. The notion that employers should bear legal responsibility for harms caused by their employees while they are doing their jobs—called vicarious liability or *respondeat superior* liability—was commonplace in other areas of the law then, and remains so today. Vicarious liability recognizes that employers should be financially responsible for harms caused by their employees while doing their bidding; allows people who are injured to be paid from employers' deep pockets (instead of employees' shallow ones); and expects that employers faced with the financial consequences of their employees' misconduct will take steps to prevent similar harms from happening in the future.

In *Monroe*, the ACLU argued that these same values would be advanced if cities were held vicariously liable for the constitutional violations of their officers. As the ACLU wrote in its brief to the Supreme Court, "the community receives the benefits" of the police and other government operations and "should therefore pay the cost and spread the risk of injury from torts resulting from such municipal operations." It would also be unjust to require the officers who terrorized the Monroes to pay these costs themselves, argued the ACLU, because they were simply doing what was expected of them: assaulting suspects and holding them for hours at a time without the opportunity to consult a lawyer or judge was common practice in the Chicago Police Department. Holding the city liable was additionally important, the ACLU argued, because Frank Pape and the other officers who arrested and assaulted the Monroes were unlikely to have enough money to satisfy any settlement or judgment entered against them. And holding the City of Chicago responsible for the officers' conduct would, in the ACLU's words, "appl[y] deterrent pressures at the only level where they can be truly effective—the level of policy decision and command."

When the Supreme Court issued its landmark decision in *Monroe v. Pape*, it gave the Monroes only part of what they asked for: the opinion recognized a right to sue individual officers under Section 1983 but held that the City of Chicago could not be named as a defendant. In the Court's view, the 1871 Congress that enacted the Ku Klux Klan Act did not intend for cities and counties to be named as defendants under Section 1983.

Seventeen years later, in a case called *Monell v. Department of Social Services*, the Court reversed itself, reasoning that they got the legislative history wrong in their decision in *Monroe* and that cities and counties *could* be sued for constitutional violations. But the Supreme Court's decision in *Monell* still did not give the ACLU and the Monroes quite what they had wanted. Justice Brennan, writing for the majority, explained that local governments could not be held vicariously liable for constitutional violations committed by their officers. Instead, the local government had to have, in the Supreme Court's words, a "policy or custom" that "caused" the constitutional violation in order to be held responsible under Section 1983.

In its *Monell* decision, in 1978, the Supreme Court did not explain what amounted to a "policy or custom" that "caused" a constitutional violation, and wrote that it was "expressly leav[ing] further development" of Section 1983 claims against local governments "to another day." As the Supreme Court began to work out the standards for local government liability under *Monell*, the justices were "deeply divided"—as one Supreme Court opinion characterized it—about what the scope of liability should be. Disagreement about the benefits and risks of holding local governments accountable for the constitutional violations of their officers appears to have fueled this division on the Court.

The justices' disagreement about how easy it should be to sue cities was already apparent in a case decided in 1980, just two years after *Monell*. In that case, *Owen v. City of Independence*, the Supreme Court ruled that cities were not entitled to the protections of qualified immunity. Justice Brennan, writing for a five-justice majority, described the benefits of imposing liability on cities in the same optimistic terms as had the lawyers for James and Flossie Monroe:

> The threat that damages might be levied against the city may encourage those in a policymaking position to institute internal rules and programs designed to minimize the likelihood of unintentional

infringements on constitutional rights. Such procedures are particularly beneficial in preventing those "systemic" injuries that result not so much from the conduct of any single individual, but from the interactive behavior of several government officials, each of whom may be acting in good faith.

But the four dissenting justices in *Owen* envisioned a far bleaker picture when they imagined the effect *Monell* claims could have on local governments. Justice Powell, who authored the dissent in *Owen*, predicted that holding cities liable under Section 1983 without the protections of qualified immunity would allow "excessive judicial intrusion" into local government decision-making and "restrict the independence of local governments and their ability to respond to the needs of their communities"—the same concerns about federal courts intruding into state and local affairs that objectors to Section 1983 raised back in 1871. Justice Powell also feared that "many local governments lack the resources to withstand substantial unanticipated liability under § 1983" and that "ruinous judgments under the statute could imperil local governments."

These concerns appear to have won the day. Over the next forty years, the Supreme Court issued several opinions that developed the contours of Section 1983 claims against local governments. The standards the Court has set for *Monell* claims are as difficult to meet—and nonsensical—as the standards it has developed for qualified immunity. Justice Brennan's hopes that *Monell* claims might be used to prevent "'systemic' injuries" appear to have been drowned out by Justice Powell's fears of excessive judicial intrusion into local government decision-making and ruinous judgments.

———

THE SUPREME COURT'S *MONELL* CASES HAVE BEEN UNDERSTOOD TO support three different theories of municipal liability. First, local governments can be held liable under Section 1983 if they enact unconstitutional policies. Second, local governments can be held liable if a policy maker violates the Constitution in an area where they have "final policy-making authority." Third, local governments can be held liable under Section 1983 if they have an informal custom or policy so "persistent and widespread as to practically have the force of law" that causes the constitutional violation.

The first two theories of municipal liability are relatively straightforward, but because they require proof of wrongdoing by those at the highest levels of government, they are uncommonly relied upon. *Monell* itself involved an unconstitutional policy that required female New York City employees to take maternity leave. But local governments do not usually adopt policies that are unconstitutional on their face—a policy requiring officers to use excessive force, for example, or requiring officers to arrest people who exercise their First Amendment free speech rights. Final policy makers are also unlikely to violate the Constitution themselves—at least in the policing context. Police chiefs, for example, who make final policies for their departments, rarely are the ones arresting people or using force against them. Instead, it is usually police officers, sergeants, lieutenants, and detectives who do the searching, arresting, and assaulting complained of in Section 1983 lawsuits.

This is where the third theory of municipal liability comes in. When it is someone on the front lines—not the police chief—who has violated the Constitution, the Supreme Court has said that the government can be held liable only if a persistent and widespread policy or custom caused the violation. These types of *Monell* claims often allege that the government failed to properly screen, train, supervise, or discipline its officers. But to prove that these failures amount to a municipal policy or custom, the Supreme Court has said that the need for better hiring practices, training, supervision, or discipline must be so obvious that the government's failure to do more amounts to "deliberate indifference" to the rights of its citizens. A plaintiff must also show the government's failure was the "moving force" behind the constitutional violation. In the Court's 1989 decision announcing this standard, *City of Canton v. Harris*, Justice Byron White explained that a "lesser standard" would pose all the risks anticipated by Justice Powell in his 1980 dissent in *Owen*: it "would open municipalities to unprecedented liability under § 1983," "result in *de facto respondeat superior* liability on municipalities," and "engage the federal courts in an endless exercise of second-guessing municipal employee training programs."

In a footnote in *City of Canton v. Harris*, Justice White offered two ways a person might show that a police department's need for better training was so obvious that it amounted to deliberate indifference. First, a person can show deliberate indifference with evidence that "the police, in exercising their discretion, so often violate constitutional rights that the need for further training must have been plainly obvious to the city policy makers, who, nevertheless, are 'deliberately indifferent' to the need." In the alternative, if there is not a pattern of prior constitutional violations, the need for training can be obvious given the nature of the officer's responsibilities. For example, the *City of Canton* footnote explained, officers are given guns and know "to a moral certainty" that they will have to arrest fleeing felons. As a result, "the need to train officers in the constitutional limitations on the use of deadly force . . . can be said to be 'so obvious' that failure to do so could properly be characterized as 'deliberate indifference' to constitutional rights."

Twenty-two years later, in 2011, in a case called *Connick v. Thompson*, a slim majority of the Supreme Court interpreted that *City of Canton* footnote in a way that made these types of claims nearly impossible to prove.

———

IN 1985, TWENTY-SIX YEARS BEFORE THE SUPREME COURT DECIDED *Connick v. Thompson*, the New Orleans district attorney, Harry Connick Sr.—father of the singer Harry Connick Jr.—prosecuted John Thompson for a robbery and a murder he did not commit. The son of a prominent New Orleans business executive was shot and killed in front of his home on the morning of December 6, 1984. A man approached the family—after they announced a $15,000 award for information leading to the murderer's conviction—and accused Thompson of the crime. Thompson was arrested for the murder based on this tip, even though an eyewitness had described the shooter as a six-foot-tall Black man with "close cut hair" and Thompson was five feet, eight inches tall and had a large Afro. When Thompson's photo was published in the paper, three siblings who had been robbed at gunpoint on December 28, 1984, identified Thompson as their assailant. So Connick's office prosecuted Thompson for that robbery as well.

Connick's team of prosecutors decided to take the robbery case to trial first. They predicted that Thompson would not take the stand in the murder trial if he was convicted on the robbery charge because prosecutors could use the robbery conviction to impeach his credibility, and that the robbery conviction would strengthen the prosecution's case for the death penalty if Thompson was convicted of the murder.

The prosecution's strategy had one major flaw: forensic evidence that Thompson was not the robber. A blood sample taken from the pant leg of one of the robbery victims showed that the robber had a different blood type from Thompson. Prosecutors have a constitutional obligation to turn over exculpatory evidence—evidence that is favorable to a criminal defendant—and this obligation is clearly set out in a 1963 Supreme Court decision called *Brady v. Maryland*. But Connick's prosecutors never shared this critically important exculpatory evidence with Thompson's legal team. One of the prosecutors checked the fabric swatch out of the property room on the morning of the first day of trial but never produced it at trial or returned it to the property room. The swatch has never been found.

Thompson was convicted of robbery. As the prosecutors had hoped and expected, he did not take the stand in the murder trial, and he was convicted and sentenced to death. In 1999, just one month before Thompson was scheduled to be executed, his lawyer's investigator came across a microfiche copy of a lab report that showed it was not Thompson's blood on the fabric swatch recovered from the scene of the robbery. Based on this lab report, Thompson's robbery conviction was vacated. Because the murder conviction relied heavily on the robbery conviction, the murder conviction was reversed as well. Connick retried Thompson for the murder, and the jury deliberated for just thirty-five minutes before finding him not guilty. Thompson then sued for his years of wrongful imprisonment.

Thompson brought a Section 1983 case against Harry Connick Sr. in his official capacity as Orleans Parish district attorney—equivalent, in legal terms, to bringing a *Monell* claim directly against the government. A jury ruled in Thompson's favor and awarded him $14 million—as *The New York Times* put it, "$1 million for every year he was isolated for 23 hours a day in a windowless cell, awaiting his execution." But a five-justice Supreme Court majority overturned the jury's $14 million jury verdict in 2011.

In 1989, in the *City of Canton* footnote, the Supreme Court had explained that a local government's decision not to train its armed police officers about the limits of deadly force would amount to deliberate indifference to the constitutional rights of its residents. Thompson showed at trial that Harry Connick Sr.'s office had done next to nothing to educate his prosecutors about their obligations under *Brady*—among the most critical constitutional protections prosecutors must abide. The sum total of its guidance about *Brady* was four sentences in the office's policy manual, and even those sentences were inaccurate, incomplete, and out-of-date. But Justice Clarence Thomas, writing for the majority in *Connick*, concluded that it was not "obvious" that the district attorney needed to train his prosecutors about their *Brady* obligations given that prosecutors were accustomed to researching the law and had ethical obligations to research the law when they had questions.

Justice Thomas's reasoning was clearly tinged with the concern, first raised by opponents of Section 1983 in 1871, that a more lenient standard for *Monell* liability would allow too much federal court intrusion into local decision-making. As he wrote, the fact that "additional training would have been helpful in making difficult decisions does not establish municipal liability," because Section 1983 "does not provide plaintiffs or courts *carte blanche* to micromanage local governments throughout the United States."

The only other way Thompson could show deliberate indifference by the prosecutor was if he could show a pattern of prior, similar constitutional violations. And, in fact, Thompson showed at trial that the District Attorney's Office had a pattern of failing to turn over evidence to defendants; *Brady* violations had resulted in four overturned convictions out of Connick's office over the ten years preceding Thompson's armed robbery trial. But, according to Justice Thomas and the other four justices in the majority, those four overturned convictions were not enough to put Harry Connick Sr. on notice of the need for better training, because the other *Brady* violations were not similar enough to the *Brady* violation in Thompson's case. As Justice Thomas explained, "None of those cases involved failure to disclose blood evidence, a crime lab report, or physical or scientific evidence of any kind."

Connick's interpretation of the "failure to train" standard has disturbing conceptual parallels to the Court's qualified immunity decisions. The Supreme Court has instructed courts to grant qualified immunity to officers unless the plaintiff can find a prior court decision holding nearly identical conduct to be unconstitutional. Local governments are not protected by qualified immunity, but cannot be held responsible under Section 1983 for inadequately training their employees unless equally elusive evidence of nearly identical prior constitutional violations would have put city officials on notice of the risk of future violations. Both standards—for municipal liability and for qualified immunity—have exceptions for "obvious" constitutional violations, but in both cases the Supreme Court has described those exceptions as so narrow that they appear, for all practical purposes, not even to exist.

———

THE SUPREME COURT'S *MONELL* CASES HAVE MADE IT EXTREMELY DIF-ficult to prove that local governments should be held responsible for the constitutional violations of their officers. But the challenges of proving local government responsibility shape every stage of the case.

First, think about drafting the complaint. Before getting to discovery—where a plaintiff might be able to unearth evidence about prior misconduct or hiring decisions—they first must set out sufficient facts that state a "plausible" entitlement to relief, according to Justice Kennedy's majority decision in *Iqbal*. It is not enough to say that there is an unconstitutional policy, practice, or custom. The plaintiff also has to include evidence of a policy unconstitutional on its face, or a decision to hire someone whose past conduct made it highly likely that they would violate the Constitution in the manner that they did, or past incidents of misconduct so similar that they made the need for additional training or supervision obvious. But at the complaint drafting stage, a person who claims their rights have been violated does not have access to evidence of internal policies, or hiring decisions, or past allegations and investigations of misconduct. That is precisely what discovery is for.

Some people have gotten past this standard at the motion-to-dismiss stage by including evidence in their complaint that a number of civil rights lawsuits were filed in the past. But there can be troubled departments without a long record of civil rights lawsuits—particularly in parts of the country with few lawyers willing to take these types of cases. And, even if a number of lawsuits have previously been filed, a person who does not have a lawyer is going to have a difficult time trying to find them.

Now, think about the challenges of discovery and proof if the plaintiff can make it past the pleading stage. To win a *Monell* claim, a plaintiff must first show that their constitutional rights were violated by the officer. Then they must show that the local government's policy or custom caused that violation. Often, the *Monell* theory is that the local government was deliberately indifferent to the need to better train, supervise, or discipline that officer—which nearly always requires finding a pattern of prior, similar constitutional violations. And to establish that pattern, the plaintiff must find evidence of prior, similar conduct *and* evidence that that prior conduct was unconstitutional.

The Supreme Court has not clarified what can serve as evidence of prior constitutional violations sufficient to put police chiefs on notice that their officers need better training or supervision. But there are not that many options. In most cities, internal affairs divisions rarely sustain allegations of officer misconduct. Officers are even less likely to be convicted of crimes. Proof of prior constitutional violations could come from past Section 1983 lawsuits. But how can these lawsuits be used as proof of constitutional violations? The complaint that begins the case contains allegations of unconstitutional conduct, not proof. When a plaintiff "succeeds" in their civil rights case, it is usually through a settlement, and settlement agreements tend to include provisions that the defendants do not acknowledge any wrongdoing. Judges rarely issue decisions that rule one way or another about whether an officer's conduct was unconstitutional; instead, court opinions tell the parties whether the plaintiff has done enough to get to the next stage of litigation. Most often, when there is an announcement that an officer's conduct is unconstitutional, it comes from a jury, but civil rights cases rarely go to a jury, and even more rarely do those jury trials result in plaintiffs' verdicts.

———

IN ONLY ONE OF THE EIGHTY-FIVE SECTION 1983 LAWSUITS ALLEGING constitutional violations by the City of Vallejo filed between 2010 and 2020 did a *Monell* claim withstand a summary judgment motion; the case settled before trial. Even in Vallejo, the challenges of proving an unconstitutional policy or custom of failing to train and supervise officers have been too great.

The lawyers retained by Joseph Johnson and the family of Mario Romero, who were shot by Vallejo officers Kenney and Joseph while sitting in Romero's white Thunderbird in September 2012, tried admirably to prove their *Monell* claim. They hired Berkeley Law School professor Franklin Zimring to examine all available data about Vallejo. Zimring concluded that the rate of shootings in Vallejo was far higher than most cities, including much larger cities like New York and Chicago. According to Zimring,

> The volume of killings in the spring and early summer [of 2012] was astonishing for a city of 117,000. A fatal shooting by police on May 24, 2012 was followed four days later by a second police killing on May 28, 2012. The next killing by on-duty police was recorded on June 30 and yet another killing five days after that on July 4, 2012. Four separate fatalities within three months in a city of 117,000. All of these events were unilateral in that no shots were fired or other wounds inflicted by the targets of the police shootings.

As troubling to Zimring as the high number of shootings was the fact that Vallejo's police chief did not seem to think that they indicated a broader problem. The chief testified during his deposition that he had reviewed each of the shootings but had made no changes in training in response to any of them and disciplined none of the officers involved. Zimring explained that the chief

> didn't see a pattern in this collection of events because he wasn't open to noticing a pattern. He testified in deposition he would only consider each event individually rather than possibly as a pattern involving large numbers of officers with changes in attitudes and practices. His reaction to a fatal shooting was to encourage the

officer who was responsible to see a marriage and family therapist with a clinical background in post-traumatic stress disorder.

By failing to see a broader pattern in the shootings, and by failing to discipline or retrain the involved officers after the shootings, the chief, plaintiffs argued, was deliberately indifferent to the risk of more violence and shootings, and this deliberate indifference caused the shooting of Romero and Johnson.

But federal judge John Mendez, after reviewing all of this evidence, granted summary judgment to Vallejo. Judge Mendez acknowledged "evidence of some systemic issues" within the Vallejo Police Department and appeared troubled by the fact that Vallejo officers "shot and killed four people in the span of just three months in the middle of 2012" yet the department "deduced no pattern and made no changes in training in response." But Judge Mendez found that that evidence did not "meet the extremely stringent legal standards required for claims under *Monell*." Why? Because the Vallejo Police Department's internal affairs investigations of each of those shootings found no constitutional violation. None of the officers were criminally prosecuted. And none of the other lawsuits brought by the victims of the people killed by Vallejo officers had resulted in a jury verdict for the plaintiff. So Joseph Johnson and Mario Romero's family could not prove that the past shootings and killings by Vallejo police officers were unconstitutional. And, as a result, they could not show that the Vallejo police chief's failure to train his officers differently following these shootings and killings amounted to a "deliberate indifference" to the risk that his officers would violate the Constitution in the future.

Judge Mendez recognized "the difficult task facing Plaintiffs who wish to bring a claim for failure to train" because it is difficult to find proof that the prior shootings were unconstitutional absent a court's ruling. "The constitutionality of police conduct is often not determined by an unbiased entity until years after the conduct has occurred," he explained. "Nevertheless," he concluded, "some evidence of constitutional violations is required to maintain the *Monell* claim in this case." And evidence of the extremely high number of shootings and the failure to discipline or retrain the officers was not, in the judge's mind, sufficient.

In addition to the evidence offered by the plaintiffs in opposition to summary judgment in *Johnson v. Vallejo*, Judge Mendez had firsthand knowledge of a pattern of substantial claims of constitutional violations by Vallejo police. Between 2010 and 2020, Mendez was the presiding judge for eighteen of the eighty-five civil rights cases filed against the City of Vallejo and its officers. Between 2010 and April 14, 2015, when he granted Vallejo summary judgment in the *Johnson* case, ten civil rights cases against the City of Vallejo were assigned to him—including the case brought by the family of Jared Huey, Mario Romero's seventeen-year-old friend who was shot and killed by Vallejo police a few months before Romero was, and which ultimately settled for $160,000.

At the time Judge Mendez granted summary judgment to the City of Vallejo in *Johnson*, he was also presiding over civil rights suits brought by the families of Anton Barrett and Jeremiah Moore—the two other people Officer Sean Kenney shot and killed in 2012, in the months before and after he shot and killed Mario Romero. When he granted the City of Vallejo summary judgment in *Johnson*, on April 14, 2015, Judge Mendez had already found that the case brought by the family of Jeremiah Moore adequately stated a claim against Kenney and the City of Vallejo, and was almost certainly drafting the summary judgment decision in the case brought by the family of Anton Barrett, denying Officer Kenney summary judgment. The case brought by Anton Barrett's family settled for $235,000 three months after Judge Mendez granted summary judgment to the City of Vallejo in *Johnson*, and the case brought by Jeremiah Moore's family settled a year later for $250,000. Judge Mendez did not reference either of these cases—or any of the other civil rights cases against Vallejo and its officers that he had heard—when he granted the City of Vallejo's summary judgment motion in *Johnson v. Vallejo*. In ignoring this other evidence, Judge Mendez was following the law.

TWO AND A HALF MONTHS AFTER JUDGE MENDEZ ISSUED HIS DECI-
sion in *Johnson v. Vallejo*, dismissing the case against the City of Vallejo,
Joseph Johnson and Mario Romero's family settled their Section 1983
claims against Officers Kenney and Joseph for $2 million. California—
like many states across the country—has what is called an indemnification statute that obligates local governments to pay settlements and
judgments entered against their officers. So, Vallejo indemnified their officers and paid their $2 million settlement. If Johnson and Romero's fam-
ily received $2 million from Vallejo, does it actually matter that their
Monell claim was dismissed? Does it actually matter that the standard for
proving *Monell* claims is so difficult to meet? It does, for several reasons.

Sometimes it is impossible to win a judgment or settlement against
the people who directly violate the Constitution. In *Connick v. Thompson*,
the prosecutors who withheld evidence could not be sued personally under
Section 1983, because prosecutors are afforded absolute immunity—
meaning that they cannot be sued for *anything* they do in their role as
prosecutors. In other words, when Thompson's *Monell* claim was dismissed
by the Supreme Court, there was no one else he could recover from. The
same is true when officers are granted qualified immunity: If the claims
against the officers are dismissed because there is no prior court opinion
with nearly identical facts, the only way to recover is through a *Monell*
claim. And if the *Monell* claim is dismissed because there is no pattern of
prior, similar conduct that has been proven unconstitutional, then there
is no way to recover under Section 1983.

A *Monell* claim can also be a person's only hope when a city refuses
to indemnify the officer who violated the Constitution. Although officers
are almost always indemnified, governments do sometimes turn their backs
on officers who have egregiously abused their power. When they do, victims are often left empty-handed. When, for example, four Latina women
sued a Houston police officer who raped them in late 2010 and early 2011,

the City of Houston refused to indemnify the officer. The officer did not appear in court to defend himself, and the judge entered a default judgment against him for $3.6 million, awarding $900,000 to each of the four women he raped. But the officer—who is serving two life sentences and is not eligible for parole until 2042—presumably will never have the money to pay those judgments.

The women also sued the city and had plenty of evidence of sexual misconduct by other Houston police officers to support their *Monell* claim. In the six years before the officer had raped the four women, the city had received at least fifty complaints of sexual misconduct against Houston police officers, including twenty complaints involving "forcible sexual assault by an on-duty officer," and eight of those complaints were sustained by the department. In the view of the judge who heard the case, "the facts that the City hired [the officer] and that his crimes went undetected for so long provoke anger" and the plaintiffs and the public "deserve the City's answers to the questions this lawsuit raises, such as how this was allowed to happen and whether there are ways to make it less likely." But these questions would not be answered through the plaintiffs' civil rights suit: the judge concluded that there was not enough evidence to support a *Monell* claim "under current case law." After the officer's criminal conviction, the prosecutors publicly thanked one of the four women who had been the first to come forward and had testified against the officer for three days at his criminal trial. "Without her, who would know the extent of the damage to the city?" one of the prosecutors told the *Houston Chronicle* in October 2012. But because the city refused to indemnify the officer, and the judge dismissed the *Monell* claim against the City of Houston, she and the other three women recovered nothing for the violation of their constitutional rights.

The challenges of proving a *Monell* claim also matter because a judgment against the government may have a greater impact. As the ACLU argued in its brief to the Supreme Court in *Monroe v. Pape*, holding a city responsible for its officers' conduct may be the only way to encourage high-ranking city officials to take action. Even though indemnification requirements mean that the City of Vallejo already bears the financial consequences of successful Section 1983 suits against its officers—it paid an estimated $16 million between 2010 and 2020 to resolve lawsuits against its police officers—those payouts do not seem to be having enough of an effect. A ruling that Vallejo has a custom or policy of violating people's constitutional rights could be the basis for a court order requiring Vallejo to change its policies and practices. Even without this type of court order, a finding that Vallejo violated the Constitution might create additional political pressures that could help hasten meaningful change.

———

ON JUNE 2, 2020, AS PROTESTS OF GEORGE FLOYD'S MURDER WERE taking over the streets and airwaves, Vallejo officers were called to a local Walgreens where there were reports of looting. As soon as Vallejo police officer Jarrett Tonn arrived, he shot and killed Sean Monterrosa, a twenty-two-year-old Latino man who was kneeling with his hands raised in the Walgreens parking lot. Officer Tonn had been sitting in the backseat of an unmarked Vallejo police truck and shot Monterrosa five times through the windshield with an AR-15 rifle. Monterrosa was struck once in the back of the head. After the shooting, body camera recordings captured Officer Tonn shouting, "Fucking stupid! This is not what I fucking needed tonight." A captain at the scene can be heard telling Tonn, "You're going to be all right. We've been through this before." It was the fourth time Officer Tonn had shot someone while on duty.

The captain's confidence that everything would be all right for Officer Tonn was understandable but mislaid. Public outcry led the California attorney general to open an investigation and the police department to commission an independent review of Monterrosa's killing. In December 2021, the independent investigators issued a report concluding that Officer Tonn violated department policy when he shot Monterrosa, and the chief notified Tonn that he would be fired. In May 2022, the decision to fire Tonn was overturned in a mandatory appeal hearing, and he got his job back.

Of course, Vallejo's problems would not have been solved by firing or prosecuting Officer Tonn. It is not enough to discard a rotten apple when there is a rotten tree. And there are continuing efforts to get at the root causes of the problems that plague Vallejo's police. The California Department of Justice is overseeing police department reforms in Vallejo. City council meetings are filled with people who are calling for change, including family members of those killed and hurt by Vallejo officers. There have been profiles of Vallejo in *The New Yorker* and *The Guardian* and on CNN, drawing public attention to the problems in this Northern California city.

Several civil rights attorneys continue to bring *Monell* claims against Vallejo in an effort to pressure reforms in its police department and some of those cases describe the officers' "badge of honor" ritual and the city's "decades long pattern and practice of misconduct among its officers" as proof of an unwritten policy or custom of impunity. It may be that the mountain of evidence against Vallejo has grown so precipitously that plaintiffs will be able to meet the *Monell* standard in the Section 1983 lawsuit brought by Sean Monterrosa's family or in some other case in the future. But people have been bringing *Monell* claims against the City of Vallejo for a long time, and as of yet no judge or jury has found a constitutional violation by the city.

Even if a judge does allow a *Monell* claim against Vallejo to move forward in the future, it will have been too late for the people already abused and killed by its officers. The Supreme Court's *Monell* standard has let police shootings, bent badges, and gratuitous violence continue without legal consequences for Vallejo—and excuses similarly deep-seated dysfunction and corruption in departments across the country.

CHAPTER 7

JUDGES

The twenty-nine-page complaint in *Tolan v. Cotton* was filed in Houston's boxy federal courthouse on Friday, May 1, 2009. Its pages told a story that had made headlines around the country four months earlier: Robbie Tolan—a Black minor-league baseball player and son of the Major League center fielder Bobby Tolan—had been shot by a white police officer in front of his home.

Bobby Tolan was a member of the St. Louis Cardinals when they won the World Series in 1967, batted second behind Pete Rose for the Cincinnati Reds, and played for the San Diego Padres, the Philadelphia Phillies, and the Pittsburgh Pirates before coaching in the major and minor leagues. In the early 1990s, Bobby retired from professional baseball and, with his wife, Marian, and son, Robert—whom everyone calls Robbie—moved to Bellaire, Texas, a city of eighteen thousand people set within the sprawl of Greater Houston. It has an upscale, small-town feel and an abundance of parks. It was, the Tolans thought, a great place to raise their only child.

Robbie followed in his father's footsteps. A star baseball player at Bellaire High School, he played for Prairie View A&M and then signed with the Washington Nationals and played on their minor-league team in 2007 and 2008. During the off-season, Robbie worked as a waiter at a Houston seafood restaurant and lived with his parents in Bellaire.

The allegations in *Tolan v. Cotton* focus on the early morning of December 31, 2008. On the evening of December 30, Robbie reported to work at the restaurant but learned he was not needed, so he and his cousin, Anthony Cooper, who also lived with the Tolans, went out for the evening. They played some pool, got a bite to eat, and bought some champagne for their planned New Year's Eve celebration with the family the next night. At about 2:00 a.m., Robbie and Anthony pulled up to their home in the family's SUV. As they were walking to the front door with their bags of food and unopened champagne, Bellaire police officer John Edwards approached with his gun drawn and ordered them to get on the ground. When Robbie and Anthony asked why, Edwards accused them of having stolen their car.

Bobby and Marian, hearing the commotion, came out of the front door of their home, still in their pajamas. Bobby told his son and nephew to get on the ground as the officer had ordered and to let him and Marian handle the situation. Robbie and Anthony got on the ground. Then Bobby raised his hands in the air and tried to reason with Officer Edwards, telling him that this was their home, that was their car, Robbie was their son, and Anthony was their nephew. Officer Edwards either did not believe him or did not care. He pointed his gun at Bobby and told him to lean against his Chevy Suburban, which was parked in his driveway.

At around this time, Bellaire sergeant Jeffrey Wayne Cotton arrived on the scene and emerged from his patrol car with his gun drawn. Sergeant Cotton ordered Marian Tolan to get against the wall. She responded by saying that they had done nothing wrong and that the officers were making a big mistake. Sergeant Cotton approached Marian, grabbed her by the arm, and threw her against her own garage door.

Robbie got to his knees and yelled, "Get your fucking hands off my mom!" Without warning, Cotton shot Robbie in the chest. Cotton had been on the scene for approximately thirty-two seconds when he fired his gun.

An ambulance was called for Robbie. Anthony was put in handcuffs, and he, Bobby, and Marian were put in separate patrol cars. As Marian was praying for the life of her son, a Bellaire police officer told her to "keep it down." Robbie was conscious as he was being wheeled into the ambulance and heard Sergeant Cotton say to other officers on the scene, "We have to get our stories straight."

Robbie Tolan survived the night but would spend almost a month in the hospital. Cotton's bullet is still lodged in his liver. He will never play professional baseball again.

Marian's sister worked for an attorney, and the morning after Robbie was shot, Marian met with that attorney and two of his colleagues in a conference room at the hospital. She asked the lawyers, "Are you ready to fight? Because I'm not taking this lying down." They assured her that they were.

The Tolans' Section 1983 complaint alleged that the officers' stop, arrest, and use of force violated the Fourth Amendment rights of Robbie, his parents, and Anthony. The complaint also alleged that what happened to Robbie and Anthony was part of a broader pattern.

The Tolans had never had bad experiences with the Bellaire police. But, at the time, fewer than 2 percent of Bellaire's population was Black, and many of the 270 or so Black residents of the predominantly white town had stories to tell—of police pulling them over for expired inspection stickers (when they were not expired), unlit license plates (when the light above the license plate worked), or not wearing seat belts (when they were). In December 2008, a Bellaire police officer approached a Black man putting Christmas lights on his home and asked if the "owner" knew what he was doing. As lawyers for the Tolans wrote in their complaint, "Bellaire police officers have a pattern, practice, and custom of approaching any African-American male found within the city limits and asking them some variation of, 'What are you doing here?'"

On May 1, 2009, when the complaint was filed, it was randomly as-signed to a federal district court judge named Melinda Harmon, an ap-pointee of President George H. W. Bush's. As Robbie Tolan recounts in his memoir, *No Justice*, his lawyers told him that "she had a reputation of throwing out just about every civil rights case she ever received." Accord-ing to the Tolans' lawyers, "If you were looking for someone to advocate for the civil rights of citizens over the police, then this was a worst-case scenario."

———

TRIAL COURT JUDGES ARE AMONG THE MOST POWERFUL PLAYERS IN litigation. It was not always so. One hundred years ago, either judges dis-missed cases at the get-go, or the cases went to trial. The role of judges was to clear out the cases that could not make it over the first hurdle of pleading, and then juries generally took on the task of deciding who had the stronger case. With the advent of the Federal Rules of Civil Procedure, in 1938, there became much more for judges to do.

Since its 1961 decision in *Monroe*, the Supreme Court has issued de-cisions that make it more difficult for people bringing Section 1983 cases to succeed. But these decisions are not self-executing. Instead, the Court's pleading standards in *Iqbal*, its interpretations of the Fourth Amendment, and its qualified immunity and *Monell* decisions are interpreted and ap-plied by hundreds of federal judges across the country each year. The ways in which judges apply these rules in civil rights cases can mean the differ-ence between victory and defeat.

The influence of judges over the path of civil rights litigation is not limited to these big-ticket issues. Judges are charged with making all sorts of decisions that cannot formally end a case but can make a huge differ-ence in how and whether it moves forward. They decide whether a wit-ness can be deposed, whether a party can get all the documents that they have requested from the other side, and who bears the burden of paying for the costs of retrieving those documents. They decide whether to allow plaintiffs to amend their complaints to add new claims or defendants. Judges decide the questions prospective jurors should be asked before they are impaneled. They decide which witnesses should be allowed to testify and what evidence juries can hear. They decide what instructions jurors should be given before settling in to deliberate. Judges decide whether to overturn a jury's verdict, reduce a jury's award, or order a new trial. They decide how much to award in attorneys' fees to plaintiffs who win their cases—how many hours were reasonably spent by the lawyers, and what the lawyers' reasonable hourly rates should be.

Trial court judges have tremendous discretion when making these momentous decisions. The Federal Rules of Civil Procedure are filled with "mays" and "shoulds," not "musts" and "wills." And, once made, these decisions are very difficult to challenge. Most decisions in civil rights cases—besides denials of qualified immunity—cannot be appealed until the end of the case. Once an appeal is filed, the standard for reversal is hard to meet; the losing party often must show that the trial court judge abused their vast discretion and that the result of the case would be different if the court had ruled the other way. Appeals can also be expensive, which can mean more money down the drain for a plaintiff's lawyer representing a client on contingency. For all of these reasons, what the trial court says often goes.

And judges' views vary. How a trial court rules on both momentous and mundane issues may depend a great deal on which judge you happen to get. Given recent fights on Capitol Hill about Supreme Court appointments, this should come as no surprise. Whenever a new justice is confirmed, and particularly when that justice is replacing another with a different ideological bent—as when Amy Coney Barrett took the seat previously occupied by Ruth Bader Ginsburg, or when Clarence Thomas took the seat previously occupied by Thurgood Marshall—the Supreme Court's stance on abortion, religious liberties, voting rights, criminal justice, and a whole range of other hot-button issues are thrown into question. Trial court judges' perspectives can vary as widely as have Thurgood Marshall's and Clarence Thomas's, and trial court judges decide cases on their own, without having to convince any other judge of the sensibility of their decision (except, perhaps, if it is appealed).

For many plaintiffs' civil rights lawyers, finding out which judge has been assigned to their case is among the most momentous pieces of information they learn about their case. As a lawyer practicing in Florida explained to me, "If you get a certain judge, you think, 'All right, I'm going to survive summary judgment.' Other judges you get, you think, 'All right, I know . . . I'm going to have a summary judgment against me and I'm going to have to file at [the court of appeals] and get it reversed.'"

Studies of judicial decision-making bear out this impression. Analysis of thousands of qualified immunity decisions revealed that judges appointed by Republican presidents are more likely to grant qualified immunity than judges appointed by Democratic presidents, and judges located in more Republican-leaning regions of the country are more likely to grant qualified immunity. Studies have also found that judges' personal characteristics may influence their decisions: white judges grant summary judgment to defendants in employment discrimination cases more often than judges of color, and court of appeals judges with daughters are more sympathetic to female plaintiffs in employment discrimination cases than are those without.

Beyond which president nominated them, or where in the country they sit, or their gender or race, what judges believe about the way the world works may influence how they rule in Section 1983 cases. For example, in 2021, during an oral argument, Supreme Court Chief Justice John Roberts mused that "if somebody, you know, takes off and runs away when you say you're going to, you know, arrest them for littering . . . he's got something to hide." Five years earlier, in 2016, the highest court in Massachusetts reached the opposite conclusion. Relying on a report documenting racial profiling in Boston, the Massachusetts Supreme Judicial Court concluded that running from the police does not necessarily give officers good cause to think something is amiss: a Black man might as easily be motivated to run from the police "by the desire to avoid the re-curring indignity of being racially profiled as by the desire to hide crimi-nal activity." Different judges can reach different conclusions about the implications that can reasonably be drawn from the same facts, and those differences in perspective can lead one judge to grant a summary judg-ment motion that another judge would deny.

What a judge believes about the dynamics of civil rights litigation also likely matters. Remember Marvin Aspen, an attorney for the City of Chicago, who, in 1966, warned Northwestern law students that plaintiffs' attorneys were bringing frivolous Section 1983 cases against the Chicago police with the hope of "making a quick buck"? Thirteen years after of-fering this warning, Aspen became a federal trial judge in Chicago, em-powered to rule on the merits of these cases. Remember Judge Ruggero Aldisert, who, in 1973, wrote with concern that Section 1983 had "made the federal court a nickel and dime court"? Aldisert was a federal court of appeals judge from 1968 to 2014 and must have ruled on hundreds of is-sues that arose in Section 1983 cases. Remember Judge Paul Niemeyer, who wrote in a 1998 article that more than 80 percent of litigation costs are spent on discovery—a commonly cited figure he acknowledged had no empirical basis, but nevertheless raised concerns for him that "the sys-tem pays too high a price for the policy of full disclosure in civil litiga-tion"? Niemeyer became a federal judge in 1988 and remains on the bench. If a judge believes that most civil rights suits are frivolous, they may be more likely to grant a motion to dismiss because the complaint does not state a plausible entitlement to relief. If a judge believes Section 1983 has turned federal courts into "nickel and dime" courts, they may be ungenerous in their assessment of reasonable attorneys' fees under Section 1988, especially when the jury's award was modest. If a judge be-lieves that plaintiffs' lawyers regularly abuse tools of discovery to force defendants to settle, they may be less likely to order defendants to turn over documents that they argue should be kept private.

In many instances, it is impossible to know what judges believe about the fundamental nature of policing or civil rights litigation, and impossible to track the role that those beliefs play in their rulings. But as a civil rights case makes its way from beginning to end, there are many moments when judges can exercise their discretion and power in ways that may lead to different opinions and different outcomes, depending on the judge. For judges skeptical of Section 1983 suits against law enforcement, there are countless opportunities to erect additional shields or strengthen shields that already exist in ways that protect officers from discovery, trial, and liability.

———

ON MAY 28, 2009, FOUR WEEKS AFTER THE TOLANS FILED THEIR COM-plaint, the defendants filed what is called an answer—a response to each of the plaintiffs' allegations. In their answer, the defendants acknowl-edged that Sergeant Cotton had shot Tolan but claimed that the shooting was justified because Tolan was threatening the officers. Cotton and Ed-wards also made clear that they were not seeking to get the claims against them dismissed on qualified immunity, but that they reserved their right to raise that defense at a later time.

In early June 2009, the Tolans' lawyers sought Cotton's and Edwards's personnel records from their former police employers, records from the state agency that trains and accredits law enforcement officers, and rec-ords concerning Cotton's service in the U.S. Navy. The Tolans' lawyers had learned that Cotton had served in the navy for ten months—shorter than the shortest enlistment obligation, suggesting that he might have been dishonorably discharged. Under Texas law, people cannot serve as law enforcement officers if they have been discharged from the military under less than honorable conditions, so if Cotton had been prematurely discharged from the navy and was then hired by Bellaire, that fact could support the Tolans' *Monell* claim against the city.

Cotton's and Edwards's lawyers asked Judge Harmon to rule that the Tolans were not entitled to any of this information because the officers might raise a qualified immunity defense in the future. This was a highly unusual request. The Supreme Court has described qualified immunity as intended to shield defendants from the costs and burdens of discovery. Judges sometimes halt discovery while a qualified immunity motion is pending. But Cotton and Edwards had not even argued that they were entitled to qualified immunity, only that they might make that argument in the future. What's more, the Tolans were requesting records that were not in the officers' possession, so there would be no litigation-related cost or burden to Edwards or Cotton if their former employers produced that information. And the evidence the Tolans' sought was relevant to their *Monell* claim against Bellaire, not their claims against the officers.

Judge Harmon referred the matter to a magistrate judge named Frances Stacy. Magistrate judges assist district court judges with their cases, and often resolve these types of discovery disputes, as well as settlement conferences and various motions. Although district judges have the final say, magistrate judges issue what is called a "report and recommendation" offering their preliminary ruling, and the district judge can overturn that decision only if they find it to be "clearly erroneous."

Magistrate Judge Stacy ruled that the Tolans could get the information they sought about Cotton's and Edwards's training and past employment. Although protections of qualified immunity are intended to shield defendants from the burdens of discovery, Magistrate Judge Stacy reasoned that those protections do not extend to documents in the possession of third parties. It would place no burden on Cotton and Edwards for these agencies to turn over records to the Tolans. The records were relevant to the Tolans' claims against Bellaire and should be allowed.

But Judge Harmon rejected Magistrate Judge Stacy's report and recommendation, concluding that the documents should not be disclosed. According to Judge Harmon, "the disputed discovery is burdensome to defendants asserting qualified immunity because the discovery is of information about those defendants, and this burden of litigation is of the sort to which the Supreme Court refers" in its qualified immunity cases. Even though the officers had not yet raised a qualified immunity defense, even though the information was not sought from the officers directly, and even though the information was relevant to the Tolans' claims against the City of Bellaire (which does not enjoy the protections of qualified immunity), Judge Harmon ruled that the Tolans could not access records about the officers' training and prior employment.

Soon after the Tolans' case was filed, it was put on hold. Officer Cotton had been indicted for shooting Robbie Tolan, and the defendants asked that the judge suspend discovery in the civil lawsuit until the criminal case was resolved. Magistrate Judge Stacy agreed to suspend discovery regarding Cotton for up to 180 days but ordered that other discovery could continue while the criminal case made its way through court. When Judge Harmon reviewed Magistrate Judge Stacy's report and recommendation, she found it clearly erroneous and granted the defendants' request not to move forward with discovery from Cotton indefinitely, until the criminal case was resolved.

On May 11, 2010, the jury in Sergeant Cotton's criminal trial deliberated almost four hours before finding him not guilty. Sergeant Cotton, who had been on paid leave from the Bellaire Police Department while the criminal case was pending, went back on the force and was soon promoted from sergeant to lieutenant.

With the criminal trial over, discovery started up again in the civil rights case. The parties exchanged documents and deposed key witnesses. On January 1, 2011, Officer Edwards and Lieutenant Cotton asked Judge Harmon to grant them summary judgment. They argued that the evidence showed that Cotton and Edwards did not violate the Constitution and that, even if they did, they were entitled to qualified immunity. According to the defendants, Officer Edwards saw Robbie driving in a suspicious manner, and so started to follow his car. Officer Edwards typed the SUV's license plate into his computer—mistakenly inputting a "6" instead of a "5"—and the computer registered that the vehicle was stolen.

Officer Edwards then called for backup, got out of his car, and told Robbie and Anthony to "come here." According to Officer Edwards, the men did not comply.

When Cotton arrived on the scene, he testified, Marian was walking through the yard and protesting the officers' behavior. In Cotton's assessment, "establishing some degree of control over Marian Tolan was necessary to maintain security at the scene," so he decided to "exert a minimal degree of physical restraint on her movements in order to guide her out of harm's way" by "us[ing] his hand to guide Marian Tolan toward the garage door of the residence." According to Cotton, Robbie then yelled, "Get your fucking hands off my mom," "pushed himself up very quickly from the prone position he had been in, and angrily spun his entire body toward Sergeant Cotton in a quick and admittedly aggressive motion."

In their opposition to summary judgment, the Tolans presented evidence supporting a very different version of the same story. In contrast to Cotton's testimony that he used minimal force to move Marian toward the garage door, Marian testified during her deposition that before Cotton shoved her against the garage door, he grabbed her with such force that it left bruises on her arm. The Tolans included photos of Marian's bruised arm in their submission to the judge. In contrast to the defendants' testimony that Robbie had stood and turned toward Cotton, Robbie testified during his deposition that he remained on his knees when he yelled for Cotton to get his hands off his mother.

Judges are instructed to view the facts "in the light most favorable to the party opposing the [summary judgment] motion"—in this case, the Tolans—and decide whether there is a "genuine" factual dispute that should be left to a jury to decide. According to Judge Harmon, even viewing the facts in the Tolans' favor, the officers' conduct was constitutional. Judge Harmon explained that the decision to stop Robbie and Anthony was based on a reasonable—even if erroneous—suspicion that their car was stolen and so did not violate the Fourth Amendment. Judge Harmon also concluded that the force used against Marian was justified. "Forcefully and intentionally shoving or pushing a woman into a metal garage door could be excessive force under other circumstances," Judge Harmon concluded, "but the circumstances here were tense and unusual."

Finally, Judge Harmon concluded that Cotton's decision to shoot Robbie did not violate his Fourth Amendment rights "because Sergeant Cotton feared for his life and could reasonably have believed the shooting was necessary under the totality of the factual circumstances." Whether Robbie rose up and looked ready to pounce (as Cotton testified) or was on his knees (as Robbie testified), Cotton's decision to shoot was reasonable— in other words, constitutional—in Judge Harmon's mind.

The Tolans wanted to appeal Judge Harmon's decision. Their attorneys, who had a contingency-fee arrangement with the Tolans, and so would be paid nothing for their time if they lost, did not want to invest more money and time into the case. So the Tolans found a new attorney who agreed to take the case but wanted to be paid by the hour for his work. Against their new lawyer's advice, the Tolans decided to sell their home in Bellaire and use that money to pay for the appeal.

The three-judge panel of the appeals court affirmed Judge Harmon's decision, describing it as "extremely detailed and well-reasoned." The court of appeals ruled that even if Cotton had used excessive force, he would be entitled to qualified immunity. It was clearly established, the court of appeals ruled, that "an officer had the right to use deadly force if that officer harbored an objective and reasonable belief that a suspect presented an 'immediate threat to [his] safety.'" Robbie could not overcome qualified immunity in the view of the court of appeals, because he could not show that "every 'reasonable official would have understood' Sergeant Cotton's using deadly force was objectively unreasonable under the circumstances and clearly-established law."

The Tolans' request for a rehearing by all of the judges on the court of appeals was denied. Next, the Tolans asked the Supreme Court to hear their case. It was a long shot: the Supreme Court is asked to hear thousands of cases each year and grants review to fewer than one hundred.

But the Court granted the Tolans' request in 2014 and reversed the lower courts.

The Supreme Court's unsigned decision explained that Judge Harmon and the Fifth Circuit had ignored evidence that supported the Tolans' claims. There were disputes about how well lit the front yard of the Tolans' house was, the tone with which Marian spoke to the officers, and whether Robbie had gotten to his feet or was on his knees when he was shot. The Supreme Court's opinion suggested that a jury who believed the Tolans' side of the story would conclude that Cotton's conduct was unreasonable, and that it should be left to a jury to decide which side's story was more credible. As the Court's opinion explained,

> The witnesses on both sides come to this case with their own perceptions, recollections, and even potential biases. It is in part for that reason that genuine disputes are generally resolved by juries in our adversarial system. By weighing the evidence and reaching factual inferences contrary to Tolan's competent evidence, the court below neglected to adhere to the fundamental principle that at the summary judgment stage, reasonable inferences should be drawn in favor of the nonmoving party.

The Supreme Court sent the case back to the court of appeals, and the court of appeals reversed itself—ruling that there *was* a factual dispute about whether Cotton used excessive force against Marian and Robbie—and sent the case back to district court.

At this point, Robbie and his case had received a great deal of attention, and Ben Crump—who had also made headlines for his work on behalf of the family of Trayvon Martin, and later represented the families of Michael Brown, George Floyd, Breonna Taylor, and many others—agreed to take the Tolans' case to trial.

In Texas, when a district judge is reversed and the case is sent back, the same judge is assigned to hear the case. So the Tolans were once again before Judge Harmon, who set a new schedule for the case to move forward.

Back when Judge Harmon had ruled that Cotton and Edwards did not violate the Tolans' constitutional rights, the parties agreed that the Tolans would dismiss their *Monell* claim against the City of Bellaire while they appealed Judge Harmon's decision, but that the city would not oppose the Tolans' request to add Bellaire back as a defendant if their appeal was successful. Yet, when the case returned to Judge Harmon and the Tolans tried to amend their complaint to renew their *Monell* claim against Bellaire, the defendants opposed the motion. Magistrate Judge Stacy granted the Tolans' motion to amend over the defendants' objection, and Judge Harmon let that decision stand. But allowing the city to be added back into the case did not mean that Judge Harmon found the Tolans' *Monell* claim compelling, as she soon made clear.

On June 30, 2015, Cotton and the City of Bellaire moved for summary judgment. The defendants maintained that Cotton did not use excessive force and argued that, even if he did, the city's policies, training, and supervision of officers were "constitutionally sound."

The Tolans did not immediately respond to the summary judgment motion; instead, on July 15, they asked for additional time to complete discovery regarding their claims against Bellaire. The Tolans argued that more time was necessary because the defendants had opposed many discovery requests while the officers' entitlement to qualified immunity was being decided by the trial court and on appeal, and had not responded to these discovery requests once the case returned to the district court.

On August 14, 2015, Judge Harmon denied the Tolans' request. After describing in detail the back-and-forth between the parties, Judge Harmon concluded that it was the plaintiffs' fault that they did not have the information they needed to prove their *Monell* claim. As she wrote,

> The Plaintiffs argue that because of the Defendants' "stonewalling" them on discovery they were not able to conduct the discov-

ery necessary to obtain facts to justify its opposition [to summary judgment]. The arguments do not establish Defendants were stonewalling Plaintiffs on discovery. The facts to oppose the summary judgment are facts that Plaintiffs should have discovered for their case in chief. If they do not have those facts it is not because Defendants have been stonewalling them, but because they have been dilatory in acquiring the facts.

Judge Harmon gave the Tolans ten days to respond to the defendants' summary judgment motion.

Two and a half weeks after the Tolans submitted their brief, on September 11, 2015, Judge Harmon called the parties in for a status conference. She told them that she was granting Bellaire's motion for summary judgment and dismissing it from the case. She also told the parties that she had not ruled on Cotton's summary judgment motion. Regarding that motion, Judge Harmon said,

> I'm very tempted to grant it, but I'm not going to grant it because I just—if I could just be candid, I think the Supreme Court sent it back to the Fifth Circuit so that they could reanalyze my case. The Fifth Circuit didn't want to do that so they punted it to me, and I don't think there is any way they would ever be satisfied if I did not—we didn't take this case to trial.

Two days later, September 13, the Tolans asked Judge Harmon to recuse herself from the case, arguing that her comments at the September 11 status conference reflected "a deep seeded [sic] and pre-determined opinion of the evidence and the outcome in this case" against Cotton, and that a new judge should be assigned to preside over the trial.

The next day, September 14, Judge Harmon denied the request to recuse. She cited a court of appeals case making clear that "a judge who presides over a case is not recusable for bias even if he is 'exceedingly ill disposed towards [a party],' if that opinion was acquired during the proceedings." Judge Harmon explained that her statements at the September 11 hearing reflected her view of the merits of the case but were "not sufficient to support a claim of 'deep-seated favoritism or antagonism that would make fair judgment impossible.'"

That same day, Judge Harmon excluded from trial five of the Tolans' experts, who would have testified about Robbie Tolan's lost potential earnings as a baseball player. This decision overruled yet another report and recommendation by Magistrate Judge Stacy. And Judge Harmon had several decisions left to make—about what questions could be asked of potential jurors when deciding who should sit on the jury, which requests to limit evidence should be granted, and what instructions the jury should hear before deciding the case.

Trial was set to begin the next day, September 15. But, as Robbie explains in his book, "the prospect of going to trial in Judge Harmon's courtroom, and almost certainly coming out with nothing, seemed like a foregone conclusion." Robbie concluded that it was "time to settle." Marian wanted to keep fighting. But Robbie had spent most of the past decade fighting this case, and he was not willing to dedicate another five years of his life to it. Marian reluctantly agreed.

As jury selection was about to begin, the parties announced that they had settled the case for $110,000. As Robbie explained in his book, "It was a pittance compared to the medical and legal fees, totaling almost a million dollars, that were drowning me, and I don't look at the settlement as a victory. It was simply a conclusion to a long personal nightmare."

———

THE LITIGATION OF *TOLAN V. COTTON* SHOWS THE MANY MOMENTS IN a lawsuit when judges can exercise their discretion, and the ways in which their decisions can vary. The magistrate and district court judge disagreed about whether the Tolans could access records from the officers' former employers. They disagreed about whether the civil case should be suspended for 180 days or indefinitely while the criminal case was ongoing. They disagreed about which experts should be allowed to testify. Different decisions at each of these junctures could have changed the trajectory of the case. What would the Tolans have found if they were allowed to review Cotton's military and prior employment records? Would Robbie have chosen to go to trial before a judge who let his experts testify?

The case also shows diverging views by judges in areas where they are not supposed to be exercising their discretion but, instead, applying the law. The point of summary judgment is to allow judges to dismiss cases only if no reasonable jury could find in favor of one side. Twenty-six different jurists considered whether summary judgment was appropriate in *Tolan v. Cotton*. In the view of fourteen of those judges—Judge Harmon, the three appeals judges who affirmed Judge Harmon's decision, and ten appeals judges who voted against rehearing the appeal—a reasonable jury could not rule in favor of Robbie Tolan. Twelve judges—three judges on the court of appeals who voted to rehear the appeal and the nine-justice Supreme Court—looking at the same facts, were of the view that Cotton's use of force was unreasonable if the jury believed Tolan's version of events.

The Tolans' case is yet one more example of judges looking at the same facts and drawing different conclusions. Just as Chief Justice Roberts and the Massachusetts Supreme Judicial Court could disagree about whether a Black man running away from the police is acting suspiciously or sensibly, these twenty-six jurists could not agree about whether, assuming the facts as the Tolans described them, Cotton's decision to shoot was reasonable.

Ultimately the case *was* allowed to go to trial, but it *didn't*—illuminating another important lesson. Even when judges' decisions do not formally end a case, they can cause a case to end. Robbie Tolan's view that he was bound to lose his jury trial before Judge Harmon is a significant part of the reason he decided to settle.

The point is not to relitigate each judge's and justice's decisions in

Tolan v. Cotton, or to diagnose their motivations. The point is this: who the judge is matters. And, if so inclined, judges have countless opportunities to interpret the legal rules and exercise their vast discretion in ways that make it especially difficult for plaintiffs bringing Section 1983 cases to get relief.

CHAPTER 8

JURIES

The night of August 12, 2014, Rob Liese was panhandling in down-town Orlando, Florida, when a man he did not know invited him out for a drink and a sandwich. Liese, a forty-year-old white man, gladly accepted; he had no place to stay and did not know where his next meal would come from. One drink turned into many drinks, but the presumed Good Samaritan slipped out of the bar without telling Liese and left him with a $60 tab he could not pay. When the bartender refused Liese's offer to wash dishes or scrub the bathrooms as payment, Liese said they should call the police; he simply did not have money to take care of the bill.

Orlando police officer Peter Delio arrived at the scene, handcuffed Liese, and told him to get into his police car. Liese said it would take him a minute; he was drunk, and he had hurt his knee and ankle a few days before when a car ran into him on another drunken evening. Officer Delio apparently lost patience, kicking Liese in the stomach and sending his body into the backseat.

At the station, Liese was handcuffed behind his back and left in a holding cell. He headbutted the window of the cell a few times, hoping to get someone's attention, and the glass broke. Then, as he returned to sit on a bench, Officer Delio opened the door and kneed Liese in the gut. The pain was so extreme Liese felt as if he were going to die. He ended up blacking out. When Liese woke up, he was in the hospital and a nurse was telling him that he was about to go into emergency surgery. Liese's spleen was removed that night. He ended up with forty-two staples in his chest and belly, a thirteen-day hospital stay, and more than $85,000 in medical bills.

Liese began looking for a lawyer to represent him while he was still in the hospital. Several declined his case, telling Liese that juries in Orlando were staunchly pro-police. Liese eventually found William Ruffier, an attorney who used to defend local governments in civil rights cases before starting his own practice. About ten years before he met Liese, Ruffier represented his first plaintiff in a civil rights case—someone who was arrested and assaulted by police in a manner too outrageous to turn away, in Ruffier's mind. By the time he met Liese, Ruffier was spending about a quarter of his time on civil rights cases and the rest on personal injury and medical malpractice cases. He was and remains very particular about the civil rights cases he takes and generally will not represent someone who has ever been arrested or spent time in jail for fear that Florida judges and juries will not be sympathetic to their claims.

Ruffier violated this rule of thumb when he accepted Rob Liese's case. Liese had been arrested countless times, starting when he was a teenager, and had served time in prison. He drank too much. He did not have a home. He did odd jobs in exchange for room and board for a night or two or for money he could use to get a bed at the Salvation Army. But there was surveillance video from the station that clearly showed the assault by Officer Delio, and Liese's injuries were so severe Ruffier decided to take a chance.

Ruffier and Liese brought a Section 1983 lawsuit against Officer Delio and the City of Orlando, alleging that Delio used excessive force against Liese and that the city did not adequately train or discipline its officers. At summary judgment, Orlando tried to get the *Monell* claim dismissed, arguing that there was no pattern of excessive force that would have put the city on notice of the need to better train its officers. But the city's police officers had used force against at least two other handcuffed people before Delio kneed Liese, and at least two people since. And after Delio kneed Liese, the police chief supplemented the department's training to focus on the use of force against people in handcuffs. This was enough, in the judge's mind, for a jury to conclude that the chief was on notice of the need for better use-of-force training. Given the surveillance video, Delio did not even attempt to argue that the claims against him should be dismissed. So, all of Liese's Section 1983 claims survived summary judgment. But getting past summary judgment did not mean victory; it meant only that Liese's case was headed for trial.

—

ALTHOUGH PLAINTIFFS SOMETIMES WIN BIG IN POLICE MISCONDUCT trials, they lose at trial far more often than they win. When I reviewed 1,183 police misconduct cases across the country, 79—less than 7 percent of cases filed—went to trial. Juries entered verdicts for plaintiffs in just 12 of those 79 cases—about 1 percent of the 1,183 cases filed, and about 15 percent of the cases that went before a jury. The other 85 percent were defense verdicts. And even when plaintiffs won at trial, they did not necessarily win much. Two of the 12 juries who entered verdicts for plaintiffs in the cases I studied awarded plaintiffs $1 in compensatory damages. Another 6 of the juries awarded plaintiffs less than $20,000. Other studies have similarly found that Section 1983 plaintiffs win less often, and win less money, than plaintiffs not seeking to vindicate the violation of their constitutional rights.

Why do plaintiffs lose trials against the police so often? And why are they often awarded relatively little when they win? Plaintiffs sometimes lose because the facts are simply not on their side or their lawyer has not been an effective advocate. But all the barriers to relief in civil rights cases mean that weak cases should get weeded out well before trial—either because no lawyer will take the case, or because a judge finds no evidence of a constitutional violation, or because the judge grants the officer qualified immunity, or because there's no evidence implicating the city. If plaintiffs can overcome all of these barriers, you would think they would win at trial more than 15 percent of the time.

Unlike judges, juries do not have to offer reasons for the decisions that they make. They deliberate in private and render a verdict with no explanation. But lawyers who regularly bring civil rights cases believe that many jurors, like many judges, put a thumb on the scale in favor of law enforcement officers, and are skeptical of claims made by people who have had run-ins with the police. Everything we know about people's beliefs about the police, the ways in which jurors are selected, and what evidence jurors hear supports this view.

———

FOR MORE THAN TWO DECADES, GALLUP HAS POLLED THE PUBLIC about their confidence in various institutions, and more than 50 percent of respondents have reported "a great deal" of confidence in just three institutions—the military, small business, and the police. When asked about the police officers in their area, respondents' confidence levels jumped even higher—to 76 percent in 2016. In June 2020, in the wake of the murder of George Floyd, Gallup announced that public confidence in the police had dipped below 50 percent for the first time in several decades, prompting a flurry of headlines about changing perspectives about law enforcement. But trust in the police had only dipped to 48 percent. And it had only moved from the third to the fourth most trusted institution; in the midst of the coronavirus pandemic, the medical system had taken third place.

Of course, not all people trust the police, and the demographics of differences of opinion on this point are noteworthy. Gallup's 2020 poll found that 82 percent of Republicans had confidence in the police, as compared with 28 percent of Democrats. Fifty-six percent of white adults expressed confidence in the police, but only 19 percent of Black adults did.

Differences in perspective are not only limited to broad survey questions about trust in the police. Just as different judges can draw opposite inferences from the same set of facts, different jurors can look at the same evidence and reach starkly different conclusions about what they saw, and those differences in perspective are correlated with their race, gender, education, region, and political leanings.

In 2007, the Supreme Court issued an opinion in a case called *Scott v. Harris* that unintentionally illuminated the dramatically different ways in which different people can perceive the same events. *Scott v. Harris* involved a police pursuit of nineteen-year-old Victor Harris, who had been clocked going seventy-three miles per hour in a fifty-five-mile-per-hour zone. A Georgia deputy sheriff, Timothy Scott, who led the chase, pushed his bumper into the rear of Harris's car, causing Harris to drive off the road, down an embankment, and flip over. Harris was rendered a quadriplegic. He sued Scott and other officers, arguing that the force used against him violated his Fourth Amendment rights.

Key to the case was whether Victor Harris was driving in a way that posed a threat to the officers or the public. The Fourth Amendment excessive-force standard turns on whether the "officers' actions [were] 'objectively reasonable' in light of the facts and circumstances confronting them," which depends in part on whether Harris was posing a risk to the officers or the public. If so, then the use of force was justified. If not, it was excessive. But proof was not limited to the witnesses' conflicting descriptions of what happened; there was video of the pursuit.

When the defendants moved for summary judgment, the trial court denied the request, concluding that a reasonable jury could find that Harris did not pose a threat and that Scott's decision to ram his car was unreasonable. The defendants appealed the trial court's decision, and the court of appeals agreed with the trial court.

But eight justices on the U.S. Supreme Court reviewed the video and saw something different. During oral argument, Justice Alito said that it seemed to him that Harris "created a tremendous risk [to] drivers on that road." Justice Scalia quipped that "he created the scariest chase I ever saw since 'The French Connection.'" Justice Breyer described his reaction as "somewhat similar to Justice Alito's." In an 8–1 opinion reversing the lower courts, Justice Scalia wrote that the video foreclosed any possible argument by Harris that he was driving safely. But one justice, Justice Stevens, saw something different from his eight colleagues when he watched the same video. He wrote in his dissent that the video, in his view, "actually confirms, rather than contradicts, the lower courts' appraisal of the factual questions at issue."

The Supreme Court posted the video on its website, and Justice Scalia wrote in his majority opinion that the Court was "happy to allow the videotape to speak for itself." Law professors Dan Kahan, David Hoffman, and Donald Braman took the Court up on this suggestion. The professors showed the video to approximately 1,350 people and asked them what they saw. The professors found that Black people had a more pro-plaintiff view than did white people; as did Democrats relative to Republicans, liberals relative to conservatives, and those who had more of an egalitarian rather than a hierarchical worldview. These differences in perspective led to differences of opinion on the ultimate question in the case. Approximately three-fourths of the people who watched the video agreed that the use of deadly force was warranted, and one-fourth believed that the use of force was excessive.

Kahan, Hoffman, and Braman argued that this evidence of variation in perspective should make judges hesitant to dismiss cases at summary judgment, knowing that exactly the same evidence could be viewed differently by different judges. This evidence also makes clear something that attorneys know very well: who is selected to sit on a jury matters a tremendous amount to the outcome of a trial.

The Seventh Amendment to the U.S. Constitution establishes the right to a jury trial in civil cases, and Congress and the Supreme Court have both recognized that juries must be drawn from "a fair cross section of the community." The Court has said that this type of representative jury is necessary "as assurance of a diffused impartiality"—a concept that makes particular sense given evidence that different groups of people see the world in different ways. Studies have found that diverse juries make better decisions: they deliberate for longer, discuss more information, make fewer factual errors, and are more open-minded. But federal juries are constituted in ways that disproportionately exclude people of color, people with low income, people with criminal records, and people who have had negative experiences with the police—people who might find it easier to see the world from the perspective of plaintiffs in Section 1983 cases.

———

JURORS' TENDENCY TO SYMPATHIZE WITH GOVERNMENT DEFENDANTS in Section 1983 cases is partially baked into the way in which jury pools are constituted. Before 1968, federal courts used what is referred to as a "key-man" method of assembling a jury pool: community leaders and organizations would recommend people who they thought would make good jurors. Concerns that this system would not truly result in a jury of one's peers led Congress to pass laws requiring that federal courts enact plans for the random selection of jurors that reflect a "fair cross section of the community" and that they not exclude people on the basis of "race, color, religion, sex, national origin, or economic status." The aim was to make juries more representative, and they almost certainly improved on the key-man method. But jury selection in federal court still stacks the deck against plaintiffs in civil rights cases.

People who have felony charges pending against them or have been convicted of a felony—any crime that is punishable by more than a year in prison—cannot serve on a federal jury. This restriction limits the ability of people with firsthand experience in the criminal justice system to serve as jurors and has a disproportionate effect on Black people and, particularly, Black men. Best estimates are that 8 percent of all adults and one-third of Black men have felony convictions that bar them from federal jury service.

Two-thirds of federal districts—including the Middle District of Florida, where Rob Liese's case against the City of Orlando and officer Peter Delio went to trial—further limit the jury pool to registered voters. This limitation also disproportionately excludes people of color in many parts of the country. In Florida, white people are overrepresented on the voter rolls: they make up 53.2 percent of the population but 62.3 percent of registered voters. In contrast, Latinx and Black people are underrepresented: Latinx people make up 26.4 percent of the population but 16.9 percent of registered voters, and Black people make up 16.9 percent of the population but 13.4 percent of registered voters.

Federal law allows district courts to supplement voter registration lists with other sources of names—like lists of people with drivers' licenses and state identification cards—where necessary to produce juries that reflect a fair cross section of the community. But federal courts have rejected challenges to jury pools drawn only from registered voters because the registered voter criteria is "neutral" and "random" and so does not "systematically exclude" people of color—even if it disproportionately excludes them—from jury service.

The geographic boundaries and demographics of federal juries make it even more difficult for Section 1983 cases to be heard by a fair cross section of the community where the case arose. When a case is tried in state court, the jury is drawn from the county where the court is located. Federal juries, in contrast, are drawn from federal districts that can include several counties. In 1871, when Section 1983 became law, supporters of the legislation believed that a federal jury was more likely to be fair because jurors drawn from a wider area would not have strong sympathies for local government officials named as defendants. But today, plaintiffs' attorneys report that federal jurors are often less diverse and less sympathetic to plaintiffs in civil rights cases than are state court juries, particularly in cities. Orlando, Florida, is almost one-quarter Black, but the

Middle District of Florida—the federal district where Orlando is located and Liese's case went to trial—is more conservative and less racially diverse.

The process of notifying prospective jurors of their upcoming jury service and getting them into the courthouse ends up excluding still more potential jurors likely to be sympathetic to plaintiffs in civil rights cases. People are notified of federal jury service when they are sent a jury questionnaire in the mail. But, as a Washington State task force observed, "African Americans, Native Americans, and Latinos are more likely to be economically disadvantaged, have unstable employment, experience more family disruptions, and have more residential mobility"—meaning they may move more often, making it more difficult to get the juror questionnaire sent to the correct address. Even when a questionnaire is sent to the right address, a prospective juror in unstable economic circumstances may not take the time to fill it out or be able to afford to leave work to appear once they are summoned. Studies have shown that Black and Latinx people are disproportionately likely to be culled at these stages of the jury selection process.

One such study was conducted in the Middle District of Florida—where Rob Liese's case went to trial—on behalf of a criminal defendant named Robert Pritt, who argued that the grand jury that indicted him and the jury that would imminently try him were not drawn from a fair cross section of the community. Pritt's legal team showed that in 2009 Black people in the Middle District of Florida made up 12.5 percent of the adult population, 11.4 percent of registered voters, but just 7 percent of the people who received and returned their jury questionnaires and were deemed qualified to serve. Latinx people made up 15.3 percent of the adult population, 13.7 percent of registered voters, but just 9.5 percent of qualified jurors who had received and returned their questionnaires. Under the Middle District of Florida's jury selection process, 44.4 percent of the adult Black population and 37.8 percent of the adult Latinx population had been excluded from service.

Pritt argued that the Middle District of Florida's clerk should address this underrepresentation of Black and Latinx people by supplementing voter registration lists with other sources to create the pool of eligible jurors, and that the clerk should do more to get juror questionnaires filled out and returned—by verifying proper addresses for questionnaires that were returned as undeliverable, following up on unreturned questionnaires, and completing incomplete questionnaires when possible. The judge rejected each of these challenges to the composition of the jury pool in the Middle District of Florida, concluding that the clerk's process reflected no "systematic exclusion" of Black and Latinx people. "It is rather," the judge wrote, "the private choices of individuals that cause any underrepresentation"—referring, presumably, to people's "choices" to not register to vote, to not have a stable address, and to not have time to fill out and return a juror questionnaire.

There is a final moment in the jury selection process when people who might be sympathetic to plaintiffs in Section 1983 cases can get excluded. Once a group of potential jurors receives their notice of jury service and shows up at court, there is the question of who will actually be selected. Before being seated on a jury, prospective jurors are asked questions by the judge and lawyers during what is called voir dire. In voir dire for police misconduct cases in federal court, potential jurors are often asked whether they have had past experiences with law enforcement that would prevent them from fairly evaluating a case. Prior arrests, brushes with the police, or family members' negative experiences with law enforcement can all be the basis to excuse someone from sitting on a jury in a police misconduct trial.

———

FEDERAL JURIES ARE SELECTED IN WAYS THAT EXCLUDE PEOPLE MORE likely to see the world as civil rights plaintiffs do. During trial, federal juries are allowed to hear things that will make them even less sympathetic to plaintiffs in civil rights cases.

Juries are allowed to hear any evidence that would undermine the plaintiff's credibility—including alcohol and drug use (which could impair their ability to perceive events around them) and prior convictions (which, if for fraud or another crime involving untruths, would suggest that they might intentionally lie on the stand). Jurors also can hear information about the plaintiff's life that might limit their assessment of the value of the harms they suffered. Juries can rely on evidence of prior injuries to reduce awards for pain and suffering. If a person is bringing a Section 1983 claim for false arrest and has previously spent time in prison or jail, juries can reduce the amount of damages they award if they presume that going to jail is less traumatizing for a person who has already spent time there. Juries can rely on evidence of the plaintiff's unemployment to discount the damages associated with not being able to work.

In 1955, six years before *Monroe v. Pape* was decided, legal scholar Caleb Foote argued that civil remedies were a potentially valuable tool to keep police in check. But at the time, civil actions against police could only be brought in state court for false arrest, assault, battery, and other non-constitutional claims, and juries were disinclined to award much in the way of damages to the types of people who typically filed these cases. As Foote explained,

> Very few of them are persons who are respectable in the sense that they have some measure of status and financial security in society and have acquired the kind of reputation which will be "damaged" by illegal police activity. Most police action operates at lower levels of society and the great majority of persons who are subjected to illegal arrests or searches and who are therefore potential tort plaintiffs come from the lowest economic levels, or minority groups, or are criminals or suspected of criminality. . . . It is not surprising that attorneys are reluctant to take their cases because of the small chance of recovery "sufficient to justify the action."

At the time Foote published this article, lawyers around the country—including those who ultimately took *Monroe v. Pape* to the Supreme Court—were arguing that people whose constitutional rights were violated by police should be able to file Section 1983 claims in federal court. But, Foote feared, if damages in Section 1983 cases were measured the same way they were measured in other types of cases, then plaintiffs' prior criminal history, social standing, race, and class would continue to limit their awards. As Professor Foote wrote, "to the extent that the plaintiff can be shown to be one of 'the outcast, the disdained, and the powerless,' it will be very easy to establish that there has been no damage in any conventional sense," and "the same blackening of the plaintiff's character which is such a characteristic defense in state actions will negate much of the usefulness of the civil rights action as a sanction."

In order to protect the constitutional rights of all, Foote argued that there should be liquidated damages in civil rights cases—meaning an amount set based on the importance of the constitutional right at issue, instead of the damages that each person can prove. But in the years after it decided *Monroe v. Pape*, the Supreme Court rejected this notion out of hand, explaining that damages under Section 1983 should be measured the same as any other case—the same award for a busted spleen and hospital stay, emotional injuries, and lost wages regardless of whether the injuries were caused by a random person walking down the street or by a police officer employed by the city to protect and serve. The Court's decisions did not indicate any concern that marginalized people would receive inadequate compensation, as Foote had feared. But Professor Foote was right to be concerned.

———

IN ROB LIESE'S CASE, THE ATTORNEYS SELECTED SIX JURORS AND ONE alternate. Although the judge asked most of the questions, Ruffier did ask a few questions about the jurors' prior engagements with the police. Three or four people in the jury pool were excused because they reported that they had had negative interactions with officers after being pulled over. All of the jurors seated for the trial were white, none had arrests or convictions, and none reported ever having had an unpleasant experience with law enforcement.

After the jury was selected and the parties' lawyers gave their opening statements, Ruffier put on his case. He first questioned Officer Delio, who admitted that he kicked Liese when he was getting into the patrol car and then kneed him in the station, conceding that he used excessive force. The head of Orlando's internal affairs division testified that Officer Delio had violated policy in at least three ways: by engaging in excessive force, by using abusive language, and by failing to give Liese prompt medical aid. When the chief of police was asked whether Delio used excessive force against Liese, he testified, "Absolutely."

Then Ruffier called Dr. Joseph Ibrahim to the stand. Dr. Ibrahim testified that Liese was brought to his hospital on the night of August 12, 2014, clutching his stomach and saying that it was difficult to breathe. A CT scan revealed that he was bleeding in his abdomen and his blood pressure was dropping, so he was taken in for emergency surgery. Dr. Ibrahim found bright red blood coming from Liese's spleen—indicating active bleeding caused by blunt-force trauma—and so he removed the spleen. Dr. Ibrahim also testified about the spleen's role in fighting off infections and the health challenges Liese was likely to continue to suffer because of its removal.

Ruffier's last witness was his client. Ruffier knew that a Florida federal jury might hold Liese's criminal history, alcoholism, and homelessness against him. So he decided not to wait for the defense attorney to bring up these aspects of his client's life during cross-examination. Instead, he got it all out in the open when Liese first took the stand.

Ruffier: Tell the jury a little bit about yourself, where you grew up and, you know, through, say, age eighteen, just briefly, if you can.

Liese: I actually grew up with a houseful of alcoholic parents, physically, sexually abused. And right before my thirteenth birthday, I was twelve, I ended up in the system. The courts felt that I was not being taken care of properly. I was there until I was eighteen. From that point on, all my decisions—I want everybody to know that my decisions were my decisions. It is not because of the way I was raised.

Liese told the jury about each of the times that he had been arrested and the time that he served in jail and prison. He also told the jury about various jobs that he had gotten and lost around the country, doing sales and construction, including a job based in Orlando that he lost in August 2014. Then Ruffier asked Liese about his alcohol use.

Ruffier: Sir, do you drink?

Liese: Yes, sir.

Ruffier: All right. Do you have a problem with alcohol?

Liese: I have had a—a pretty—pretty big problem with it, yes.

Ruffier: All right. Describe that to the jury for us.

Liese: I've never been one to talk or deal with feelings or issues very well. So I figured I can either drink them away or at least drink them to where I don't have to deal with them now. And my intention is never to go out and get drunk but to go out and have just enough, and we all know that doesn't happen. I tend to drink in excess quite often, and a lot of times it's—you know, I go home and I pass out.

Liese told the jury about panhandling for food and money to stay a night or two at the Salvation Army in August 2014. He described all of the events of August 12, 2014—first speaking with the man who offered to buy him a sandwich and a beer and then being left with the bill and having the bartender call the police. He described trying to get into Officer Delio's patrol car, hearing him say, "I don't have time to deal with you drunks," and getting kicked into the car by Delio. Liese testified about being driven to the station, being put in the holding cell, banging on the door, and having Delio come in and knee him in the stomach. Then Ruffier asked Liese questions about the pain he felt immediately after.

Ruffier: What did—what did the knee strike to your abdomen feel like, if you recall?

Liese: You ever see those big balls that they use in construction to knock down buildings? That's pretty much what it felt like. I mean, I lost my breath and I couldn't—I couldn't grab my breath. It felt like somebody had just cut off my air, boom . . .

Ruffier: Do you recall asking for medical attention?

Liese: Repeatedly. At some point—at one point I had finally caught my breath, but I just—I couldn't—the pain was so, so severe, I actually started crying, literally asking for somebody to get me medical attention. . . .

Ruffier: Mr. Liese, can you describe for the jury what you were physically feeling during this ninety minutes or so that you were laying in that position?

Liese: I—honestly, I thought I was going to die. I just felt—I just felt like somebody was just trying to rip my insides out. It was just a sharp, constant pain.

Liese described passing out and waking up to learn that he was about to go into surgery. He described the thirteen days he spent in the hospital. Ruffier then asked Liese about how he was doing in April 2016, at the time of the trial. Liese had found a house to live in, was taking college classes online, and was trying to start a business refurbishing people's lawn ornaments. But the loss of his spleen was still affecting him.

Ruffier: How has the surgery and the blow to your abdomen, how has that affected you physically?

Liese: Physically, I mean, I get sick a lot more. I didn't used to get sick, you know, as much. If I did, I was able to pretty much fight it off pretty quick; but, you know, I just—as a matter of fact—in the last month I've spent two weeks fighting off walking pneumonia. I actually currently have an obstruction in my bowels. I have—some days I have a hard time using the bathroom. Other days, I can't stop. I just take it day by day. You know, I do the best I can with what I've got.

Ruffier: Do you have a scar as a result of the surgery?

Liese: I do.

Ruffier: Describe the scar for the jury.

Liese: It's about a half inch below my belly button and it comes all the way up to about the center of my chest, forty-two staples.

Ruffier: How have you been affected mentally from this circumstance?

Liese: It's been frustrating. More depression than frustrating but, I mean, I've been out of work for the majority of the last year and a half, two years. When I start, you know, I try to start working or, you know, getting out there to try to find a job with somebody, I'm good for a few days and, you know, I end up overexerting myself. I start getting sick and then I'm laying in my house for, you know, a few days. So that's kind of kept me from gaining employment with someone else.

Ruffier: Sir, do you still drink alcohol to excess?

Liese: No, not to excess. I do still drink, you know, but I don't drink anywhere nears what I used to, and when I do, I'll get a six pack or a twelve pack and I'll stay home. I don't leave my house. I lock it up and that's it.

After Liese testified, both Delio and the City of Orlando asked the judge to dismiss the claims against them. The judge granted Orlando's motion, describing it as "an exceptionally difficult and close decision" but concluding that Liese had not met his burden of showing that the chief was deliberately indifferent to the need to better train his officers. The judge denied Delio's motion, finding that a jury could conclude he had used excessive force.

Then it was time for Delio to put on his case. Given the surveillance video from the Orlando holding cell, clearly showing Delio kneeing Liese and Liese falling to the ground, there was no way the defense could dispute that Officer Delio assaulted Liese while he was handcuffed. Given the medical records, there was no way to dispute that Liese lost his spleen that night. Every law enforcement official who testified—including the Orlando chief of police—had concluded that Officer Delio used excessive force.

Instead, the defense's strategy was to argue that the damage to Liese's spleen was not caused by Officer Delio kneeing him. The defense attorney argued that Liese could have been injured when a car ran into his knee a few days prior, or some other time when he was drunk. The defense attorney argued that the jury should not believe Liese's testimony because of who he was. At one point, defense counsel said, "Mr. Liese is not a credible person. There is no evidence in this case that he has been a credible person throughout his lifetime." And defense counsel argued that Liese's checkered past meant that he had suffered nothing in the way of damages. In his closing, the lawyer for Officer Delio told the jury,

The first award for damages are for pain and suffering, mental anguish, inconvenience, and loss of reputation. Well, you have to take all the evidence in. I didn't bring this up. Plaintiff brought this up, the history of his life. He said he was subjected to sexual abuse, had alcoholic parents, was transferred back from homes, lived in a youth detention area, lived on the street, was admitted to jail, came in and out of jail, been charged with all types of crimes, had a short business for a short period of time, was homeless during these events when it happened. In fact, just before August 11, [2014,] he was living in an RV in a park in here and was thrown out of that and now he had to live on the street and was on the street for at least the next three days until he was admitted to the hospital.

What's his reputation? What harm did this do to his reputation? What mental anguish has this caused his life the way he has lived it, all the way up until the point that he encountered Officer Delio? We say none.

After hearing closing arguments, and being instructed about the law, the jury began its deliberations. As Liese and Ruffier sat outside the courthouse, waiting for the jury's verdict, Ruffier's phone rang. It was Peter Delio's attorney, who said that Delio's parents, who had been in the courtroom every day of the trial, felt terrible about what had happened to Liese and would pay him $50,000 to settle the case. After consulting with Ruffier, Liese turned down their offer: $50,000 wouldn't begin to cover his medical bills and attorney's fees.

After a couple of hours, Ruffier's phone rang again: the jury had reached a verdict. When Liese and Ruffier returned to the courtroom, they learned that the jury had found that Delio used excessive force, in violation of Liese's Fourth Amendment rights. But the jury awarded him zero in damages. Not a cent for a kick so hard that Liese felt that he was going to die, blacked out in pain, and had his spleen removed in an emergency surgery.

Although Ruffier was not allowed to interview the jurors about their decision, the judge followed his usual custom of going back into the jury room to speak with the jurors after they rendered their verdict. Ruffier later heard through the grapevine that the jurors were reportedly reluctant to award Liese money because they thought he would spend whatever he received on alcohol. As Ruffier explained to a journalist after the verdict, "Mr. Liese has a very humble background and circumstances, and I think that perhaps society doesn't feel those people deserve compensation."

———

AS IT TURNS OUT, PETER DELIO DID NOT ESCAPE CONSEQUENCES FOR his misconduct. The Orlando Police Department investigated Delio and gave him a forty-hour suspension for violating the city's policy against using unreasonable force. The "suspension" was not really a suspension; instead, the hours in his paid-time-off bank were reduced by forty. But the department later fired Delio for not monitoring Rob Liese or immediately calling the paramedics after kneeing him in the stomach. The city then referred the incident to the Florida Department of Law Enforcement, and Delio was criminally prosecuted. Delio went to trial in his criminal case and was found guilty.

At Delio's sentencing in November 2016, seven months after the jury entered its verdict in Rob Liese's Section 1983 case, Delio apologized to Liese, and Liese said that he forgave Delio. In fact, Liese told prosecutors that he did not want Delio to serve time in prison. After the judge sentenced Delio to fifty-one weeks in jail, two years' probation, and anger management classes, Liese took it upon himself to write to the judge to ask that Delio's jail time be reduced. As Liese explained in his letter to the judge, he knew from personal experience that sitting in jail would only hurt Delio and prevent him from moving forward with his life.

Liese also sought $40,000 in restitution from Delio after the sentencing—a financial award that can be ordered in a criminal proceeding to the victim of a crime—for two years of missed work. Despite Delio's apologies to Liese, and Liese's efforts to get Delio's sentence reduced, Delio's attorney opposed Liese's request for restitution, arguing that Liese was lying when he said his injuries had caused him to lose work. The judge denied Liese's request; given his spotty employment history, the judge said he did not find evidence that Liese had missed out on any jobs as a result of the injury.

I tracked down Rob Liese in August 2022. After the civil and criminal trials were over, Liese left Florida for Indiana, and then Missouri. When we spoke, Liese was living in Macon, a small town equidistant from St. Louis and Kansas City. In the eight years since his spleen was removed, Liese's health issues had kept piling up; he had seizures, strokes, depression, stomach issues, and needed oxygen twenty-four hours a day. As he explained it, other parts of his body overcompensated for the loss of his spleen and were starting to shut down. Liese was managing a Burger King but didn't know how long the job would last. He had no trouble finding jobs, but his health issues made it difficult to keep them. Delio's assault on Liese has resulted in catastrophic physical and emotional pain, medical bills, and economic hardship; Liese has been left to bear those burdens entirely on his own.

———

CONTRARY TO TALL TALES ABOUT RUNAWAY JURIES, JURIES IN FEDeral civil rights cases are far more likely to run away from a finding of liability than toward it. Jurors, like judges, view evidence through the filters of their own experience and beliefs. It is for this reason that juries are supposed to be made up of a fair cross section of the community. As Supreme Court Justice Thurgood Marshall wrote in 1972,

> When any large and identifiable segment of the community is excluded from jury service, the effect is to remove from the jury room qualities of human nature and varieties of human experience, the range of which is unknown and perhaps unknowable. It is not necessary to assume that the excluded group will consistently vote as a class in order to conclude . . . that its exclusion deprives the jury

of a perspective on human events that may have unsuspected importance in any case that may be presented.

The ways in which federal juries are constituted mean that people inclined to see the world from the perspective of plaintiffs in civil rights cases are excluded from jury pools at several points in the process. Even after plaintiffs manage to get past all of the other shields protecting law enforcement, the jury can raise one final shield, and they often do.

CHAPTER 9

COURT-ORDERED REFORMS

Remember the last time that you drove to a friend's house to pick them up for a night out. Remember what the traffic was like on the way, what the air smelled like when you got out of the car. Remember walking toward your friend's front door, your mind filled with the song you were listening to on the radio, or the question you wanted to make sure to ask during a quiet moment in the evening. Now imagine a police officer coming toward you, gun drawn, ordering you to get on the ground.

James Campbell had just parked in front of his friend's house on the early evening of June 14, 2002, when he heard that order shouted by Indianapolis police officer Frank Miller. Officer Miller was on the lookout for a Black man with braids who had run from a robbery. Campbell is Black, but he had an Afro, not braids. He was not running. He was not out of breath. He had just gotten out of his car. And he did not have—and had never had—reason to run from the police.

James Campbell grew up in Indianapolis and served in the U.S. Marines for four years after high school. He had been working for the Perry Township School District, near Indianapolis, for six years and, at thirty-one, was its transportation and security supervisor. That made him responsible for making sure that thousands of children traveled safely to and from school in the district's more than 150 buses, including children from some of the roughest neighborhoods in the area—a responsibility that he took to heart. Once, a driver radioed Campbell to say a second grader would not get on the bus because her parents were nowhere to be found and she and her baby sister were in the house alone. Campbell went to the house himself, changed the baby's diaper, arranged for protective services to get the baby, and got the second grader to school. Campbell worked closely with the Indianapolis and Marion County police; officers sometimes provided backup for him when he was dealing with a fight on campus. Campbell had even graduated from the Indianapolis police academy in 2000 as part of his training for the job. He never expected to find himself looking into the barrel of a police officer's gun.

That afternoon, Campbell had come home from work and gotten changed into dress clothes before driving over to the home of Kimo Parham, a friend since high school who was an insurance product analyst. The two were headed out to the Indianapolis jazz festival. It had recently rained, and getting on the ground would ruin Campbell's sweater and pants. So he leaned against a car, and Officer Miller handcuffed him.

Kimo Parham was working on his computer in the basement when he heard his eleven-year-old son shout that a police officer was pointing a gun at James. Parham ran outside and watched from his front porch as Officer Miller patted his friend down, running his hands around Campbell's waist and legs and pulling everything he had—money, identification, and keys—out of his pockets.

Two more officers—Scott Wolfe and Andrew Lamle—arrived on the scene. Officer Wolfe told Officer Miller that Campbell did not meet the description of the suspect they were looking for because he did not have braids. Another officer, Kevin Duley—who had been the officer pursuing the suspect—came to the scene and confirmed that Campbell was not the person they were looking for. But Officer Miller kept Campbell in handcuffs. Officer Lamle patted Campbell down a second time. Officer Wolfe asked Campbell why he was dressed up and accused him of being a drug dealer. Campbell told the officers that he was a marine, that he had served overseas in Somalia, that he had medals to show for it. "Yeah, right," he remembers them scoffing.

Campbell watched as Officer Wolfe walked down the long driveway of Parham's house toward the street, leaned down, picked up a small plastic bag, and said, "Look what we have here." The bag contained marijuana. The bag did not belong to Campbell. He did not use drugs. But Officer Miller told Campbell he was under arrest for marijuana possession. Then Officer Miller reached into his back pocket and pulled out a pair of latex gloves.

When Campbell saw the gloves, he asked Officer Miller what was going on and what he was planning to do with the gloves. Officer Miller said that he was going to strip-search Campbell. Campbell asked to speak to a supervisor. Officer Miller told Campbell no supervisor was coming to the scene; this was the policy of the Indianapolis Police Department, and it was something he had to do.

Officer Miller took Campbell, still handcuffed, to Parham's unfenced backyard. Miller loosened Campbell's belt and his trousers fell. Officer Miller pulled down Campbell's boxers and ordered him to bend over. Miller, with a flashlight in his hands, spread Campbell's buttocks. Parham, his young children, his neighbors, and anyone curious about what police cars were doing in the area could see Campbell with his dress pants and underpants pulled down, and with Officer Miller examining his private parts. Officer Miller found nothing. After the search, Campbell was uncuffed, issued a summons, and told he could go. He was never charged with any crime.

When the officers left, Campbell was in shock. He stayed at Parham's house for a while, trying to pull himself together, called his parents to tell them what happened, and then went home. "Being a former marine and having been in wartime situations," he told me, "I consider myself to be pretty tough. But nothing can prepare you for a moment like that."

Campbell wanted the officers to be punished and to make sure that something similar would not happen to him or anyone else again. He filed a complaint against Officer Miller with the police department's citizens' complaint board. He expected that the officers would be disciplined or fired after an investigation of what he considered an egregious violation of his rights. Campbell was interviewed by someone but never heard back about the outcome of the investigation. When he attended a meeting of the board, Campbell learned that his complaint had been closed without any consequences for the officers.

Campbell then contacted Michael Sutherlin, one of the few civil rights attorneys in Indianapolis, whom his mother, a public school teacher, had found. Sutherlin met with Campbell and Campbell's mother and agreed to file a Section 1983 suit on Campbell's behalf. The complaint demanded money for the fear and humiliation Campbell felt as a result of the arrest and search. It also demanded something else—a court order prohibiting the Indianapolis Police Department from strip-searching people in public in the future. This type of court order is called an injunction, and it has been available to plaintiffs for centuries.

During a hearing on Campbell's request for an injunction, the judge heard evidence that Indianapolis had a policy of strip-searching all arrestees and that its officers regularly strip-searched the people they arrested in public because their jail was overcrowded. Officer Miller testified that he had strip-searched twenty or thirty people in public since he joined the force two years before, and had observed other officers perform strip searches in public another twenty or thirty times. The Indianapolis police chief testified that officers had little guidance about how they were supposed to conduct "thorough body searches" of people charged with non-violent misdemeanors; instead, the policy left it up to the "reasonableness and discretion of the officer, based on the totality of the circumstances."

After hearing this evidence, the judge refused to order the Indianapolis Police Department to stop strip-searching arrestees in public. She did not refuse James Campbell's request because Officer Miller behaved appropriately or because Indianapolis's policy was constitutional. Instead, the judge ruled that Campbell was not entitled to an injunction because he could not establish a "real and immediate threat . . . that Defendants would again arrest him for possession of marijuana or for any other offense necessitating a public 'thorough body search.'" In other words, because Campbell could not prove that the Indianapolis police would violate his constitutional rights in just this way in the future, he could seek money damages but not a court order to change their strip-search policy.

———

THE U.S. CONSTITUTION ANTICIPATED A SYSTEM OF GOVERNMENT where federal and state authority could be both independent and overlapping, an arrangement of separate spheres and mutual respect. But in the aftermath of the Civil War, the federal government gave itself greater powers to police the states; Section 1983 was part of that shift. Congressmen opposed to Section 1983's passage in 1871 expressed concern that the statute disrupted the balance of power between the federal government and the states; they did not want federal courts in the business of managing counties, cities, and towns in ways that would intrude on the decisions of local government officials. But the congressmen who supported Section 1983's passage intended that federal courts would deploy all available remedies to combat unchecked racial terror in the South. As the Supreme Court explained in 1972, "The very purpose of § 1983 was to interpose the federal courts between the States and the people, as guardians of the people's federal rights."

For much of the century after Congress passed Section 1983, the Supreme Court's interpretations of Reconstruction-era legislation and the Fourteenth Amendment were so narrow that the right to sue was virtually never exercised. But as the Supreme Court became more hospitable to

civil rights cases, it appeared to have no compunction about courts granting injunctive relief as a remedy for constitutional violations. In 1939, the
Supreme Court's decision in *Hague v. Committee for Industrial Organization* affirmed a lower court's decision that the mayor of Jersey City violated the First Amendment when he prevented a labor organization from
meeting and distributing literature and the lower court's grant of a sweeping injunction to prevent future interference. In 1954, in *Brown v. Board
of Education*, the Supreme Court ruled that racial discrimination in public education was unconstitutional and, in 1955, in a decision commonly
referred to as *Brown II,* the Supreme Court ordered states to integrate
their schools. Even if the Court's allowance in *Brown II* that states act
"with all deliberate speed" robbed that order of much of its power, it
marked the beginning of widespread federal court injunctions issued to
cure constitutional violations by local governments.

In the decade after the Supreme Court's 1961 decision in *Monroe v.
Pape*, the Court looked approvingly on court-ordered injunctions in school
desegregation and voter apportionment cases. As the Court explained in
1971, in *Swann v. Charlotte-Mecklenburg Board of Education*, one of several Supreme Court cases addressing states' resistance to desegregating
schools, "Once a right and a violation have been shown, the scope of a district court's equitable powers to remedy past wrongs is broad, for breadth
and flexibility are inherent in equitable remedies."

During this period, some lower court judges granted injunctive relief
in lawsuits challenging local police department practices. In Baltimore, a
hunt for two suspects led the police department to search more than three
hundred homes, primarily of Black people, in December 1964 and January 1965. Police would enter these homes—with machine guns but without warrants or probable cause—terrorizing the families awakened in
the middle of the night in much the same way James Monroe and his family had been terrorized less than a decade earlier. One of the families, the
Lankfords, brought a lawsuit challenging these practices. By the time
the case had made its way to federal court, the suspects had been caught

and convicted. But the Lankfords wanted a court order preventing the police from doing something similar in the future. The trial court denied their request, reasoning that this kind of order was unnecessary because the police had already enacted a new policy prohibiting these types of searches.

In 1966, the court of appeals in *Lankford* reversed. According to the appeals court, damages awards were unlikely to prevent future misconduct from occurring: individual officers likely did not have the money to pay any award, there was no promise that the city would pay on their behalf, and there was no assurance that, even if money changed hands, that money would discourage police from doing something similar in the future. Given "the grave character of the department's conduct," the court of appeals wrote, there was "a strong obligation on the court to make sure that similar conduct will not recur."

The court of appeals' rationale in *Lankford* echoed the views of the supporters of Section 1983 in the Reconstruction Congress ninety-five years earlier: injunctive relief was an appropriate tool to address past misconduct and ensure similar harms were not inflicted again. But other courts, faced with similar cases during the same period, were more sympathetic to the types of concerns offered by critics of the Civil Rights Acts in the Reconstruction debates—that federal courts should be wary of interfering with local governments except under the most egregious circumstances. As the court of appeals for the District of Columbia explained in 1972, when it denied a request for injunctive relief in a case challenging police officers' practice of unconstitutionally stopping and frisking pedestrians, "A court should not bind the hands of the police on the mere possibility that certain conduct may be repeated. To do so would unnecessarily involve the courts in police matters and dictate action in situations in which discretion and flexibility are most important."

Justices on the Supreme Court were similarly divided about the power federal courts could exercise to order local governments to stop violating the Constitution. During the 1960s, the weight of the Supreme Court's decisions favored the view that injunctive relief was necessary to secure constitutional rights. But as the Supreme Court's leadership passed from Chief Justice Warren to Chief Justice Burger to Chief Justice Rehnquist, and the makeup of the Court became more conservative, this type of injunctive relief became increasingly difficult to attain.

———

THE SUPREME COURT BEGAN TO BEAT THIS RETREAT IN *YOUNGER V. Harris* in 1971. John Harris Jr. was indicted for distributing political leaflets and argued that the law he was prosecuted under violated the First Amendment. Harris asked a federal judge to order the state to stop prosecuting him. Three additional plaintiffs joined the case; they had not been prosecuted under the California law but feared that they might be in the future.

In an opinion authored by Justice Hugo Black, the Court ruled that the three people who had not yet been prosecuted could not sue because they had only "imaginary or speculative . . . fears of state prosecution." Harris had been indicted and his fears were real. But Harris could not seek an injunction for a different reason: because federal law prohibited people from bringing civil suits attempting to invalidate ongoing state criminal prosecutions. Rather, someone in Harris's position must challenge the constitutionality of the law as part of their defense in the criminal case. Justice Black could have resolved the case quickly and narrowly based on this well-established precedent. Instead, his opinion described in sweeping terms the importance of protecting local governments from undue federal oversight, describing the "ideals and dreams of 'Our Federalism'" that required state institutions "be left free to perform their separate functions in their separate ways."

Justice William O. Douglas, dissenting in *Younger*, offered a very different vision of federal courts' past and present powers. "Whatever the balance of the pressures of localism and nationalism prior to the Civil War," Justice Douglas wrote, those powers were "fundamentally altered by the war" and by the constitutional amendments and legislation enacted during Reconstruction, including Section 1983, that "made civil rights a national concern." In Justice Douglas's view, federal courts needed to be able to flex their powers over state and local governments in cases like *Younger*, particularly in that historical moment: "In times of repression, when interests with powerful spokesmen generate symbolic pogroms against nonconformists, the federal judiciary, charged by Congress with special vigilance for protection of civil rights, has special responsibilities to prevent an erosion of the individual's constitutional rights." But Justice Douglas was alone in his dissent.

Three years later, in 1974, the Supreme Court applied the rationale of *Younger* in a decision, *O'Shea v. Littleton*, that prevented a federal court from entering an injunction to stop widespread criminal justice abuses in Cairo, Illinois. In the late 1960s, Cairo was what a local civil rights lawyer later called a "racial powder keg." Cairo's Black residents had long sought equal pay and opportunity in employment, housing, and education without success. Then, in 1967, Robert Hunt Jr., a Black passenger in a car pulled over for a defective taillight, was arrested because he was "verbally abusive" and was later found hanged in his jail cell. Days of protest followed, and in response hundreds of white people formed a vigilante group—led by the county prosecutor—who, for the next year, "roamed freely, armed and aggressive, intimidating the black community." In the spring of 1969, Black people boycotted Cairo's white-owned businesses to press for an end to employment discrimination. The next year was marked by protests and picketing by Black community members and searches, arrests, and beatings by the police.

The situation in Cairo had gotten so combustible that in 1969 the Illinois state legislature recommended that a special prosecutor investigate the city. In 1970, the International Association of Chiefs of Police described the Cairo Police Department as "ill-trained" and without "the necessary leadership to accomplish its mission." In 1973, the U.S. Commission on Civil Rights recommended that Illinois state officials take over the city's police department. These findings and recommendations were effectively ignored.

In 1971, residents of Cairo sued the county prosecutor and two local judges, seeking damages and injunctive relief. Their complaint alleged that the prosecutor refused to bring charges against white people, while seeking higher bonds, more serious charges, and longer sentences for Black people. According to the complaint, the judges who were named as defendants granted the prosecutor's discriminatory requests.

In 1974, the Supreme Court ruled that the plaintiffs could not seek a court order to stop the prosecutor's and judges' misconduct. According to Justice White, who wrote the majority opinion, the plaintiffs in *O'Shea* could not prove that they would be mistreated in the future, just like the plaintiffs in *Younger*. But, Justice White reasoned, even if they could point to imminent prosecutions, the federal courts should not interfere. Citing *Younger*, Justice White explained that the "recognition of the need for a proper balance in the concurrent operation of federal and state courts counsels restraint against the issuance of injunctions against state officers." Instead, he reasoned, if residents of Cairo were prosecuted unfairly in the future, they could raise those objections as a defense in their criminal case, or seek criminal charges against the judges and prosecutors themselves.

Justice Douglas again dissented. In *Younger*, Douglas had dissented alone. In *O'Shea*, he was joined by Justices Brennan and Marshall. Justice Douglas argued that Section 1983 authorized injunctive relief to address the very types of injustices leveled at Black residents of Cairo—a version of the familiar refrain "If not now, when?"

> What has been alleged here is not only wrongs done to named plaintiffs, but a recurring pattern of wrongs which establishes, if proved, that the legal regime under control of the whites in Cairo, Illinois, is used over and over again to keep the blacks from exer-

cising First Amendment rights, to discriminate against them, to keep from the blacks the protection of the law in their lawful activities, to weight the scales of justice repeatedly on the side of white prejudices and against black protests, fears, and suffering. This is a more pervasive scheme for suppression of blacks and their civil rights than I have ever seen.

Justice Douglas's dissent also offered a version of "If not us, who?" Getting Cairo's state court judges to overturn a racially motivated prosecution, or persuading a prosecutor to bring criminal charges against the local judges who had applied the law in discriminatory ways, would be "difficult, if not impossible." The only way to address the problems in Cairo was through the type of injunction that the majority ruled the plaintiffs could not seek.

Then came *Rizzo v. Goode* in 1976, a decision in which the Supreme Court, relying on *Younger* and *O'Shea*, held that a trial court could not award injunctive relief to address widespread mistreatment of Black people by the Philadelphia Police Department. After twenty-one days of hearings at which 250 witnesses testified, the judge in *Rizzo* wrote a meticulous opinion finding that the department had no "conscious departmental policy of racial bias, or of discriminatory enforcement on racial lines," but that "such violations do occur, with such frequency that they cannot be dismissed as rare, isolated instances; and that little or nothing is done by the city authorities to punish such infractions, or to prevent their recurrence." The judge ordered that Philadelphia Police Department officials help draft new policies to accept and review complaints against police officers. The policies ultimately approved by the judge were "more nearly in accord with the defendants' position than with the plaintiffs' position" and "did not go beyond what the defendants had always been willing to accept." The court of appeals affirmed the injunctive relief granted by the trial court.

The Supreme Court did not contest the trial court's findings in *Rizzo*. Indeed, the Supreme Court described the trial court as having "carefully and conscientiously resolved often sharply conflicting testimony, and made detailed findings of fact." But Justice Rehnquist, writing for the majority, ruled that the trial court could not order the Philadelphia Police Department to adopt the new policies the department helped draft.

In Justice Rehnquist's view, the plaintiffs in *Rizzo* had even less right to seek a court order than the plaintiffs in *O'Shea*. At least the plaintiffs in *O'Shea* had named as defendants the very judges and prosecutor who had brought charges against and sentenced people in a discriminatory manner. In contrast, according to Justice Rehnquist, the *Rizzo* plaintiffs' "claim to 'real and immediate' injury rests not upon what the named petitioners might do to them in the future—such as set a bond on the basis of race—but upon what one of a small, unnamed minority of policemen might do to them in the future because of that unknown policeman's perception of departmental disciplinary procedures." Justice Rehnquist also criticized the trial court for issuing an injunction that overly intruded on local government prerogatives. The trial court's order, according to Justice Rehnquist, amounted to "a sharp limitation on the department's 'latitude in the dispatch of its own internal affairs'"—even though the department had a hand in crafting the revised police procedures adopted by the court.

It was Justice Blackmun who wrote in dissent this time, joined by Justices Brennan and Marshall. (Justice Douglas had retired in 1975.) Justice Blackmun rejected the notion that the named officials had to be directly involved in the wrongdoing; after all, the legislative history of Section 1983 made clear it was intended to address constitutional violations by government officials as well as violations allowed to occur "by reason of . . . neglect." And, in another invocation of the imperative to take action, the dissent concluded that *Rizzo* was "one of those rightly rare but nevertheless justified instances . . . of federal court 'intervention' in a state or municipal executive area."

———

THE SUPREME COURT COMPLETED CRAFTING THE SHIELD TO PRO-
tect police from injunctive relief in 1983, in *City of Los Angeles v. Lyons*.
Adolph Lyons, a twenty-four-year-old Black man, was pulled over by two
Los Angeles police officers at two thirty in the morning on October 6,
1976, because, they said, he had a burned-out taillight. As Lyons exited
his car, the officers drew their revolvers and told him to face his car and
spread his legs. He did. He was then told to put his hands on the top of his
head. He did. After one of the officers patted Lyons down, Lyons dropped
his hands to his sides. An officer slammed Lyons's hands back on his head.
Lyons complained about pain caused by the keys he held in his hands, and
within seconds the officer put Lyons in a chokehold. Lyons blacked out.
When he regained consciousness, he had urinated and defecated on himself and was spitting up blood and dirt. Lyons was given a traffic citation
and sent on his way.

Adolph Lyons's experience was not unique. At the time, the Los Angeles Police Department trained officers that they could use chokeholds
to "subdue *any* resistance by suspects" and were "taught to maintain the
chokehold until the suspect goes limp." Between February 1975 and July
1980, Los Angeles police officers used chokeholds at least 975 times—
more than any other type of physical restraint. Between 1975 and when
Lyons's case was heard by the U.S. Supreme Court in 1982, Los Angeles
police officers killed sixteen people after putting them in chokeholds.
Black people were twenty times more likely to be put in a chokehold than
white people, and were more likely to be killed by chokeholds as well;
although Black people made up just 9 percent of the Los Angeles population, 75 percent of the people killed by police chokeholds in Los Angeles
were Black.

Lyons sought money to compensate him for his injuries and the pain
and suffering caused by the chokehold used against him. He also sought
a court order that the Los Angeles Police Department change its policy to

prohibit officers from using chokeholds except in situations that called for deadly force.

The trial court assigned to Lyons's case entered a preliminary injunction—an order prohibiting chokeholds except in situations requiring deadly force that would be in effect while the case was being litigated. In support of this decision, the court found that Los Angeles's use of chokeholds in situations where deadly force was not required was "unconscionable in a civilized society" and violated the due process clause of the Fourteenth Amendment. The court of appeals agreed.

But when the Supreme Court decided the case in 1983, it reversed the decision awarding injunctive relief. The Supreme Court did not disturb the lower court's conclusion that the officers had violated Lyons's constitutional rights. But it held that Lyons could only seek money for his injuries; he could not seek forward-looking relief.

Once again, the majority invoked the principle that federal courts should tread lightly when it comes to local governments. Justice White, writing for the majority, explained that "the need for a proper balance between state and federal authority counsels restraint in the issuance of injunctions against state officers engaged in the administration of the states' criminal laws in the absence of irreparable injury which is both great and immediate." And, according to the majority, irreparable injury would be "great and immediate" only if Lyons could show that he would be stopped in the future by a Los Angeles police officer and that he would be illegally choked by that officer "without any provocation or resistance on his part"—a showing that would require proof that "*all* police officers in Los Angeles *always* choke any citizen with whom they happen to have an encounter." Justice White recognized that Los Angeles police officers might unconstitutionally choke others in the future, writing that "it may be that among the countless encounters between the police and the citizens of a great city such as Los Angeles, there will be certain instances in which strangleholds will be illegally applied and injury and death unconstitutionally inflicted on the victim." But unless Adolph Lyons could some-how show that this particular fate would befall him, he was "no more entitled to an injunction than any other citizen of Los Angeles."

In *Lyons*, the Supreme Court decision was split 5–4, with Justices Marshall, Brennan, Blackmun, and Stevens in dissent. Justice Marshall, whose legal advocacy at the NAACP Legal Defense Fund had relied heav-ily on forward-looking relief, penned the fiery dissent, which began,

> The Court today holds that a federal court is without power to en-join the enforcement of the City's policy, no matter how flagrantly unconstitutional it may be. Since no one can show that he will be choked in the future, no one—not even a person who, like Lyons, has almost been choked to death—has standing to challenge the continuation of the policy. The City is free to continue the policy indefinitely as long as it is willing to pay damages for the injuries and deaths that result.

The majority's ruling, Justice Marshall wrote, "removes an entire class of constitutional violations from the equitable powers of a federal court" and "immunizes from prospective equitable relief any policy that autho-rizes persistent deprivations of constitutional rights as long as no indi-vidual can establish with substantial certainty that he will be injured, or injured again, in the future."

Imagine what the Reconstruction Congress in 1871 would have made of Justice White's analysis in *Lyons*. During Reconstruction, Black men, women, and children were assaulted, raped, lynched, and shot. Local gov-ernments had no laws explicitly allowing this conduct, but were doing nothing to protect victims. According to the rationale in *Lyons*, the fam-ily members of those killed and those who managed to survive could not seek injunctive relief forcing state and local governments to take action, because they could not prove that they would be assaulted or murdered in the future. Instead, they could seek money damages only for past harms or for the loss of their family member when a similar atrocity occurred again.

There are some types of cases that are able to overcome these barriers to injunctive relief. In confined places, like prisons and schools, it is easier for people to predict what will happen in the future; after all, prisoners and students are certain to be in the same facilities day after day, interacting with the same coterie of guards and teachers. But most people have the freedom of movement, and it is more difficult to know whether, when, and under what circumstances they will have a run-in with government officials.

Courts have allowed people to seek injunctive relief against police in cases where they can show that they will repeatedly be subjected to the same behavior—for example, in cases challenging stop and frisk programs, the use of extreme weapons and tactics to disperse protesters, and the treatment of people living on the street. But less frequent interactions—such as assaults, shootings, or strip searches in public—are more difficult targets for injunctive relief. Not because injunctive relief is unimportant in these cases, but because the plaintiff cannot show with certainty that they will be harmed in these ways again.

In 1991, Congress tried to sidestep the Supreme Court's decisions in *Rizzo* and *Lyons*—and respond to the national furor over the video of Los Angeles police officers assaulting Rodney King—by passing a bill that would authorize the U.S. attorney general and individual victims of police abuse to seek injunctive relief against police departments engaged in a pattern or practice of misconduct. But pressure from police groups and opposition from George H. W. Bush's Justice Department led the House to drop individual victims' right to seek injunctions from the bill. Following a veto threat and a filibuster from Senate Republicans, the bill was abandoned. It was reintroduced in 1993—still allowing the Department of Justice but not individuals to seek injunctive relief—and was passed and signed into law by President Bill Clinton in 1994.

Since 1994, the Department of Justice has investigated scores of police departments for racial bias, excessive force, and other constitutional violations. In the settlements and consent decrees it has entered into with law enforcement agencies, the Department of Justice has negotiated for better collection of data, more stringent use-of-force policies, improved assessment of problem officers, and better civilian complaint procedures, investigations, and discipline. These agreements have been applauded for meaningfully improving police departments.

But granting the Department of Justice power to investigate and sue police departments has not adequately made up for *Lyons*'s and *Rizzo*'s restrictions on individuals' ability to seek injunctive relief. The Department of Justice's commitment to these types of investigations depends entirely on who is sitting in the Oval Office. And even under President Barack Obama, whose Department of Justice aggressively exercised this authority, the DOJ did not have anywhere near the resources it would have needed to take action against more than a small sliver of the approximately eighteen thousand law enforcement agencies across the country. Each investigation can take thousands of hours of attorney time over several years, and during the Obama administration there were just eighteen attorneys in the DOJ's Civil Rights Division who investigated the practices of law enforcement agencies. If the original bill had passed, countless people like James Campbell would have been empowered to bring lawsuits seeking forward-looking relief. Instead, people like Campbell are left with two unsatisfactory options—try to overcome the seemingly insurmountable barriers imposed by *Lyons* and *Rizzo*, or hope that money damages will force the changes they seek.

———

WHEN CAMPBELL GOT THE TRIAL COURT'S ORDER DENYING HIM THE right to seek an injunction to stop public strip searches in Indianapolis, he and Michael Sutherlin, his lawyer, decided to appeal. The court of appeals affirmed the trial court's decision. Channeling the concerns of opponents to Section 1983 back in 1871, the court of appeals explained that courts should be wary of granting injunctive relief to change police practices because "erroneous grants of injunctive relief that hamper enforcement of the criminal law have the potential to cause havoc." Better, in the minds of the judges on the court of appeals, to risk the harms that might result from denying injunctive relief to stop an unconstitutional policy than to "incur the risk of premature or overbroad injunctive relief." And, regardless, the court of appeals wrote, Campbell could not meet the standing requirements imposed by *Lyons*. Campbell had never been arrested before and testified that he did not use drugs. That meant, the court of appeals reasoned, that it was unlikely he would be arrested and strip-searched again. Campbell was allowed to seek money damages but could not seek a change to the department's strip-search policies.

So James Campbell and Michael Sutherlin pursued a case for money damages against Officer Miller, the City of Indianapolis, and several other officers who were on the scene. After discovery, the officers and the city moved for summary judgment. Officer Miller argued that he did not violate the Fourth Amendment: he had probable cause to arrest Campbell for marijuana possession, he had reason to believe that Campbell might be hiding additional drugs, and looking inside his boxer shorts was a "reasonable attempt to discover the presence of additional evidence." Even if he did violate the Constitution by strip-searching Campbell in public, Officer Miller argued, he was entitled to qualified immunity.

The judge dismissed the claims against the officers not directly involved in the search but denied the other motions. In the judge's view, crediting Campbell's description of events, "the search he was forced to undergo clearly violated his established rights." Testimony from Officer Miller and others that strip-searching arrestees in public was Indianapolis Police Department policy meant that the city's motion for summary judgment on Campbell's *Monell* claim should be denied as well.

Campbell managed to get past most of the pretrial shields put in his way, but when the case went to trial, the jury found in favor of the defendants. The jury's verdict form said that they believed Officer Miller had reasonable suspicion that he would find drugs when he searched Campbell and that the scope and manner of the public search was reasonable. When Michael Sutherlin asked the trial court judge to reverse the jury's verdict she denied the request in a terse opinion. But when Campbell appealed, the court of appeals reversed the trial court, finding that no reasonable jury could have concluded that "the search performed on Campbell, involving as it did public nudity and exposure of intimate body parts, was reasonable." The appeals court sent the case back for a retrial.

In Indiana, when a trial court's decision is reversed on appeal and the case is sent back for a new trial, it is assigned to a different judge. So, while Robbie and Marian Tolan had to return to Judge Melinda Harmon's courtroom after the Supreme Court reversed her, James Campbell was assigned a new judge who was, in Sutherlin's view, going to be more sympathetic to Campbell's claims than was the judge originally assigned to his case. As the trial date neared, the parties settled for $200,000.

Campbell got something else through settlement as well—a commitment by the Indianapolis Police Department that they would not strip-search people in public in the future. Although the courts refused to allow Campbell to seek an injunction as part of his lawsuit, the city was willing to change its policy as a condition of the settlement. When Michael Sutherlin ran into Officer Miller a few years later, they talked a bit about Campbell's case. According to Officer Miller, the policy change had stuck. Some of the other officers in the department teased him about it, calling the prohibition on public strip searches the "Miller Rule." But, Officer Miller told Sutherlin, the officers were following the Miller Rule, and the new way of doing things was working out just fine.

In 2009, just one year after Campbell settled his case, and six years after he was denied an injunction because he could not show a "real and immediate" threat that his rights would be violated again, he was stopped on another summer evening by a different group of Indianapolis officers. Campbell was driving his neighbor home from a nearby McDonald's when he saw a police car following him. After Campbell parked in front of his house, the police car's emergency lights and spotlights lit up, and an officer yelled, "Keep your hands on the wheel or you'll be shot." Campbell and his passenger were pulled from the car at gunpoint and forced facedown in the street. An officer asked if he could search Campbell's car and told him that if he said no, he would be forced to stay on the ground until the officers got a warrant. Campbell agreed to the search. Nothing illegal was found. When Campbell was finally allowed to stand, he was told that his car matched the description of a car involved in a "shots fired" 911 call—although the 911 records revealed that Campbell's gold Mercury Sable did not, in fact, fit the description of the car police were searching for. After fifteen minutes, Campbell was released. Campbell was not arrested; we will never know whether the officers would have followed the Miller Rule if he had been.

Campbell contacted one of the lawyers who had worked with Michael Sutherlin on his first case, who agreed to represent him. So, Campbell filed a second lawsuit.

Campbell and his lawyer agreed that they wanted to fight, again, for some sort of policy change. Given the state of the law, they decided against trying to get an injunction in court. Instead, they met with police officials and told them that Campbell would withdraw his lawsuit if they made policy changes that would prevent something similar from happening in the future. Campbell never heard back from the police representatives about his offer.

The defendants moved to dismiss Campbell's complaint because it did not include enough factual detail; the court denied the motion. After discovery, the defendants moved for summary judgment because, they argued, the officers did not violate Campbell's constitutional rights and were entitled to qualified immunity; the court denied this motion as well. After Campbell's case had been pending for almost two years, they settled.

Campbell does not even remember how much he was paid; he just remembers that it wasn't much. Money had never been the goal for him.

———

SOME CRITICS OF CIVIL RIGHTS LITIGATION ARGUE THAT PLAINTIFFS and their lawyers are just in it for a payday. In fact, many people want their lawsuits to help prevent something similar from happening in the future. But the Supreme Court's decisions have forced people to seek money instead of forward-looking relief. People who are seeking to change police practices can try—as James Campbell and his lawyers did—to negotiate policy changes as part of the settlement of their damages case. Otherwise, their hopes must be placed in the prospect that a damages award will translate into systemic changes. But, as you will soon learn, the ways in which damages awards are budgeted for and paid out often mute their power.

CHAPTER 10

Officers' Bank Accounts

When someone manages to overcome all of the barriers to victory in a Section 1983 case and recovers money against a police officer, who pays the bill? Since *Monroe v. Pape* was decided in 1961, the Supreme Court has apparently assumed that those settlements and judgments are paid by the police officers themselves. That is one of the key justifications for qualified immunity; without it, officers would too easily be held personally liable for settlements and judgments entered against them. But the threat of officers' personal financial liability is pure myth.

The Supreme Court's qualified immunity decisions have ignored a web of state laws, local policies, and government practices that combine to ensure that police officers almost never have to pay anything toward settlements and judgments in lawsuits brought against them. Spurred by the same concerns that have fueled qualified immunity doctrine, state legislatures, city councils, local government officials, and government defense attorneys have created additional shields to protect officers' bank accounts. Like the other shields erected to protect the police, they end up harming the people whose rights have been violated along the way.

—

CLAY TIFFANY WAS THE FIRST PERSON WHO GOT ME WONDERING where the money came from. In the village of Briarcliff Manor, a tony suburb outside New York City, everybody knew Tiffany. Growing up in the 1960s, Tiffany was a Briarcliff Manor High School basketball legend; his name is still etched on a plaque in the trophy case that commemorates the school's thousand-point scorers. By the time I met Tiffany, in 2002, he was in his fifties, and Briarcliff Manor residents knew him as the village gadfly. High school friends remembered Tiffany as funny and light-hearted. But by the early 1990s, longtime friends noticed a change. As one friend recalled, "He seemed to have become agitated and almost glowed with indignation over problems involving race, politics—gosh, you name it."

Over six feet tall, white, and with an unruly crown of curly red hair, Clay Tiffany spent his days as a self-proclaimed independent journalist, uncovering local practices he considered unfair or unlawful and complaining about them to local officials and at village council meetings. He complained about Briarcliff Manor's country club. He complained that a local judge was engaged in illegal gambling because he played poker with friends. Tiffany shared the fruits of his investigative labor on his remarkably named public access television show, *Dirge for the Charlatans*. In 1993, after Tiffany had criticized Briarcliff Manor officials one too many times, the village manager prohibited him from entering the village's municipal building without an appointment, and Tiffany was arrested twice for violating that rule. In 1995, Tiffany sued the village, arguing that the limits on his ability to enter the municipal building violated his First Amendment rights. In 1999, he took his case to trial—without a lawyer—and won $85,000.

On a March afternoon in 1997, while his First Amendment lawsuit against the village was pending, Tiffany was pulled over by a Briarcliff Manor police officer he did not recognize. The officer, Nick Tartaglione, had recently been hired by the department. With bulging muscles and a deep tan, Tartaglione stuck out as much as Tiffany did in Briarcliff Manor. According to Tiffany, Tartaglione approached his car and said, through the open window, that he heard Tiffany liked *moulinyans*—derogatory Italian slang for Black people—and then said, "I'm connected with the Mob. I can have you taken care of anytime I want." Officer Tartaglione then took Tiffany's driver's license and registration and walked back to his patrol car. Feeling threatened, Tiffany got out of his car and, standing several feet away, said that he was afraid of Tartaglione and was going to flag down the next car he saw and give the driver the name of a friend to call. When Tiffany got a car to stop and began speaking to the driver, Officer Tartaglione grabbed Tiffany, slammed him into the police car, and handcuffed him.

Tiffany quickly turned his investigative attentions to Tartaglione. And it turned out there was a lot to investigate. Tiffany learned that Tartaglione had beaten up people while employed as a police officer in neighboring jurisdictions and had left those jobs under suspicious circumstances. He then started reporting what he found out about Tartaglione on *Dirge for the Charlatans*. That apparently got under Tartaglione's skin.

Over the next two and a half years, Officer Tartaglione assaulted Tiffany three more times—the assaults growing more extreme with every encounter. In May 1998, Tiffany called the village police department, reporting that he saw Tartaglione "lollygagging" while on duty. Tiffany went to the police department to file a written complaint about Officer Tartaglione. As Tiffany sat in his car, filling out the complaint, Tartaglione approached, ordered Tiffany out of his car pushed him against it, handcuffed him, threw him over his shoulder, and carried him into the police station. In December 1998, Tiffany went to a DMV hearing where Officer Tartaglione was testifying. After the hearing ended, Tiffany drove away and Tartaglione followed him. Tiffany was in a nearby parking lot when Tartaglione approached, drew his gun, and threw Tiffany to the pavement, breaking Tiffany's nose. After each of these incidents, Tiffany complained to the mayor, village manager, and police chief about Tartaglione.

He kept a portable tape recorder in his jacket pocket to document each of his complaints as he made them. Tiffany then reported about these run-ins on *Dirge for the Charlatans.*

On July 15, 1999, another Briarcliff Manor officer told Tiffany that Tartaglione was going to "get" him one night, in Scarborough Park, where Tiffany regularly went during summer months to swim in the Hudson River. The next day, Tiffany reported the threat to the police chief, who assured him that he would not be bothered by Tartaglione. One day after Tiffany received this assurance, Officer Tartaglione was stationed on nighttime patrol at Scarborough Park. When Tiffany got out of the water, Officer Tartaglione was waiting for him. Tartaglione maced Tiffany repeatedly, then punched him and ordered him to the ground, where he kicked Tiffany in the face and body, yelling, "You can't tell lies about me on your television show!" Officer Tartaglione broke Tiffany's orbital bone and several ribs, landing him in the hospital.

In March 2000, Clay Tiffany sued Nick Tartaglione for repeatedly assaulting him and sued the Village of Briarcliff Manor and local government officials for knowing Tiffany was in danger and doing nothing to protect him. Tiffany had a strong case; the injuries he suffered were severe. It is often difficult to prove a *Monell* claim against a local government, because it is difficult to show that those in charge were deliberately indifferent to the danger of future constitutional violations. But, here, in this small-town case, Tiffany had told Briarcliff Manor's final policy makers—the mayor, city manager, and police chief—very clearly that he was at risk. And Tiffany had recorded himself putting those officials on notice.

Two sets of attorneys agreed to represent Tiffany, but each quit his case within a few months; perhaps unsurprisingly, Tiffany rubbed a lot of people the wrong way. My firm ended up taking on Tiffany's case in late 2002. Just a few months into my career as a civil rights attorney, I ended up doing much of the legwork on the case. That meant listening to and transcribing countless mini audiocassettes of muffled conversations between Tiffany and village leadership. And it meant spending many hours talking with Tiffany in my cramped office and on the phone.

During litigation, the Village of Briarcliff Manor did all it could to distance itself from Tartaglione. The village argued that Tartaglione had acted "outside the scope of his employment" when he assaulted Tiffany, so it was not responsible for his conduct. Briarcliff Manor tried to distance itself from Tartaglione in other ways as well. One month after Tartaglione assaulted Tiffany for the final time, Briarcliff Manor suspended and then fired Tartaglione for perjuring himself in an unrelated drunk-driving case. Briarcliff Manor additionally referred the perjury case to the district attorney's office; Tartaglione was criminally prosecuted but acquitted after a bench trial. In response to his firing and criminal prosecution, Tartaglione filed two lawsuits against the village and its officials. In one case, filed in state court, Tartaglione sued to get his job back. In the other, a Section 1983 suit filed in federal court, Tartaglione alleged that village officials violated his constitutional rights by fabricating the perjury charge against him.

As we were litigating Tiffany's lawsuit against Tartaglione and the village, the village was simultaneously defending itself against these two lawsuits brought by Tartaglione. Tartaglione's Section 1983 case was dismissed by the trial court, and that dismissal was affirmed on appeal. But he had better luck in state court: after a four-year battle with the village, Tartaglione was reinstated to the police force and awarded $300,000 in back pay.

Shortly after he returned to the force, and in the midst of discovery in Tiffany's case, Tartaglione offered to pay Tiffany $200,000 to resolve the claims against him. Attorney-client privilege means I cannot disclose information about the private conversations we had with Tiffany about this offer or anything else. But I can relate that we wrote a letter to defense counsel, explaining that Tiffany wanted to know where the money was coming from—Tartaglione himself, or from the village.

I assumed that if Tiffany accepted Tartaglione's settlement offer, the money would be paid from his back-pay award. But in the end, after Tiffany had accepted the money, Briarcliff Manor revealed that its insurer had written the check. I was shocked. Why would Briarcliff Manor's insurer pay to settle a civil rights case against an officer the village had fired? Why would it pay to settle a case on behalf of an officer who the village argued was acting outside the scope of his authority when he assaulted my client?

———

TEN YEARS AFTER I REPRESENTED TIFFANY, AFTER I JOINED THE FAC-ulty at UCLA School of Law, I decided to try to figure out whether Briarcliff Manor's decision to settle a case on behalf of an officer it had fired from the force was an anomaly. Despite statements by courts, legislators, and law enforcement officials that officers are always just one lawsuit away from bankruptcy, there was no good evidence about how frequently officers were actually held financially responsible in civil rights lawsuits. So, I sent public records requests to 150 law enforcement agencies across the country, large and small, to find out how frequently officers personally paid settlements and judgments entered against them. After a year of emails, letters, and phone calls to follow up on these requests, I was able to coax information from 44 of the largest law enforcement agencies in the United States, and from 37 smaller agencies.

The findings were as stark as they were surprising. In the forty-four large jurisdictions, over a six-year period, plaintiffs had received more than $735 million to resolve the police misconduct cases they'd brought. Officers were made to contribute just 0.02 percent of that $735 million. The remaining 99.98 percent of the awards came from the pockets of taxpayers, not police officers. And in the thirty-seven smaller agencies in my study, no officer contributed to any settlement or judgment in a police misconduct case—not one dime.

In just two of the forty-four large agencies in my study—Cleveland

and New York—could I confirm that officers had personally contributed to a settlement or judgment during the six-year study period: 34 cases (out of 6,887) in New York, and 2 (out of 35) in Cleveland. But, even in these two cities, the likelihood that an officer would be required to make a financial contribution to a settlement or judgment entered against them was remote. Extrapolating from the study data, an officer employed by the NYPD had a 1 in 308 chance of contributing to a settlement during a twenty-year career. In Cleveland, an officer had a 1 in 242 chance of doing so over the same time frame. In the other forty-two largest jurisdictions and all thirty-seven smaller jurisdictions in my study, officers were more likely to be struck by lightning than pay anything from their pockets in a police misconduct case.

Even in the rare event that an officer was required to contribute to a settlement or judgment, officers were not threatened with bankruptcy—not even close. Officers' contributions in my study ranged between $250 and $25,000, with an average payment of $4,194 and a median payment of $2,250.

I also learned that the Village of Briarcliff Manor was not an outlier in its decision to pay a settlement on behalf of an officer who seemed to cross way over the line. During the span of my six-year study, juries awarded more than $9 million in punitive damages—damages awards specifically intended to punish officers when they have acted recklessly or maliciously. Yet officers did not pay a penny of these awards. Police officers did not contribute to settlements and judgments even when they were disciplined, fired, criminally prosecuted, or sent to prison.

———

A WEB OF STATE LAWS, LOCAL POLICIES, AND GOVERNMENT PRACTICES combine to ensure that police officers virtually never have to pay anything in lawsuits against them. Although laws, rules, and informal practices have changed over time, the outcome—that officers rarely pay—appears always to have been true.

On March 6, 1959, just four days after the Monroes filed their Section 1983 suit against Frank Pape, his fellow officers, and the City of Chicago, the *Chicago Daily News* published a story describing how Chicago typically paid awards entered against its police officers in successful state suits. People who had been assaulted, battered, or falsely arrested by the police could not sue Chicago directly for its employees' misconduct under state law. But, the *Daily News* reported, most officers did not have the money to satisfy a settlement or judgment against them, and local law prohibited municipal employees' salaries from being garnished to pay off a legal liability, so officers were, essentially, judgment-proof unless they happened to be independently wealthy.

This meant that a person seeking compensation had to file two lawsuits. After obtaining a judgment against the individual officer, the plaintiff had to bring a claim against the city to get it to pay the award. The city would sometimes agree to pay, particularly when the police officer had the ear of city hall, but would more often object on the ground that the officer acted in a "malicious" manner.

Charles Pressman, among this early generation of civil rights attorneys in Chicago who served as a director of the Chicago ACLU in the 1950s and 1960s, told the *Chicago Daily News* that the city played both sides strategically in this serial litigation. The city would represent the officer in the first case, arguing that he had not acted negligently. Then, if a judgment was entered against the officer, the city would take the opposite position in the second case—arguing that the officer acted maliciously as a way of avoiding having to pay the judgment. Even when the judge accepted that argument and the city was relieved of the obligation to pay, the police officer was allowed to remain on the force.

In the years after the Supreme Court's 1961 decision in *Monroe v. Pape*, the number of Section 1983 suits against law enforcement increased dramatically. But even more dramatic than the increase in cases was the rhetoric used to describe the potentially ruinous effects that these suits would have on police officers' willingness to vigorously do their jobs and local governments' ability to hire and retain officers. These concerns inspired the Supreme Court to create and to repeatedly strengthen qualified immunity doctrine.

As it turns out, state and local governments were concerned by this possibility as well. In response, legislatures across the country passed indemnification statutes—statutes providing that if an officer is sued, any settlement or judgment will be paid by the city, county, or state employer. Although the term "indemnification" may be unfamiliar, it describes a concept that is, likely, extremely familiar: if someone does something that causes harm while at work, their employer must pay any legal judgment entered against them. So, if a driver for ABC Foods hit your car, you would not expect the truck driver to pay the settlement or judgment in that case. They were driving an ABC Foods truck, doing ABC Foods' work. Assuming they weren't driving recklessly or drunk, ABC Foods would pay.

Descriptions of legislative intent motivating indemnification for law enforcement officers and other government officials echoed explanations offered by the Supreme Court to justify qualified immunity doctrine: indemnification was necessary in order to "assure the zealous execution of official duties by public employees," to "avoid placing a burden on state employment," and to "create a working environment wherein employees do not feel paralyzed in the performance of their duties for fear of being sued." In other words, the Supreme Court and state legislatures across the country simultaneously took up the concern of protecting the police but through different approaches—one through indemnification and the other through qualified immunity.

Like qualified immunity, state indemnification statutes were not—at least initially—intended to be watertight. Just as qualified immunity was first created only to protect officers acting in good faith, most states' indemnification statutes set out that governments were not obligated to indemnify officers for malicious or willful behavior, or for conduct outside the scope of the officers' employment, or for punitive damages. Legislatures did not want to shield officers from liability for these types of misconduct. As the sponsors of an indemnification bill in Nassau County, New York, made clear, their objective was not to provide officers with "blanket immunity" but to "alleviate [officers'] concern that their actions, although proper, may subject them to personal liability."

Given these exceptions and limitations, scholars long assumed that government indemnification was "neither certain nor universal." But my study of lawsuit payouts revealed the opposite: officers could be almost certain that they would not be required to pay even when they acted willfully or outside the scope of their employment, and even when punitive damages were awarded against them.

In part, this is because local governments have strong interests in indemnifying their officers, even if the law allows them not to. Local officials may believe, as did state legislators when they passed indemnification statutes, that protecting officers from liability sends the message that they support their officers. And some local officials seem to believe that they should send this message by shielding officers from liability even when they have done something plainly wrong. Officials in Greenwood Village, a Denver suburb, apparently hold this view.

In the wake of George Floyd's murder, Colorado passed a bill authorizing cities to require officers to contribute up to $25,000 to a settlement or judgment if they were found to have acted in bad faith. In response, the Greenwood Village city council passed a resolution promising that it would never make a bad-faith finding "no matter what." As the Greenwood Village mayor explained, the city passed the resolution because it did not want "our police officers to worry about us throwing them under the bus." The fact that a financial contribution could only be required of officers found by the village to have acted in bad faith apparently was not assurance enough.

Local government officials also may exercise their discretion to indemnify officers—even when they have been criminally charged or punitive damages have been awarded against them—because they do not believe their officers have done anything wrong. New York City has indemnified every punitive damages award against the police officers it has represented since at least 1996. A former attorney for the city defended these decisions in 2019, explaining that the city represents and indemnifies its officers only if it believes that the officers did not engage in misconduct. As he explained, a jury's conclusion that an officer "got it wrong" does not and should not change the city's decision.

It may also be that cities sometimes choose to pay their officers' settlements and judgments—despite evidence of clear misconduct—because the contrary decision would cause more trouble than it is worth. Local governments have different grievance procedures when officers are denied indemnification that usually involve multiple stages of review. In Minneapolis, as just one example, the city attorney makes a preliminary decision about whether the city is obligated to pay; the officer can request a hearing before an administrative law judge if he or she is denied indemnification; the city council will make a final decision; and then the city council's decision will be reviewed by a judge.

If the Village of Briarcliff Manor had denied indemnification to Officer Tartaglione, he would likely have objected to the decision and then sued. Remember, the village ended up having to pay Tartaglione $300,000 in back pay after he sued to get his job back—far more than the $200,000 its insurer spent to settle Clay Tiffany's claims against Tartaglione. With the village having faced three lawsuits involving Tartaglione, its insurer's decision to pay Tiffany $200,000 as a means of avoiding a fourth suit starts to make sense.

———

DESPITE A NEARLY AIRTIGHT SHIELD FOR OFFICERS' BANK ACCOUNTS, the fiction that officers face financial liability in police misconduct suits has been used to scare courts and legislators from removing some of the other shields against civil rights suits—including qualified immunity. But this is just one of its strategic benefits to police. It can also be used by government lawyers to hinder people from ever seeking justice, or to reduce plaintiffs' winnings if they manage to prevail.

Some cities have a policy of denying officers indemnification as a way of discouraging plaintiffs from filing civil rights lawsuits. A deputy city attorney in El Paso, Texas, told me that it had a policy of never indemnifying officers. But no El Paso officer contributed to a settlement or judgment during my six-year study period. As the deputy city attorney further disclosed to me, plaintiffs' attorneys are less likely to file cases against officers who they believe are judgment-proof and who will not be indemnified. If a plaintiff decided to file a lawsuit despite the city's no-indemnification policy, the city could pay to settle the claim before trial if it decided that it was in its best interest. Paying to settle a case where both the officer and the city were named as defendants did not violate El Paso's no-indemnification policy; that policy only prevented it from satisfying a judgment entered against an officer by a jury.

Local governments also use the threat that they will not indemnify their officers during settlement negotiations. A risk manager employed by San Bernardino, California, told me that the county made an initial decision about whether to indemnify a deputy when he was sued but did not make a final decision until the case was over. The risk manager reported that he routinely sent officers a reservation-of-rights letter at the beginning of a case—stating that the county had decided to indemnify the deputy but that it reserved the right to reverse its decision. Sometimes, a deputy would call after receiving the letter, anxious that he might not be indemnified. The risk manager told me that during those calls he calmly explained that withholding a final decision on indemnification was part of the process that benefitted both officers and the department and that the county would pay in the end.

Government attorneys also gain tactical advantage during trial by withholding indemnification decisions. Although New York City always indemnifies punitive damages awards entered against the officers it defends, the city's attorneys categorically state during litigation that they do not make indemnification decisions until after trial. The officers' attorneys use the possibility that the city will refuse to pay its officers' liabilities as justification for arguments that courts should give jury instructions implying that officers will have to pay and permit the questioning of officers on the witness stand about their salaries, mortgages, and child support obligations—questions that (falsely) suggest to the jury that the officers' personal finances are at stake.

The California Highway Patrol has also used the threat that it would not indemnify officers to its benefit during and after trial. In 1997, Steven Grassilli, a forty-four-year-old water tank installer living in a small community near San Diego, called the California Highway Patrol to complain about CHP officer Richard Eric Barr. Officer Barr had ticketed Grassilli's friend for removing the catalytic converter from his car. But Grassilli knew Officer Barr had removed the catalytic converter from his own truck so it would have more towing power. After Grassilli complained about Officer Barr, Barr began a campaign of harassment against Grassilli. Over the next five years, Officer Barr and his supervisor, Michael Paul Toth, pulled Grassilli over more than a dozen times and issued him more than thirty citations. They ticketed one of Grassilli's suppliers so many times that the supplier stopped doing business with him. Grassilli sued the California Highway Patrol officers who had retaliated against him. At trial, the jury found that Barr and Toth had violated Grassilli's constitutional rights and awarded Grassilli $500,000 in compensatory damages.

CHP was obligated to indemnify Barr and Toth for this $500,000 compensatory damages award as a matter of California law. But California law gives governments discretion to deny officers indemnification for punitive damages awards—awards intended to punish individual defendants for egregious misconduct.

During the punitive damages phase of trial, Officer Barr and Sergeant Toth testified about their limited financial resources—suggesting that the defendants would personally satisfy any punitive damages verdict. Defense counsel even falsely indicated, during the closing argument in the punitive damages phase of trial, that defendants would be personally responsible for the compensatory damages that had been awarded, saying that the officers were already "going to be punished handsomely with having to write a check" for the $500,000. Ultimately, the jury awarded $3 million in punitive damages against Officer Barr and $1 million in punitive damages against Sergeant Toth. As one juror said, after the verdict, "I feel this was a very serious case and a very serious problem. It was very eye-opening, in that I want to believe the law isn't misused."

Several months after the trial, defense counsel told plaintiff's counsel that the California Highway Patrol had decided to pay the punitive damages awards against Officer Barr and Sergeant Toth. Yet, on appeal, this same lawyer challenged the punitive damages awards in part because the trial judge had not instructed the jury that the officers' financial condition was relevant to the jury's assessment. The court of appeals reduced the punitive damages verdicts from $4 million to $55,000, based in part on the conclusion that the "punitive damages awards constitute a disproportionately large percentage of each defendant's wealth and would result in defendants' financial ruin." The appeals court disregarded evidence introduced by the plaintiff that the California Highway Patrol had already decided to indemnify the punitive damages awards against the officers. After the punitive damages verdict was reduced on appeal, the parties settled during a mediation for $2 million. The California Highway Patrol paid the entire settlement.

———

DESPITE ALL OF THE REASONS THAT LOCAL GOVERNMENTS HAVE TO indemnify their officers, police officers are sometimes denied this cover. But even in these rare events, officers' bank accounts almost always remain protected. In these cases, the shield that protects police officers from financial accountability is actually raised by the plaintiff and his or her attorney.

Few law enforcement officers could personally satisfy a large settlement or judgment entered against them. And if they were required to pay settlements and judgments in civil rights suits, the belief that they were just one lawsuit away from bankruptcy might be true. But just as people are unlikely to sue a driver who rear-ends them if the driver is uninsured, plaintiffs and their attorneys are unlikely to file a civil rights suit against an officer they know cannot pay.

So, when governments refuse to indemnify their officers, plaintiffs' attorneys tend to look for deeper pockets. If an attorney learns before filing the case that an officer will not be indemnified, they may bring a lawsuit against the city instead. If the attorney learns during litigation that an officer will not be indemnified, they may try to negotiate a settlement that resolves claims against both the city and the officer—to be paid by the city. If a jurisdiction declines to indemnify an officer after trial, the plaintiff's attorney may try to negotiate a post-trial settlement that the city will pay.

What, then, if the government refuses to pay a settlement or judgment against its officer? I have learned of some instances in which plaintiffs do pursue officers individually. But in these cases, the plaintiffs generally do not attempt to collect the entire judgment. Instead, they eke out a token amount that the officer can pay. Far more often, I hear stories of plaintiffs and their attorneys dropping cases if they cannot find a way to recover from the government. In other words, the most likely result is not that the officer will go bankrupt but that the plaintiff will give up.

When Representatives Ayanna Pressley and Justin Amash introduced a bill in June 2020 that would end qualified immunity, Tucker Carlson went on the air to excoriate the bill, arguing, among other things, that police officers "could be bankrupted, they could lose their homes. That's unfair. It would also end law enforcement. No one would serve as a police officer." But the specter of bankrupt police officers simply has no basis in reality. State and local laws, local government politics, defense attorneys' maneuvering, and plaintiffs' interests combine to ensure that police officers rarely pay a penny toward financial awards plaintiffs receive.

Clay Tiffany died in 2015. One year later, Nick Tartaglione was arrested for murdering four people and burying them in his backyard as part of a drug deal gone wrong. Tartaglione showed up in newspapers again as Jeffrey Epstein's cellmate; he reportedly cut Epstein down when he first tried to hang himself in the federal jail in New York City. Tartaglione is awaiting trial on charges that could send him to death row.

As it turned out, Tiffany was right about Tartaglione being a crooked cop. He was also right to want to know where the money came from.

CHAPTER 11

LOCAL GOVERNMENT BUDGETS

On a frigid Monday night in February 2007, on the Northwest Side of Chicago, the jukebox at Jesse's Shortstop Inn was playing Johnny Cash's version of "Sunday Morning Coming Down"—the sixth-saddest country song of all time, according to *Rolling Stone*.

> *Well, I woke up Sunday morning*
>
> *With no way to hold my head that didn't hurt*
>
> *And the beer I had for breakfast wasn't bad*
>
> *So I had one more for dessert.*

Karolina Obrycka, a twenty-four-year-old émigré from Poland, was serving a handful of patrons. Most were quietly tending their drinks. One was not.

Anthony Abbate, a veteran patrolman of the Chicago Police Department, had already been kicked out of the bar once that afternoon for throwing a customer to the ground. Four hours later, Abbate was back. In between gulps of whiskey and soda and shots of blackberry brandy, Abbate directed his ire at another unfortunate customer, whom he punched, put in a headlock, and then chased around the bar—while periodically flexing his biceps and yelling, "Chicago Police Department!"

Abbate stopped his harassment long enough to demand another drink. When Obrycka told Abbate that he had had enough, he entered the service area behind the bar. Obrycka, who was 125 pounds and half Abbate's size, tried to push him away. "Nobody tells me what to do!" Abbate yelled. He threw Obrycka against the wall and then to the ground. He kicked and punched her—"like a rag doll," she later remembered—and yanked out a handful of hair. When another bar patron pulled Abbate away, Obrycka escaped. Abbate, still yelling, threw a barstool to the ground and stomped out into the night.

As bad as the assault was, the cover-up was worse. Obrycka called 911 as soon as Abbate left the bar. Less than ten minutes later, two Chicago patrolmen arrived. Obrycka told them that a police officer named Tony Abbate had assaulted her and that the bar had video footage of the assault. The owner of the bar offered to play the video for the officers. Instead, when the bar owner went to the back room to cue up the video, the officers walked out of the bar and drove off. The officers made no effort to find or arrest Abbate. Their report identified Abbate only as "Tony," did not mention that he was a police officer, and did not indicate that there was video of the assault.

Almost immediately after the assault, Abbate and his work partner began calling dozens of friends inside and outside the department. Within an hour, two of those friends arrived at Jesse's Shortstop Inn. They told Obrycka that if she agreed not to file a complaint against Abbate, he would pay her medical bills and for time off work. Obrycka refused the offer, saying that her silence could not be bought. Later, their tactics changed. They threatened that if the videotape of the assault was not turned over or destroyed, patrons of Jesse's Shortstop Inn would be arrested for driving under the influence of alcohol and Obrycka would be in danger. A handful of days after the assault, Obrycka quit her job. "I didn't feel safe there anymore," she said. "I felt that Tony would come back or one or more of his friends. And they would do more damage."

Karolina Obrycka met with Chicago Police Department investigators and showed them the video from the bar that documented the assault, the patrolmen's quick trip to the bar after her 911 call, and Abbate's friends' efforts to buy her off. The police superintendent, the head of internal affairs, and several other high-ranking officials watched the video and agreed that the state's attorney's office should review it for possible felony charges. But before the state's attorney could get involved, officers from the department's internal affairs division presented Obrycka with a misdemeanor battery complaint and told her to sign it. No other action was taken against Abbate for the next three weeks. It was only when Obrycka's lawyer made the video public—and it was seen millions of times around the world—that the City of Chicago began to take the case seriously. The state's attorney then charged Abbate with a felony; he was convicted and sentenced to two years' probation and was fired from the department.

Obrycka and her lawyer brought a Section 1983 suit against Abbate and the City of Chicago and fought the city's efforts to dismiss the case for more than five years. During a two-week trial, Obrycka offered evidence that Abbate assaulted her and that the code of silence within the department had emboldened Abbate to beat Obrycka and fellow officers to try to intimidate her and sweep her allegations under the rug.

The jury found that Abbate had violated Obrycka's constitutional rights and that the City of Chicago's policies, customs, and practices were responsible for Abbate's conduct. The jury verdict against Chicago on the *Monell* claim was crucial in this case; the city had refused to indemnify Abbate, so she was unlikely to recover anything without a win against the city. The jury awarded Obrycka $850,000, which the city paid—along with almost $2 million to Obrycka's lawyers for their time.

The jury verdict in Obrycka's case was far from the largest awarded against Chicago and its officers in 2012, and was just a pittance compared with the almost half a billion dollars Chicago paid in police misconduct lawsuits between 2010 and 2020. That half a billion dollars—the second-highest paid by a municipality in police misconduct suits during that decade behind only New York City, which has three times as many officers—does not fully capture the financial costs of these police misconduct lawsuits. Chicago must also pay for the lawyers who defend the city and its officers. Sometimes, Chicago has its own lawyers represent officers in police misconduct cases; the city's legal department is an agency with a $40 million annual budget. When, instead, it decides to hire private lawyers to defend its officers—which it regularly chooses to do—it must pay even more. Between 2004 and 2019, Chicago paid private lawyers $213 million to defend officers in police misconduct suits. To put these costs in some perspective, in 2018 Chicago paid outside lawyers to defend officers in police misconduct suits more than twice the amount it spent to fund the city agency tasked with investigating police misconduct.

The Supreme Court has long issued rulings that assume payouts in Section 1983 cases not only compensate victims but also deter future constitutional violations. Yet the way in which governments budget for and pay settlements and judgments in civil rights lawsuits dampens their impact. Although viral videos can spur government action, and press coverage of large settlements and judgments may carry political consequences, police departments rarely feel any financial consequences of these payouts. Instead, the money to pay large settlements and judgments in police misconduct suits is often taken from central government funds. As a practical reality of government budgeting, that money often ends up being pulled from the crevices of local government budgets that are earmarked for the least powerful: the people whose objections will carry the least political weight; the same marginalized people disproportionately likely to be abused by police.

———

THE ACLU LAWYERS WHO BROUGHT *MONROE V. PAPE* IN 1959 HOPED
that local governments—not individual police officers—would pay settlements and judgments in Section 1983 suits. Police officers would rarely
have the money to satisfy settlements and judgments in cases against
them; having the government pay would ensure that people whose rights
had been violated were actually compensated for their losses. The hope
was, also, that the dollars awarded would inspire change. As the attorneys
for the Monroes explained in their petition to the Supreme Court,

> If the City must pay for the wrongful acts of its agents, the public
> will quickly know of it. The resultant pressures will be reflected
> in the policy decisions and command performance of those who
> govern the City and rule its police department. Disciplinary con-
> trols will be exercised at the top—the level where it really counts
> in a modern big city police department which more nearly resem-
> bles a large business corporation than it does an old fashioned
> town constabulary. Things will change. Not only will past injus-
> tice be redressed, but, far more important, future injustice will be
> prevented.

Yet as long as there has been the hope that placing the financial responsibility for settlements and judgments on local governments can encourage better caretaking, there has been the concern that the payment
of settlements and judgments in these cases will overwhelm local governments. The lawyers representing the Monroes anticipated that the Supreme Court might be reluctant to hold the City of Chicago liable for the
conduct of its officers for fear that the costs of civil rights liability would
be too great for local governments to bear. That concern was already in
the air. Two years before *Monroe v. Pape* was decided by the U.S. Supreme

Court, the Illinois Supreme Court had ruled that local governments could be held liable for state torts by their employees, and that had led to widespread concerns about debilitating liability costs. A *Northwestern University Law Review* study had found that those tort claims had not bankrupted local governments; instead, cities and towns across Illinois paid only pennies per capita each year. The Monroes cited this study in their brief to the Supreme Court, arguing that fears of debilitating municipal liability were not "borne out by statistics."

The Supreme Court did not address the potential costs of lawsuits against local governments in *Monroe*—perhaps because it ruled that local governments could not be sued under Section 1983, and it was unaware that local governments already often paid settlements and judgments against officers. But when the Court decided *Monell v. Department of Social Services* in 1978, ruling that local governments could be held liable under Section 1983 when their customs, policies, or practices caused constitutional violations, future Chief Justice Rehnquist wrote a passionate dissent, joined by then Chief Justice Burger, that despaired of the financial burdens that local governments would face:

> The decision in *Monroe v. Pape* was the fountainhead of the torrent of civil rights litigation of the last 17 years. Using § 1983 as a vehicle, the courts have articulated new and previously unforeseeable interpretations of the Fourteenth Amendment. At the same time, the doctrine of municipal immunity enunciated in *Monroe* has protected municipalities and their limited treasuries from the consequences of their officials' failure to predict the course of this Court's constitutional jurisprudence. None of the Members of this Court can foresee the practical consequences of today's removal of that protection.

By 1980, two years later, Justices Lewis Powell and Potter Stewart had come to share Justice Rehnquist's and Chief Justice Burger's concerns. That year, in *Owen v. City of Independence*, the Supreme Court ruled that municipalities were not entitled to the protections of qualified immunity. In his sharply worded dissent on behalf of the four justices, Justice Powell wrote that the Court's decision to allow cities to be sued in *Monell* (in 1978), in combination with its conclusion that cities were not entitled to qualified immunity in *Owen* (in 1980), "converts municipal governance into a hazardous slalom through constitutional obstacles that often are unknown and unknowable."

Some of Justice Powell's concerns were about the need to preserve states' independence from federal oversight—concerns that similarly inspired the Supreme Court's limitations on the ability to seek injunctive relief. Through Section 1983 municipal liability, Justice Powell wrote, federal courts would be imposing money damages on local governments, which would "inject constant consideration of § 1983 liability into local decisionmaking," a result that "may restrict the independence of local governments and their ability to respond to the needs of their communities." Justice Powell also feared that these financial burdens on municipalities would be too great: that "many local governments lack the resources to withstand substantial unanticipated liability under § 1983" that "could imperil local governments" and might result in "a severe limitation on their ability to serve the public."

An op-ed in *The Wall Street Journal*, published in 1986, similarly criticized civil rights lawsuits—and the attorneys' fees that could be awarded under Section 1988—as imperiling local governments' budgets and well-being:

> The fact is that suing state and local governments on virtually any far-out civil-rights theory has become a veritable cottage industry for thousands of attorneys. As a result, millions of dollars in public funds are being diverted from schools, highways and health programs into the swollen coffers of law firms, liberal activist groups (such as the ACLU), and legal-aid societies. . . . And the liberality

with which federal judges have been dispensing the public's money to litigious counsel has only encouraged others to follow the same path.

———

THE SAME DEBATE ABOUT HOW MUCH CIVIL RIGHTS LAWSUITS COST taxpayers, and whether those costs exert constructive or destructive influences, continues to be waged in courtrooms and newspapers today. Every few months, there is another news story that calculates how much a city has paid in settlements and judgments and what else those dollars could have funded—playgrounds, community centers, and the like. As a May 2021 editorial for *The Boston Globe* recounted, "In the past decade, 31 of 50 cities with the highest police-to-civilian ratios have spent more than $3 billion to settle misconduct lawsuits. That's money that could have been allocated to schools, housing, mental health, addressing substance abuse disorder, and other vital resources that go underfunded, especially in communities of color."

Sometimes these types of stories are deployed in favor of the notion that we need to reduce police misconduct. Other times, they are used to argue that we need to reduce police misconduct lawsuits. A tort reform group called Citizens Against Lawsuit Abuse has written a series of reports describing how the money spent on litigation against local governments "throw[s] budgets out of balance and lead[s] to cuts in public services." Although CALA acknowledges that "there will always be legitimate lawsuits instigated by or filed against cities and counties," it believes that "too often . . . unscrupulous attorneys and plaintiffs view public sector budgets as a coffer to be raided, and file abusive lawsuits against local governments seeking a quick payday."

Reports of the many millions of dollars spent by local governments on police misconduct lawsuits can be jaw-dropping. But these figures, in isolation, overstate the true magnitude of the dollars paid.

Police misconduct lawsuits usually account for only a modest share of local governments' annual expenditures. Chicago paid almost half a billion dollars to resolve police misconduct lawsuits between 2010 and 2020. Half a billion dollars sounds like a lot of money. But $468 million paid over ten years amounts to an average of $46.8 million annually, just 0.28 percent of Chicago's $16.7 billion budget for 2022, and approximately the same amount Chicago planned to pay to repair its sidewalks, curbs, and gutters that year. That's also about a sixth of the $275 million retroactive pay increase Chicago officers got that year, as called for in the city's contract with the police union.

In fact, the effect of ballooning police budgets on local governments' financial stability is a far more pressing budgetary concern than are payouts in Section 1983 cases. In many cities—including Atlanta, Baltimore, Chicago, Detroit, Houston, and Los Angeles—annual police spending amounts to between one-quarter and one-third of general fund expenditures. In these same cities, settlements and judgments in police misconduct suits account for between 0.06 percent and 0.64 percent of general fund expenditures.

Although things work somewhat differently in smaller cities and towns, the bottom line is usually the same. Large cities are "self-insured," meaning that they pay settlements and judgments from their budgets. In contrast, most smaller cities and towns purchase liability insurance to cover the costs of police misconduct and other lawsuits. But insurance premiums are usually just 1 or 2 percent of these small cities' and towns' budgets. There are exceptions to this general rule; in some small cities and towns, large judgments in civil rights suits have forced local governments to increase taxes and others to shutter their police departments altogether, contracting with county sheriffs' departments instead. But, in these places, the civil rights judgment was usually the last straw, instead of the first. Often, a series of expensive lawsuits has led the liability insurer to increase premiums or deny coverage; then the jurisdiction has chosen to go without insurance; then it has been sued again. These exceptional situations get far more news coverage than those that are run-of-the-mill.

Payouts in police misconduct suits—in cities and towns large and small—
are usually just a tiny fraction of their overall budgets.

———

FOR PAYOUTS IN CIVIL RIGHTS LAWSUITS TO DETER POLICE MISCON-
duct, the amount of money that jurisdictions pay is only part of the equation; another is where within the jurisdictions' budgets that money comes
from. After examining how a hundred cities, counties, and states across
the country, large and small, budget for and pay settlements and judgments in police misconduct cases, I discovered that half of the law enforcement agencies in these hundred jurisdictions were required to contribute
as a formal matter to the payment of settlements and judgments against
their officers. Some departments paid settlements and judgments directly
from their budgets, and some made annual contributions to a central government litigation fund.

But, even when police departments paid the costs of settlements and
judgments, these payouts rarely had any real consequences for police departments' bottom lines. I expected that a police department that paid
settlements and judgments from its budget would feel their costs: a spike
in payouts would presumably require the department to cut back on other
costs, and a reduction in payouts would free up money for other purposes.
But that is not the way things work in many cities.

Take Chicago, for example. Each year, Chicago's city council and mayor
come up with a proposed budget. The budget for the Chicago Police Department includes a line item for settlements and judgments against the
department and its officers. Every year, Chicago underestimates how much
it will pay in police misconduct lawsuits. During the three years of my
study, the Chicago Police Department was allocated, on average, about
$16.5 million per year for lawsuit payouts. During those three years, plain-
tiffs in police misconduct suits received more than $52 million per year.
When the police department's litigation fund ran dry—as it did in the
first quarter of one of those fiscal years—the police department was not

called upon to reduce spending in other areas. Instead, the city council took money from other parts of the city's budget to make up for the shortfall, often from parts of the budget that were earmarked for the most vulnerable members of the city. As one former attorney for the City of Chicago reflected,

> When you had to budget for more [police] tort liability you had less to do lead poisoning screening for the poor children of Chicago. We had a terrible lead poisoning problem and there was a direct relationship between the two. Those kids were paying those tort judgments, not the police officers.

A spokesperson for the Chicago Police Department confirmed for me, when I asked, that "the police department isn't forced to cut back on things like OT [overtime] or equipment purchases due to litigation costs."

I found the same practices in multiple cities where police misconduct lawsuit payouts came out of department budgets. Broward County, Florida; Columbus, Ohio; and Boston, Massachusetts, also underfunded their police department litigation budget and then took the extra that they needed from other parts of the city budgets, preserving the police departments' funds.

———

SOME STATES, CITIES, AND COUNTIES DO PAY SETTLEMENTS AND judgments from law enforcement agencies' budgets and do not simply have excess awards taken from general funds. When I interviewed officials from six of these jurisdictions, none complained about the arrangement. Several noted that paying litigation costs from their budgets helped them to identify and address risks. As the risk manager for the California Highway Patrol told me, "We are always getting feedback on what happens on the street and we know that we are going to feel it in our budget if we don't."

Paying settlements and judgments from law enforcement agencies' budgets is no cure-all. Some agencies that pay settlements and judgments from their budgets have long histories of police misconduct. And, perhaps relatedly, the financial risk that these agencies bear is slim. Although the risk manager for the California Highway Patrol reported that payouts made it more aware of lawsuits brought against it, just 0.09 percent of its budget goes to satisfy settlements and judgments in an average year. So, even when payments in Section 1983 cases come from law enforcement agencies' budgets, their deterrent impact may be more of a tickle than a punch. This is all the more reason to have the payments in these cases come from agency budgets, particularly when the alternative is taking money from funds designated to support the poorest neighborhoods.

———

REQUIRING POLICE DEPARTMENTS TO BUDGET FOR AND PAY THE costs of civil rights lawsuits might also influence the way departments go about defending these cases. Karolina Obrycka offered to settle her case against Anthony Abbate and the City of Chicago at the beginning of litigation for $400,000, including attorneys' fees. Chicago refused the offer and a team of ten city lawyers and private attorneys proceeded to fight the case on Chicago's behalf—without success—for more than five years, spending upward of $5 million along the way.

The city filed motions arguing that Obrycka was not entitled to information about its practices while criminal charges against Abbate were pending, an argument the court rejected. Then the city argued that Obrycka was not entitled to information about its practices until she could prove that Abbate violated her constitutional rights—also rejected. The city refused to turn over information about its policies and practices on the grounds that Obrycka's discovery requests were too burdensome and costly. The court rejected most of the city's objections to her requests. The city then moved for summary judgment, arguing that Obrycka did not have proof that it had a de facto policy of concealing and suppressing investigations into police officer misconduct and a code of silence. The judge rejected these arguments as well and denied the motion. With trial on the horizon, the city tried to exclude the testimony of several of Obrycka's expert witnesses, sought to exclude from trial dozens of different pieces of information, and fought about what instructions would be given to the jury.

Three days before trial began, the judge asked the city's attorney appearing before her at the final pretrial conference "one last time," in the judge's words, whether settlement was a possibility. According to the judge, the city's attorney refused to participate in a settlement conference, calling the case "a matter of principle." That principle cost the citizens of Chicago millions—not just the $850,000 awarded by the jury, and the nearly $2 million paid to the plaintiffs' attorneys for the more than fifty-three hundred hours they spent litigating the case over more than five years, but also the time and money the city's own lawyers spent filing losing motion after losing motion. The *Chicago Tribune* has found that at least eleven times Chicago has spent more than $2 million to defend against a police misconduct suit and then spent at least $5 million to settle the case.

For decades, judges and commentators have criticized plaintiffs' attorneys for filing weak civil rights cases with the hope that they will win and get their fees paid by cash-strapped local governments. But it is the attorneys hired by the City of Chicago who appear to be racking up fees and raiding the city's coffers. If the Chicago Police Department had to pay lawsuit costs from its budget, including the cost of the attorneys hired to represent it, the department and its attorneys might approach these cases differently. But they have nothing to lose; they are playing with house money—money that might otherwise have been used for lead paint testing in public housing.

News reports are right to despair of the schools and community centers that could be refurbished with the money used to satisfy settlements and judgments in police misconduct cases. But the conclusion is not that there should be fewer police misconduct lawsuits filed or payments made. Instead, local governments should rethink their budgeting practices that shield police departments from any financial consequences of their officers' constitutional violations and instead take money from those in most need of support.

CHAPTER 12

LEARNING FROM LAWSUITS

At around 1:15 p.m. on September 15, 2010, Shawn Schenck, a forty-seven-year-old Black man, entered Green Valley Deli and Pizza—a bodega on the corner of 158th Street and Park Avenue in the Bronx—to buy a pack of cigarettes. Less than a minute later, six detectives from the Bronx Narcotics Unit stormed into the bodega, grabbed Schenck and four other men, threw them to the floor, and cuffed them behind their backs. Detectives kept yelling, "Where's it at? Where's it at? Where's the stuff?" Schenck had no idea what they were talking about.

One of the detectives lifted Schenck off the floor by his handcuffs and then drove his forearm into the back of Schenck's neck, forcing his face to hit a wall. The detectives pushed Schenck and the other men outside. Then, in front of the crowd that had formed outside the bodega, one of the detectives put on a rubber glove, unbuckled Schenck's belt, pulled his pants and underwear down, and felt around his testicles and probed his anus. The detectives found nothing but put Schenck into a van anyway and drove him around for three hours, picking up other arrestees. When a supervisor watched the bodega's security footage and confirmed that the married father of two had done nothing wrong, Schenck was released.

On August 10, 2011, at about 1:00 p.m., Paul Perry was taking a walk in his Bronx neighborhood. Perry, a sixty-one-year-old Black man, had had diabetes since 1992, and the disease had limited his circulation and required him to use a cane. On his way home, he saw an old acquaintance on the sidewalk. They briefly exchanged greetings and then went on their way. A minute or two later, detectives from the Bronx Narcotics Unit jumped out of an unmarked car and arrested Perry. A detective pulled Perry's pants down to his knees and searched his genital area in full view of the busy Bronx street. Perry was handcuffed tightly, put in the back of a van, and driven around with other arrestees. The van had no air-conditioning and Perry felt ill. When Perry was taken to the Fifty-second Precinct in the Bronx, he was made to remove his clothes and squat for yet another inspection of his anus. No drugs or contraband were ever found on Perry, but he was arrested and charged with sale of a controlled substance. He pleaded not guilty and was released after more than twenty-four hours in custody. On October 3, 2011, all charges against him were dismissed.

At around midnight on July 4, 2015, London Barajona, a sophomore at Monroe College in the Bronx, was walking into his family's apartment building at 394 East 194th Street in the Bronx, when several members of the Bronx Narcotics Unit stopped him, told him to put his hands behind his back, threw him against a metal grate, and handcuffed him. The officers forced Barajona to the ground, kneed him in the neck and shoulder, and dragged him across the concrete. The officers found nothing on him but charged him with criminal sale of marijuana anyway. Barajona was held in the station for twenty-five hours until he was released. He went directly to the hospital, where he was treated for injuries to his back, neck, wrists, and femur. After multiple court appearances, all charges against him were dismissed.

Scores of lawsuits filed against Bronx Narcotics Unit officers and detectives tell versions of these nightmarish stories. Stories of people being arrested while walking down the street or standing on the sidewalk out-side their apartments, taken to the police station and held for hours or days, and then being released when no charges are brought against them. Sto-ries of people asleep in their beds or quietly tending to their lives, startled by police breaking down the doors of their homes, put in handcuffs, taken to the police station and held for hours or days, and then required to go back and forth to court for months to fight charges that are ultimately dropped for lack of evidence.

These civil rights lawsuits tend to settle for four or five figures. Shawn Schenck settled his case for $10,000. Paul Perry settled his case for $12,500. London Barajona settled his case for $20,000. But the payouts add up. In 2019, New York City paid more than $30 million to plaintiffs alleging police misconduct in the Bronx—45 percent of the approxi-mately $67 million paid by New York City to settle police misconduct suits that year.

The same officers' and detectives' names show up again and again in these lawsuits. A 2021 ProPublica report found that at least eight hundred New York Police Department officers over the prior seven years had been named in five or more lawsuits settled by the city, and about fifty officers had been named in a dozen or more cases that the city settled. In 2019, *Gothamist* found ten officers employed by the NYPD who had been sued more than twenty times. Five of those ten officers were stationed in the Bronx Narcotics Unit. One of them, Abdiel Anderson, holds the dubious distinction of having been sued more than any other NYPD officer—more than forty times. The lawsuits brought by Shawn Schenck, Paul Perry, and London Barajona each named Anderson as a defendant. New York City taxpayers have spent nearly half a million dollars on settlements in lawsuits against this one detective alone.

According to the Supreme Court, successful Section 1983 cases should motivate police chiefs to "discharge . . . offending officials" and "institute internal rules and programs designed to minimize the likeli-hood of unintentional infringements on constitutional rights." We already know that the money spent to resolve these cases doesn't come from officers' pockets or police departments' budgets. But these lawsuits could still influence officers' and officials' behavior if they took the time and effort to learn from them. In fact, lawsuits can *only* influence police officers' and officials' behavior if they gather and analyze enough information about the cases to make informed decisions about how to change their policies and practices to prevent something similar from happening in the future.

The Supreme Court's assumption that officers and officials learn about the lawsuits filed against them seems logical: If you were sued, you would presumably spend some time learning about the allegations against you. If you had employees who were sued for their performance on the job, you'd probably try to figure out what led to those cases being filed. But this logic doesn't hold up when it comes to Section 1983 lawsuits filed against the police.

In a 2016 deposition, NYPD detective Abdiel Anderson testified that he did not know how many times he had been sued or details about any of the twenty-two lawsuits that had been filed against him at the time. Many civil rights lawyers who practice in New York City have had the experience of listening to an officer testify during a deposition, under oath, that he does not know whether he has been sued before, how many times he has been sued, the allegations in those cases, or their outcomes. When another Bronx Narcotics Unit officer, Peter Valentin, who was sued at least twenty-eight times between 2006 and 2014, was asked by a reporter about the fact that the city had paid $884,000 to settle civil rights cases brought against him, he responded, "I'm not aware of that. Once it goes to court, I don't follow it."

It's not just police officers who ignore information about Section 1983 lawsuits. Too often, there is a fundamental disconnect between civil rights suits and the officials responsible for supervising and setting policy for the officers named in them. Police department officials pay attention to high-profile killings that inspire front-page news stories, candlelight vigils, and angry meetings with the mayor. Around the country, government officials have invoked George Floyd's and Breonna Taylor's names when they have enacted laws and policies limiting police power to use choke-holds and no-knock warrants. But most police officials make little effort to learn from lawsuits brought against their own officers that do not re-ceive sustained attention—like those brought by Shawn Schenck, Paul Perry, and London Barajona. Instead, government attorneys defend the officers in court, any settlement or judgment is paid out of the govern-ment's budget or by the government's insurer, and the law enforcement agency does not track or analyze the names of the officers, the alleged claims or evidence revealed, the eventual resolution, or the amount paid.

———

I FIRST STARTED THINKING ABOUT WHAT COULD BE LEARNED FROM lawsuits in 2004. I was part of a team of lawyers who sued New York City for widespread violence by corrections officers at its jail facilities on Rik-ers Island, and that year we took dozens of depositions of the officers who had beaten our clients, and those officers' higher-ups. As I prepared for the depositions I took, I reviewed each officer's personnel file but was sur-prised never to find any reference to lawsuits filed against them. I asked each of the officers I deposed whether they had been sued before. In re-sponse, they testified—like Detective Abdiel Anderson—that they had no idea whether or how often they'd been sued, what the allegations were, or the outcomes of the cases. When our legal team questioned sergeants and captains, they testified that they did not know how often the officers they supervised had been sued or how much had been paid from city cof-fers for their misconduct.

These depositions stuck with me. I became a civil rights litigator be-cause I wanted to make a difference. But what difference could lawsuits make if no one paid any attention to them?

In 2009, five years after I took those depositions in the case challeng-ing conditions on Rikers Island, I was teaching at UCLA School of Law and decided to try to figure out whether the officers I deposed had just been stonewalling me or whether they truly knew nothing about the lawsuits filed against them. I also wanted to find out if New York City was an outlier, or if officers and officials in other jurisdictions paid equally little attention to legal claims. Only a few city attorneys and police department officials were willing to talk with me about what, if anything, they learned from lawsuits, but I was able to track down additional information from news stories, investigations by the Department of Justice and Human Rights Watch, and reports by independent police auditors and bar associations.

I learned that the officers and officials we had deposed in the Rikers Island litigation weren't posturing; New York City officers and officials had access to next to nothing about the lawsuits brought against them. When a New York City police officer was sued, no information about that lawsuit—not the allegations, not the resolution, and not the amount ultimately paid to settle the case—was put into the officer's personnel file. Lawsuits were not referred to the police department's internal affairs division or New York City's Civilian Complaint Review Board, which does its own independent investigations of misconduct allegations against officers. The police department had a database that it used to track problem officers, but it did not enter any litigation information into that system. The New York City Law Department—which represents the city and its officers in these cases—did regularly provide the police department with a data printout of cases filed against it and its officers but included detailed descriptions for only the 1–2 percent of cases anticipated to result in a payment of $250,000 or more. The law department and police department rarely—if ever—analyzed the evidence developed during litigation for personnel and policy implications. And the law department and police department did not look for trends in the officers named or the claims alleged in these cases.

I also learned that New York City officials had spent decades begging the police department to gather and analyze information from the thousands of lawsuits filed against it and its officers. Much of that begging came from the city's comptroller, who oversees the city's budget and is responsible for paying to resolve legal claims against the city and its employees.

In 1992, the comptroller, Elizabeth Holtzman, issued a report recommending that the NYPD investigate claims in lawsuits to see if officers should be disciplined or fired, and use the depositions and discovery from litigation to identify personnel and policy problems. In 1999, her successor, Alan Hevesi, wrote to the police commissioner echoing Holtzman's recommendations. Even when cases are settled, Hevesi wrote, "there is enough evidence collected to convince the City that the plaintiff has a serious case. The police department should analyze these settled claims, and take steps to review the officers' performance and propensity to commit acts of excessive force." NYPD officials did not take Holtzman and Hevesi up on their suggestions.

The next comptroller, William Thompson, decided to take matters into his own hands. In 2006, Thompson created a unit made up of staff from the comptroller's office and the city's law department to review cases each week that were good candidates for a quick settlement. In 2009, an attorney at the comptroller's office told me that she would tell law department attorneys about any patterns she saw in the cases she reviewed during those weekly meetings. But when I spoke to an attorney at the law department, he reported that they had no protocols to communicate any of the information from those weekly meetings to police department officials.

The repeated efforts by New York City's comptroller's office to get the NYPD to pay attention to the information in lawsuits was unusual; the New York Police Department's inattention to lawsuits was not. In the course of my research, I found several other cities—including Philadelphia, Nashville, New Orleans, Sacramento, and San Jose—that also ignored the information in lawsuits brought against them and their officers. In these cities, as in New York, the police departments did not track lawsuits against particular officers or look for trends across cases. Lawsuits also played no role in officers' performance evaluations or discipline, and allegations in lawsuits were not investigated by internal affairs. In fact, an attorney who worked for the City of Philadelphia told me that if their police department's internal affairs division was investigating an allegation of misconduct and then learned that a lawsuit was filed regarding that same allegation, the internal affairs investigation would be suspended and remain inactive until the lawsuit was resolved. When I asked what the rationale was for this practice, I was told that it was "just part of the way it works in Philly."

———

I DID FIND A HANDFUL OF JURISDICTIONS THAT GATHERED AND ANA-lyzed information from Section 1983 lawsuits brought against their police officers, and it was almost always because they were forced to do so. Some, like the Los Angeles Police Department, agreed to adopt these policies as the condition of a consent decree it entered into with the U.S. Department of Justice. Other departments were forced to start paying attention to lawsuits because an outside auditor was appointed after high-profile incidents. These auditors decided, as part of their work, to review trends in lawsuit claims and to review the information that came out of discovery and at trial. Incidentally, Chicago's police auditor position was created in partial response to the public outcry after Anthony Abbate assaulted Karolina Obrycka at Jesse's Shortstop Inn in February 2007.

Although police officials in these jurisdictions did not always embrace the idea of reviewing lawsuits filed against them, they found a lot to learn from them. Sometimes, lawsuits are the only way for a police department to learn about allegations of misconduct. To be sure, there are other ways people can notify police departments of wrongdoing. Departments allow people to file civilian complaints, for example, that internal affairs can investigate. But civilian complaint processes do not always work as they should.

The Department of Justice has investigated civilian complaint systems in more than two dozen police departments and found fault with each one. Some departments did not do enough to solicit complaints: their forms were unclear or written only in English. In other departments, officers discouraged or harassed people trying to file complaints or refused to accept them altogether. The Department of Justice also found that officers sometimes mislabeled or misfiled complaints so that they were not investigated. People filing lawsuits face their own challenges—finding a lawyer, drafting a "plausible" complaint, and getting past all of the other legal hurdles standing in their way. But there is very little chance that a person will be harassed when trying to file a complaint in the courthouse, or that their lawsuit will be ignored by the judge assigned to hear the case.

Even when a person does file a civilian complaint and there is an internal investigation, litigation of these same allegations can reveal important and previously unknown details. The Department of Justice reviews also found that many departments had no standard procedures for investigating civilian complaints. When departments did investigate misconduct allegations, many did not follow the types of investigative strategies they would use to solve crimes: investigators did not seek out witnesses, collect evidence, interview police employees, or reconcile inconsistent statements.

When police auditors have compared closed lawsuit files with closed internal affairs investigation files of the same allegations, they have found the information in the lawsuit files to be far more complete. As an independent auditor for the Los Angeles Sheriff's Department explained in a report to Los Angeles County, when misconduct allegations are investigated internally, "inertia weighs heavily on the side of disposing of a matter quickly and moving on." In contrast, someone who has filed a lawsuit has a "strong incentive . . . to dig deeply and generate more detailed and critical information" supporting their case. "If information exists, litigation is the likeliest vehicle to ferret it out."

Portland, Oregon, is one of the few cities I studied that was willing to learn from lawsuits brought against its police department and officers. When the Portland police auditor looked for trends in lawsuits against the department and its officers, he found several lawsuits alleging that officers on the night shift at one Portland police station were hitting people in the head. Following retraining and closer supervision, allegations of head strikes in that station declined. When the Portland police auditor saw another cluster of lawsuit complaints suggesting that officers did not understand the scope of their authority to enter homes without a warrant, the city attorney's office made a training video to educate officers on this issue, and the problem nearly disappeared. And only through litigation did the city learn how a man died of blunt-force trauma two hours after being taken into Portland police custody. The night of the man's death, the involved officer and deputy were videotaped at the Portland jail describing the confrontation. Although the audio portion of the recording was unintelligible, Portland's internal affairs investigators did nothing to improve the sound. Only during litigation did the plaintiff's attorney enhance the audio, at which point it became clear that the officer said he tackled the man, contradicting his statement to internal affairs. As a report about the circumstances of the death concluded, "Plaintiff's attorney was the driving force behind [the Portland Police Bureau's] ultimate recognition of the importance of the video as evidence."

———

ONE COMMON JUSTIFICATION FOR GOVERNMENT OFFICIALS' INATtention to lawsuits is that lawsuits are not a trustworthy source of information. In 2009, New York City mayor Michael Bloomberg's deputy counselor testified in opposition to the city council's efforts to gather information about pending lawsuits and settlements on the ground that "the mere fact of a settlement in any litigation is not an acknowledgement of wrongdoing, or of the truth of the facts alleged. . . . While some settlements seem unfair or even outrageous to us, and to the public, the Law

Department's decision to settle a matter is largely separate from the merits of the litigation."

Without a doubt, settlements do not always reflect the merits of the underlying lawsuits. Sometimes, as Mayor Bloomberg's deputy counselor suggested in his 2009 statement, settlements are larger than the cases warrant. The $110,000 paid to Robbie and Marian Tolan is evidence that settlements also can be too small. Lawsuits are imperfect sources of information for all sorts of other reasons too. Many people who believe they have been mistreated by the police never file lawsuits at all. When people do file lawsuits, they may exaggerate their claims and their injuries. Defendants, for their part, may understate their conduct or lie during depositions. Lawsuits may be dismissed for any number of reasons unrelated to the strength of the underlying claims.

But the imperfections of lawsuits are no reason to ignore them. Law enforcement, as much as any other profession, should appreciate the notion that information can be imperfect but still useful. Police rely on imperfect information all the time when doing their jobs. They must contend with confidential informants who are not always reliable; smudged fingerprint evidence; witnesses with faulty memories; and circumstantial evidence that does not necessarily tell the whole story. Police departments are willing and eager to analyze imperfect data when trying to solve and fight crimes. They have proven less inclined to turn those same powers of insight to explore allegations of misconduct against them.

———

SINCE I BEGAN STUDYING THE NEW YORK CITY POLICE DEPARTMENT in 2009, there have been continuing efforts to get the NYPD to learn from the lawsuits brought against the city and its officers. When Scott Stringer became New York City's comptroller in 2014, he was more proactive than his predecessors. In July 2014, Stringer created what he called "ClaimStat"—a system to track and analyze trends in lawsuit data modeled on CompStat, a tool that had been introduced twenty years earlier in New York City to track crime trends. With CompStat, police officials gather crime statistics and other data from each precinct, then use those data to identify patterns in types and locations of crimes. ClaimStat was intended to work the same way, by identifying patterns in lawsuit allegations. The comptroller published maps with the locations of alleged misconduct and identified litigation "hot spots" for various city agencies to examine.

In 2012, New York's city council created a new office—over the objections of Mayor Bloomberg—called the Office of the Inspector General for the New York City Police Department, to "conduct independent reviews of the department's policies, practices, programs and operations." In 2014, Phil Eure, who had served a similar role in Washington, D.C., came in to lead the agency. The next year, he drafted a report that cited my research about Portland and other litigation-attentive jurisdictions and recommended that the NYPD do more to gather and analyze information from lawsuits brought against it.

In March 2015, one month before Eure was scheduled to publish this first report, the NYPD took a flurry of initial steps to begin paying more attention to lawsuits. It created the Risk Management Bureau and a unit within that bureau to collect, track, and analyze litigation data for trends. The NYPD also announced it would create an electronic database that would collect litigation and other data to support its risk-management work.

When Phil Eure published his report in April 2015, he applauded these initial efforts by the New York City Police Department. But the report also noted that the NYPD still did not have basic litigation information that it needed to learn from lawsuits. The law department had given the NYPD access to its litigation database, but NYPD officials could not search the database by the officers named in lawsuits or by the types of allegations. The law department had provided NYPD officials with monthly litigation reports, but those reports did not include detailed information about the allegations in the suits and were in a form incompatible with the NYPD's other databases.

Eure's April 2015 report made several recommendations to improve these systems. In response, the NYPD appeared to take several steps backward. The NYPD moved the unit created to learn from lawsuits out of risk management and into another division focused on defending against civil rights suits. The NYPD also redesigned its risk-management database so that it would no longer track any lawsuit information.

In 2017, the New York City Council enacted legislation that gave the OIG authority to review patterns in lawsuits filed against the NYPD and make its own recommendations about the discipline and training of officers. When the OIG did that analysis in 2018, it studied six precincts with the largest increases and decreases in claims over a two-year period and trends in the types of allegations brought against officers in those precincts. The OIG was careful to caution that these lawsuit filings were "not conclusive as to the true incidence of excessive force, false arrests, and denial of rights," but instead offered "a roadmap for more in-depth areas of inquiry that NYPD could analyze further" so that it could "see what is driving these trends."

In its 2018 report, the OIG also continued to find fault in the systems that the NYPD had in place. Its system to identify problem officers was not tracking the number, type, or outcome of lawsuits filed and was not identifying trends in types of cases and spikes in precincts. The NYPD was still not getting detailed information about these cases from its lawyers. The city's lawyers periodically gave NYPD officials a list of cases "commenced" and "disposed of" but did not offer any other information about the suits or provide the NYPD with court documents—like complaints and summary judgment motions—that had additional detail about the plaintiffs' allegations. The law department had forty employees focused on defending the thousands of claims filed against its officers each year, but only one employee was responsible for identifying trends across cases for risk-management purposes.

The OIG also found that when the NYPD's Risk Management Bureau did identify trends in cases, it did not develop new policies in response. In the NYPD's view, new policies "could expose NYPD to litigation risk" if they were made public. Instead, the Risk Management Bureau would tell police officials of the trends it identified during informal conversations and phone calls. In a further effort to limit their paper trail, they did not track whether these interventions helped reduce complaints or lawsuits. The OIG's 2018 report criticized the NYPD for not doing more.

The New York City Police Department wrote a twenty-five-page response to the OIG's report, challenging its assessment that the NYPD was not doing enough to learn from litigation. But when the OIG prepared its 2019 report, it found that the NYPD had adopted many of the OIG's recommendations. The NYPD was tracking more information about lawsuits than it had when the OIG first examined the department's practices in 2015, including details about the claims and the officers involved. The NYPD did not limit its review to cases it considered meritorious; instead, it collected information about all lawsuits and claims it received regardless of their outcomes. The OIG recommended that the NYPD track even more information about these lawsuits so that it could better make sense of the data it was collecting. But the OIG and the NYPD, in their responses, both noted that NYPD-related lawsuits alleging police misconduct had declined by 49 percent between 2014 and 2018, and attributed the decline in part to the NYPD's new attention to police misconduct suits.

Although the NYPD has begun taking steps toward gathering and analyzing information from lawsuits brought against the department and its officers, this is a cautionary tale. For decades, New York City's comptroller pushed the NYPD to do this type of lawsuit analysis to no avail. These initiatives gained momentum only when city officials took matters into their own hands—with the comptroller publishing its own lawsuit information, the city council creating the Office of the Inspector General to oversee the NYPD's efforts, and then the city council resolving to allow the OIG to analyze the NYPD's litigation information itself. Even with all of these pressures, it required sustained oversight for the NYPD to take even these most basic, commonsense steps. And there is no telling whether or for how long they will remain in place; Phil Eure resigned in early 2022, just before Mayor Eric Adams took office, and the OIG's May 2022 report noted that the NYPD had rejected or failed to implement the OIG's remaining recommendations to better track litigation data. In other jurisdictions, without these types of pressures, lawsuits too often are treated simply as the cost of doing business, with no lessons to offer.

People often file lawsuits with the hopes that they can help prevent something similar from happening in the future. But if police officials don't gather and analyze information from lawsuits, they can't possibly learn from them.

CHAPTER 13

A BETTER WAY

Join me in a thought experiment: First, imagine that we as a society agreed with the Supreme Court's most optimistic descriptions of the purposes that Section 1983 suits should serve. People whose rights have been violated should be able to recover money to compensate them for their losses, and these cases should lead officers and their government employers to take steps that make similar harms less likely to recur. Now imagine how a system of civil rights enforcement might be structured to achieve these paired goals of compensation and deterrence.

That system would look nothing like what we have in operation today. We fail to meet, or even come close to meeting, this vision of justice.

People whose rights have been violated may not be able to find a lawyer to represent them. In many parts of the country, few lawyers are willing and able to bring civil rights cases at all. And the lawyers who do bring Section 1983 cases turn down most that come their way. Because attorneys get paid only a portion of their clients' winnings, they are unlikely to accept cases they expect to lose—even if they believe a prospective client was treated unjustly. People whose constitutional rights have been violated may also have trouble finding a lawyer if they did not suffer costly injuries, or if a jury is unlikely to be sympathetic to their claims because they have a criminal record or mental health issues, or if they are not a perfect victim in some other way.

Even when a person can find a lawyer to represent them, their case may be dismissed if they don't have access to essential information at the outset. They might not know the name of the officer who arrested them, or they may not have the facts to show that their assault was part of a broader pattern or custom of mistreatment. Their complaint will be dismissed unless they have enough evidence to support a "plausible" claim— before they have access to the court-ordered discovery that would actually allow them to prove government wrongdoing.

Even when a person can find a lawyer and has enough information to draft a plausible complaint, their case may be dismissed because the harm they suffered does not reach the constitutional threshold. Because the Supreme Court defines the Fourth Amendment's protections in terms of what it is reasonable for an officer to do under the totality of the circumstances, viewed from the perspective of the officer and without the benefit of 20/20 hindsight, police can stop, search, arrest, assault, and kill people who have done nothing wrong without violating their constitutional rights.

Even people who can show their constitutional rights were violated may have their cases dismissed because they cannot find prior court decisions with nearly identical facts; without such cases they cannot defeat qualified immunity, even if the officers clearly abused their authority. Some people may have strong cases but accept middling settlements because government attorneys have threatened that the officers will not be indemnified and they cannot meet the formidable threshold for municipal liability. Some may have all the evidence they need to show their constitutional rights were violated but be denied relief or receive pennies on the dollar from unsympathetic juries.

And even when a person overcomes all of these odds, that case will not reliably influence the officer's or the department's decisions moving forward. Most officers and departments are insulated from any financial consequences of settlements and judgments, and most departments don't analyze information from the lawsuits brought against them and their officers.

This is not to say that civil rights lawsuits never compensate or deter. Alonzo and Stephanie Grant viewed the jury verdict in their favor as a vindication. James Campbell's case prompted Indianapolis to implement the "Miller Rule," instructing police officers not to publicly strip-search the people they arrest. The families of Ryan Cole and Mario Romero negotiated seven-figure settlements to resolve each of their lawsuits. But the shields erected to protect police by courts and officials at every level of government make victories far fewer and more modest than they should be.

———

TODAY, DEBATES ABOUT OUR SYSTEM OF POLICE ACCOUNTABILITY often focus, laser-like, on qualified immunity. In the weeks after George Floyd was murdered, in May 2020, protests were punctuated with handwritten signs that protesters held aloft calling for its end. These calls were echoed in bills introduced in the House and Senate to eliminate or scale back the doctrine. State legislatures across the country also considered bills that would create state-law versions of Section 1983 and prohibit the defense of qualified immunity for claims brought under these new causes of action.

Calls for an end of qualified immunity were matched in intensity by those who opposed reform. In August 2020, Indiana congressman Jim Banks introduced a bill to preserve qualified immunity in response to congressional efforts to eliminate the doctrine, threatening that ending it was simply "another way of saying abolish the police" because, without qualified immunity, "criminals would . . . open endless frivolous lawsuits against the officers who put them behind bars" and officers would be "forced to quit, because they couldn't afford to serve any longer."

As state legislatures began to consider statutes that would create state-law causes of action without qualified immunity, these same concerns were aired in statehouses. In August 2020, the editorial board of the *Albuquerque Journal* described in stark terms the dangers they imagined were associated with removing this protection for police:

> Do we really want a simple negligence standard to apply to the split-second decisions officers have to make in potentially danger-ous situations? Do we really want to take a rookie Albuquerque Police Department officer working graveyard in high-crime Albu-querque, making maybe $60,000 a year, and put his or her house on the line for doing something in response to a 911 call that in 20-20 hindsight might have been done better?

In September 2020, in response to a bill pending in the Virginia leg-islature, the executive director of the Virginia State Police Association warned that ending qualified immunity "would open the door to count-less frivolous lawsuits and most definitely become another impediment to hiring and retention."

Understanding how qualified immunity doctrine fits within the fab-ric of civil rights litigation makes clear that neither the most optimistic nor the most dire predictions about civil rights litigation without quali-fied immunity are likely to occur. Ending qualified immunity would make things meaningfully better. People whose rights have been violated would not have their cases dismissed simply because the officer violated their rights in a way that had never previously been ruled unconstitutional. Courts would no longer issue qualified immunity decisions that send the message, as Justice Sonia Sotomayor has written, that police can "shoot first, think later." The scope of constitutional protections would become clearer because courts would have to rule on whether rights protected by the Constitution were violated, and this added clarity would mean that police departments' policies could be clearer as well. Civil rights litiga-tion would become less costly, complicated, and time-consuming, because lawyers would no longer have to master the complexities of qualified immunity doctrine, spend precious hours scouring court cases for ones with similar facts, or defend against multiple qualified immunity motions and appeals.

But ending qualified immunity wouldn't usher in a golden age of police accountability. The Supreme Court's restrictions on when plaintiffs' attorneys can recover their fees would still mean that people with criminal histories, mental health challenges, or limited damages would have a hard time finding a lawyer—even if they also had strong evidence that their rights were violated. It would still be difficult to find enough facts before discovery—particularly when bringing a *Monell* case against a local government—to overcome the *Iqbal* "plausibility" pleading standard. People who were mistakenly arrested or searched, or had force used against them in ways that were unnecessary or unjust—but considered "reasonable"—would still get no relief under Section 1983 because their Fourth Amendment rights were not violated. It would continue to be tremendously difficult to meet the standards of *Monell*—to show that a constitutional violation was the consequence of an unlawful policy, custom, or practice by the local government. It would remain difficult in many parts of the country to find a jury sympathetic to these types of constitutional claims and willing to believe the word of a plaintiff against a defendant law enforcement officer.

Eliminating qualified immunity would help us move toward a system where people whose constitutional rights have been violated are better able to seek justice through the courts. But we won't be able to assure that those people are compensated for their losses—or that those suits can deter future misconduct—unless and until we address the web of other shields that make it difficult for plaintiffs to succeed in these cases.

———

WE ALSO NEED TO ADDRESS THE WEB OF SHIELDS THAT UNDERMINE Section 1983's goals of compensation and deterrence when people do manage to win in court. Indemnification laws and policies mean that officers virtually never contribute to settlements and judgments entered against them—frustrating the deterrence goals of Section 1983. Some argue that officers should be made to pay settlements and judgments from their own pockets. But when local governments deny officers indemnification, the people whose rights have been violated end up with nothing—or far from enough—frustrating Section 1983's compensation goals. If we want to make sure that people are compensated when their rights are violated, most or all of the money must come from local government budgets or insurance and not from the bank accounts of individual officers.

One way to make sure that people are paid what they are owed is to do away with *Monell* standards and hold cities legally responsible for the constitutional violations of their officers—just as private companies are held vicariously liable for the acts of their employees. Another option is to continue to rely on indemnification but make indemnification even more certain than it currently is. Today, local governments around the country have indemnification agreements and policies with exceptions if the officer has behaved recklessly, maliciously, or outside the scope of his employment. Some defense attorneys use these limits strategically, threatening to deny officers indemnification as a way of pressuring plaintiffs into accepting lower settlements, and driving down the dollar amounts that juries ultimately award, only to have the city satisfy the entirety of the award after trial. If a police officer has relied on their gun, badge, uniform, or authority to violate a person's rights, then the government should pay for the harms they cause.

If officers aren't financially responsible for settlements and judgments entered against them, how will they suffer consequences for their misconduct significant enough that they are deterred from doing something similar in the future? Some might argue that that's what internal police discipline is for. But police departments rarely discipline their officers—making it clear that we cannot rely on the police to police themselves—

even in cases where people win substantial settlements and judgments against them. I'm all in favor of improving police department investigations and discipline and more often firing officers who violate policy and the law. But until we do, we need a plan B.

One option is to have officers pay a portion of the settlements and judgments entered against them. In June 2020, one month after George Floyd was murdered, the Colorado legislature passed a bill that does just this. Colorado's bill requires that local governments indemnify their officers—unless they have been convicted of a crime—but also provides that a police officer found by their employer to have acted in bad faith can be obliged to pay 5 percent or $25,000 of the settlement or judgment, whichever is less. If the officer shows they do not have the money to pay, the city must pay the officer's share of the obligation.

I'd prefer a statute that does not exclude officers who have been convicted of crimes from governments' indemnification obligations. In my view, if an officer violates someone's rights while relying on their official authority, the government that gave them that authority should bear the costs. The carve-out in Colorado's statute means that the women raped by the Houston police officer who was not indemnified—and was sentenced to life in prison—would still get nothing for their injuries. But the Colorado statute creates a more just system in many ways. Very few people would be denied indemnification because very few officers are actually charged with and convicted of crimes. A bright-line rule requiring indemnification unless the officer has been criminally convicted should prevent government lawyers from strategically using the threat that officers will be denied indemnification. And, except for the rare instances in which an officer is criminally convicted, the statute ensures that people whose rights have been violated will be compensated and that officers can be financially sanctioned when they act in bad faith.

Although more states should follow Colorado's approach, local governments eager to advance this kind of reform don't need to wait for their state legislatures to act. When I studied police indemnification practices around the country, two cities—Cleveland and New York City—occasionally required officers to contribute to settlements or judgments. These officers weren't entirely denied indemnification. Instead, they were indemnified on the condition that they contribute a modest amount—about $4,200 dollars, on average—to the settlements entered against them. We can debate whether the officers should have been required to contribute more money, or whether more officers should be required to contribute. But these local governments ensured that people whose rights were violated received most or all of the compensation they were awarded, while creating a financial sanction for some officers. And they didn't need to go through the state legislative process to get it done.

To advance Section 1983's deterrence goals, lawsuits must influence the behavior not only of the police officers directly involved in the cases but also of the police department officials who hire, supervise, train, and discipline them. Right now, there may be political pressures when a high-profile case hits the news. But cases that are less well-known have hardly any impact at all. In part this is because police departments have very little skin in the game; settlements and judgments and legal defense costs rarely have any measurable impact on department budgets. It is also because police departments are under no obligation to learn from or take action in response to the suits that are brought against them and their officers.

How can we increase the impact of these suits on police department behavior? The Supreme Court could revisit its decisions in *Rizzo* and *Lyons*, and make it easier for individuals to seek injunctive relief that would change police department policies and practices. But, given the near impossibility of that happening anytime soon, local governments should take advantage of the leverage they have to make police departments more attentive to the lawsuits brought against them. A local government can, for example, tie the money to pay settlements and judgments—as well as the defense of these cases—to their law enforcement agency's budget. During each year's budgeting process, the department can get an allocation of money that reflects what they expect to pay that year in lawsuits; if they go over budget, they will have to reallocate money from elsewhere, and if they are under budget, they will have a surplus. Some agencies already budget and pay for lawsuits this way; although lawsuits account for only a small portion of these law enforcement agencies' budgets, it does mean that when these agencies are making hiring, training, and supervising decisions that might lead to lawsuits, and when they are defending against those suits, they have skin in the game.

Local governments can also require or pressure police department officials to learn from the lawsuits filed against them and their officers. Appointing an outsider—like the Office of the Inspector General for the New York City Police Department—to review police department practices and litigation trends across cases is one approach. Local governments can also require their police departments to review all of the lawsuits brought against them and assess trends across cases, or adopt certain policies, as a term of budget allocations or as a condition of indemnification. Some municipal liability insurers already do something like this: they condition continued coverage and reduced premiums on policies and practices that are expected to reduce liability costs. City and county councils cannot increase police departments' premiums or cut off coverage the way insurers can, but they should be able to leverage the budgetary and other powers they have in similar ways.

I don't promise that any one of these changes—or even all of them together—will get us the system of accountability we need. But they will get us closer.

———

THE FACT THAT THERE ARE SO MANY BARRIERS TO COMPENSATION and deterrence means that there is something for officials at every level of government to do to improve the current state of affairs.

The Supreme Court could do away with all of the barriers to relief that it created. It could do away with qualified immunity. Do away with the "plausibility" pleading standard created in *Iqbal*. Interpret the Constitution in ways that give less latitude to police officers. Ease the *Monell* requirements for local government liability so that police departments are more often held responsible for the acts of their officers. Allow plaintiffs' attorneys to get their reasonable attorneys' fees even if a case is settled before trial. Allow people to get injunctive relief without having to prove that they will have their constitutional rights violated again in the future. Each of these changes would help advance the compensatory and deterrence goals of Section 1983.

Thus far, the Supreme Court has proven reluctant to take any steps to remove the barriers it has created. The Court has periodically flirted with the idea of taking up qualified immunity, and has sent hints that it is stepping back from its most robust descriptions of the doctrine, but it has declined multiple opportunities to decisively limit qualified immunity's power. The Court appears to have even less appetite to pull back other shields of its creation.

Congress could also act tomorrow to remove the barriers the Supreme Court has devised. And at least some members of Congress seem to have more appetite for change than does the Supreme Court. Bills to end qualified immunity, among other wide-ranging policing reforms, were introduced in the summer of 2020 after the murder of George Floyd and were reintroduced in 2021. But after the House passed both bills, and after fifteen months of negotiations in the Senate, the George Floyd Justice in Policing Act was abandoned. Republican senators' unwillingness to limit qualified immunity in any way was a significant stumbling block in their efforts to reach compromise.

In the wake of intransigence at the federal level, states have stepped in. Since May 2020, state lawmakers have proposed bills that would limit or remove several of the barriers erected by the Supreme Court. More than half of the states proposed bills that would effectively do away with the Supreme Court's qualified immunity doctrine by allowing people to bring state law claims for constitutional violations without qualified immunity as a defense. Some of these proposed state laws also allowed for vicarious liability, essentially doing away with the requirements of *Monell*. Some also provided for attorneys' fees for lawyers bringing these state law constitutional claims. State legislatures have also proposed bills that would limit police officers' power to use force in ways that go beyond the Supreme Court's standard in *Graham v. Connor* and create bright-line rules prohibiting chokeholds and no-knock warrants, among other limitations. And states have proposed bills that would require law enforcement agencies to produce information about settlements and judgments entered against them and their officers, among other data. Although Section 1983 was enacted in 1871 to allow people to secure their constitutional rights in federal courts and sidestep the many limitations of state laws and state courts, states are now using their own laws and courts to sidestep the many barriers to relief in Section 1983 cases created by the Supreme Court.

The bill enacted in Colorado in June 2020 is, in many ways, a gold standard. Colorado's bill includes the creative indemnification provision requiring local governments to indemnify their officers but also providing that officers can be required to contribute to a settlement or judgment if they act in bad faith. The bill additionally creates a right to sue law enforcement officers for violations of the Colorado state constitution, prohibits qualified immunity as a defense, and allows plaintiffs' attorneys to recover their fees when they prevail. And the bill bans officers from using chokeholds, creating the type of bright-line limit on police officers' power eschewed by the Supreme Court in *Graham* and its other Fourth Amendment decisions.

Colorado's legislation advances compensation and deterrence in a number of ways. People whose constitutional rights are violated are more likely to win in court because they will not have to overcome the challenges of qualified immunity. Attorneys who bring these cases can get their reasonable fees if they win. Officers who've acted in bad faith can be financially sanctioned in a way that does not deny compensation to people who deserve it. And the requirement that local governments assess whether their officers have acted in bad faith might actually encourage departments to learn from lawsuits brought against them.

Local governments have also stepped up. New York City has engaged in various efforts since 2015 to encourage the NYPD to learn from lawsuits brought against it and its officers. In 2021, New York City also passed a local ordinance creating a right to sue in excessive-force cases without having to overcome qualified immunity. More cities can follow New York City's lead. And, as described above, there is much more that cities and counties can do to create financial penalties for officers who violate the law and pressure their police departments to gather and analyze information from lawsuits brought against them and their officers. In addition, if indemnification rules don't change, city attorneys can stop using the threat that they will deny officers indemnification as a negotiating tool.

Change also needs to come from outside government. More attorneys need to be willing to bring civil rights cases in parts of the country that do not currently have much of a civil rights bar. In 2020, the NAACP Legal Defense Fund announced the Marshall-Motley Scholars Program, which aims to train the next generation of civil rights lawyers. The program is funding fifty law students' legal educations if they commit to being civil rights litigators in the South for at least eight years. These types of initiatives can help jump-start civil rights bars in places where attorneys have not historically signed on to take these cases.

We also need to change the perspectives of people who are called to sit on juries, the people who come to hold the seats of local and state governments, and the people who are appointed as judges. If people in these positions of power are biased in favor of the police, or are biased against people of color, people with mental health challenges, drug and alcohol addiction, or criminal histories, then we can't have a functional system of government accountability. There is no magical solution to reduce or eliminate these biases. But we can't ignore them, and we need to find a path forward here as well.

One approach is to find different people to fill these roles. For example, we can rethink the requirements to sit on a federal jury. Today, in many federal districts, jury duty is limited to registered voters without felony charges or convictions. But some districts draw juror names from a broader pool—those with drivers' licenses or state identification cards, or those who have applied for unemployment benefits—resulting in jury pools that are more reflective of the community. More federal districts should consider this type of expansive approach to juror qualification while experimenting with approaches to address problems with undeliverable jury questionnaires and nonresponsive potential jurors. We can also change the people in charge of our states, counties, and cities. Local government politics have become ground zero for many efforts to improve police accountability, particularly as efforts in the federal government have stalled. So local political office carries great power and potential when it comes to police reform.

We can rethink who sits on the federal bench. As of 2020, federal courts did not reflect the demographics of the country: Although approximately 40 percent of the U.S. population are people of color, less than 27 percent of federal judges were people of color. Although approximately half of the people in the United States are women, only about one-third of judges were women. The federal judiciary has also historically been stacked in favor of the government: the Cato Institute found, as of 2020, that "former courtroom advocates for government (389, 44.20 percent) now outnumber former advocates for individuals against government (57, 6.47 percent) by nearly seven to one." President Joe Biden has prioritized judicial nominees who have experiences as public defenders and civil rights lawyers, women, and people of color. Appointing judges with different backgrounds will mean that when judges use their "experience and common sense" to evaluate plaintiffs' complaints in civil rights cases, they will be applying judgment borne from their experiences seeing disputes from the perspectives of those who believe they have been wronged by government.

Making civil rights lawsuits easier to bring, and making sure that the outcomes of these cases have an impact on officers and departments moving forward, are not going to solve all of the problems in policing. Many important ideas are being explored to influence who is hired to serve in law enforcement and what they are authorized to do. For example, cities have passed initiatives to have unarmed people respond to those having mental health crises, like Tony Timpa and Ryan Cole. Some cities have decriminalized low-level offenses and ended police stops for some minor traffic violations. These kinds of changes should reduce the frequency with which people interact with police and, by extension, the frequency with which people are killed or harmed in these interactions.

But no matter what changes are put in place, there will still be times when government officials overstep the authority they have been given and people are hurt in the process. No matter what policing looks like in the future, we will need tools to compensate people who have been hurt, and to prevent something similar from happening again. Civil rights lawsuits will continue serving an important role. We might as well get them working better than they do now.

———

HOW WE MOVE FORWARD WILL DEPEND—AS IT ALWAYS HAS—ON what those in power believe about the scope and severity of police misconduct and the need for accountability and reform.

In the immediate aftermath of George Floyd's murder, there seemed to be a shared understanding that something needed to change. That was the moment in which Colorado's comprehensive bill made its way through the state legislature. Leslie Herod, the bill's sponsor, had tried to get the bill through the legislature a few months earlier and had been unsuccessful. The bill was gathering dust until, in the aftermath of that tragedy, the legislature was eager to get something done. Representative Herod reintroduced the bill, and it was passed and signed within the month. There were two weeks of intense negotiations with conservative lawmakers, police union groups, and advocates for victims of police misconduct. But the legislature and the governor agreed to end qualified immunity and to create financial responsibility for officers who act in bad faith without being derailed by partisan bickering about lawsuits' power.

Despite Colorado's success, similar bills have failed in California, Washington, Virginia, and elsewhere. I've testified in legislative hearings in several states, and the terms and tone of each have been eerily and frustratingly familiar. Those testifying against the bills threaten that, absent qualified immunity, officers and local governments would face bankruptcy for reasonable mistakes made in a split second and frivolous lawsuits would flood the courts—with no evidence to support these concerns.

I testify, citing my research showing that it is indemnification rules, not qualified immunity, that shield officers' bank accounts. I cite my research showing that police misconduct lawsuits account for less than 1 percent of local governments' budgets, while police departments eat up one-quarter to one-third of those budgets. I read legislators the text of *Graham v. Connor*, which makes clear that officers do not violate the Constitution if they act reasonably from the perspective of an officer on the scene. I point to the many other tools judges can use to weed out frivolous cases. And, almost without fail, during the question-and-answer period, a legislator asks me how I can advocate in favor of ending qualified immunity when it would bankrupt officers for making split-second mistakes.

I spent one Sunday afternoon during the summer of 2020 speaking to a California state assembly member who was on the fence about a proposed bill that would expand the right to sue under state law without a qualified immunity defense. He told me that he feared limiting qualified immunity protections would dramatically increase officers' and local governments' liabilities. I emailed him studies showing that officers in California are required to be indemnified as a matter of state law, that lawsuits account for less than 1 percent of most police departments' budgets, that few cases are actually dismissed on qualified immunity grounds, and that juries most often vote in favor of police instead of plaintiffs. Opponents of the California bill had no comparable evidence of civil rights lawsuits' supposed dangers, but the assembly member remained unconvinced. He told me that when he first joined the California State Assembly, another member of the assembly explained to him that some laws get passed out of hope and other laws get passed out of fear. He said that he did not like making decisions out of fear, but that this bill scared him more than any he could remember. He was not alone: the bill died on the assembly floor.

The types of unfounded fears that swayed the California assembly member's vote have led lawmakers in other states and Congress to vote against legislation that would take tentative but important steps toward a more just system. What legislators should truly fear, though, are the harms that will come to their constituents without more robust civil rights enforcement.

Section 1983 was enacted 150 years ago to provide some measure of justice and accountability in the courts for people whose rights had been violated. Over the past century and a half, a familiar litany of overblown fears have been used as justification to limit the power of Section 1983 in multiple overlapping ways. But the courts, legislators, and local government officials who have erected these barriers to relief don't acknowledge or seem to appreciate the harms these barriers impose on people whose constitutional rights have been violated by police and whose only hope for accountability and justice is through the courts.

Unfounded claims about the dangers of too much justice have brought about a world in which Onree Norris could receive nothing more than a few repairs to his doors after Captain Cody and his team busted into the home he'd lived in for more than fifty years and forced him to the floor; a world in which the Dallas Police Department could hide information about Tony Timpa's death and then argue that his mother's complaint should be dismissed because she did not have that information; a world in which Andrew Scott could be shot to death in his own home by a sheriff's deputy who had no reason to suspect him of any crime, and his girlfriend and parents could receive nothing for their loss; a world in which Robbie Tolan could be shot outside his own home and his family could have to sell that home and spend years of their lives and more than a million dollars to recover just $110,000; a world in which a jury could find that Rob Liese deserved nothing for a police officer's kick so hard that it caused him to lose his spleen.

Overblown fears about bankrupt officers and frivolous lawsuits filling the courts must no longer distract us from the real people whose lives have been shattered by the police and then shattered again by the courts. Our system—in which those who are victims of horrific misconduct must regularly bear the costs of that misconduct themselves—desperately needs repair. The key to moving forward is being guided by hope instead of fear, by evidence instead of rhetoric. Now, armed with the facts, we must act.

ACKNOWLEDGMENTS

This book would not exist without Carolyn Savarese, my phenomenal agent, who convinced me that it needed to be written and that I was the person to write it. Carolyn has been wise, encouraging, ambitious, and levelheaded throughout.

I am incredibly lucky to have been able to work with my brilliant editor at Viking Books, Ibrahim Ahmad. Ibrahim brought tremendous vision, insight, and judgment to the table each time we met. Thanks also to Georgia Bodnar for acquiring the book, and to the entire team at Viking—including Brian Tart, Andrea Schulz, Patrick Nolan, Kate Stark, Lindsay Prevette, Carolyn Coleburn, Mary Stone, Marissa Davis, Michael Brown, and Linda Friedner—for bringing it to fruition. My daughter, Kate, was a lifesaver twice over for coming up with the subtitle to the book and snapping my author photo. Chef's kiss to Abby Weintraub, who designed one heck of a cover.

This book's foundation is fifteen years' worth of research about police misconduct litigation. Many thanks to the student editors of all of the law reviews that published those articles, including those at *Cardozo Law Review, Chicago Legal Forum, Columbia Law Review, Georgetown Law*

Journal, Indiana Law Journal, Michigan Law Review, New York University Law Review, Northwestern University Law Review, UCLA Law Review, University of Chicago Law Review, William & Mary Law Review, and *The Yale Law Journal*. Thanks also to my tremendous coauthors on two of those articles—Ingrid Eagly on one, and Alex Reinert and Jim Pfander on the other. Several research assistants provided invaluable assistance on those articles over the past decade and a half, including Blake Berich, Jack Cambou, Brian Cardile, Thomas Cochrane, Michelle Cuozzo, Richard Frye, Kenyon Harbison, Maxwell Harwitt, Tommy Huynh, Ayan Jacobs, David Koller, Karen Kwok, Daniel Matusov, Rosemary McClure, Madeline Morrison, Madeleine Mozina, Hannah Pollack, David Schmutzer, Douglas Souza, Adam Swank, CT Turney-Lewis, Rachel Vazquez, Bryanna Walker, Luke Ward, and Maggie Yates. Extra thanks to Adam, Bryanna, and Madeleine for assisting with additional research for this book. Many thanks, also, to UCLA School of Law, my intellectual home since 2006, for supporting my work; to my wonderful colleagues for engaging with me on this book and the articles that came before; and to UCLA's incredible library staff and empirical research group.

I am deeply humbled by and grateful to all of the people who have shared their experiences and insights with me over the past fifteen years, including victims of misconduct, civil rights attorneys, federal and state legislators, city attorneys, risk managers, budget officers, police auditors, and law enforcement officials. Their perspectives about how the world works have been an inspiration and a guiding force. For enlightening me about the cases that anchor the chapters of the book, special thanks to Amir Ali, Easha Anand, Cary Aspinwall, Charles Bonner, James Campbell, Mark Cannan, Nicholas Conway, Terry Ekl, Benjamin Hall, Geoff Henley, Susan Hutchison, Kris Kelley, Geoffrey King, Rob Liese, Miranda Mauck, James Montgomery, Mark NeJame, Melissa Nold, Kimo Parham, Jason Recksiedler, Katie Rosenfeld, John Ross, William Ruffier, Jesse Ryder, Darryl Scott, Eric Seitz, Houston Stevens, Michael Sutherlin, Marian Tolan, Michael Verna, and Nate Washington.

Much that I've written—in this book and elsewhere—can be traced back to questions I first asked as I was working on civil rights cases as a law student and lawyer. I am appreciative beyond words for the professors and lawyers who trained and mentored me during those years, especially Brett Dignam and Steve Bright at Yale Law School; the fabulous lawyers at what was then Clarence, Snell & Dyer LLP, in San Francisco; and the amazing team at what was then Emery Celli Cuti Brinckerhoff & Abady LLP, in New York City.

I am indebted to those who read and commented on drafts of the book proposal and manuscript—Easha Anand, Kate Aurthur, Karen Blum, Devon Carbado, Maureen Carroll, Beth Colgan, Brenda Coughlin, Ali Cudby, Kate Dyer, Ellen Fey, Barry Friedman, Kathryn Hahn, William Patrick, Jim Pfander, Alex Reinert, Stephen Yeazell, and Brad Zukerman—and am especially beholden to Kate Aurthur, Beth, Devon, William, and Steve for not only reading but also patiently and generously rereading many of these pages several times.

Deepest gratitude of all goes to my family. To my parents, Dan and Teresa, for their unconditional love, support, and encouragement. To our children, Kate and Julian, for each being their extraordinary selves, brimming with passion, integrity, courage, and heart. To our dog, Otto, who spent incalculable hours valiantly defending me from the mailman and other potential intruders while I wrote. And to Teddy, my devastatingly handsome husband and very best friend, for joining me on this and every other journey—some have been fabulous, and some have been downright harrowing, but all have been better with you along for the ride.

GLOSSARY

LEGAL TERMS

Absolute immunity. Prosecutors, judges, legislators, and witnesses are all entitled to absolute immunity—meaning that they cannot be sued under Section 1983 for misconduct related to their duties. In contrast, most other government officials—including police officers—are entitled to a qualified immunity, meaning that they can be sued only for conduct that violates "clearly established law." See *qualified immunity.*

Answer. In the world of civil litigation, a response by defendants to the plaintiffs' complaint, admitting or denying each of the plaintiffs' allegations. The answer gives the parties and the judge a better sense of what the disputed issues in the case will be.

Bright-line rule. A clearly defined rule that leaves little room for varying interpretations.

Civil Rights Act of 1871. Also known as the Ku Klux Klan Act, the Act was enacted during Reconstruction. Section 1 of the Act ultimately became Section 1983, the statute allowing people to sue when their constitutional rights are violated by state and local government officials.

Complaint. The first legal filing in a court case, setting out who the defendants are, what the plaintiffs assert the defendants did wrong, and what the plaintiffs want in terms of relief—usually, in Section 1983 cases, money and/or an injunction. See *injunction.*

Consent decree. An agreement between the parties that resolves their dispute and is approved by the judge, who will often appoint a court monitor to make sure the parties comply with the consent decree's terms. A standard settlement agreement, in contrast, is negotiated between the parties without a judge's approval and without the judge's continuing oversight.

The Department of Justice often enters into consent decrees with the local governments it investigates and sues for civil rights violations, requiring that the government take specified steps to improve their policies, training, and supervision.

Contingency fee. An arrangement between a lawyer and a client who does not want to—or cannot afford to—pay their lawyer by the hour for their time. A contingency-fee agreement provides that the lawyer will represent the client without payment, but that the client will pay the lawyer a portion of any recovery in the case if they are successful. The percentage of the contingency varies depending on the agreement between the lawyer and client, and can vary in a single case depending on the stage of the litigation at which the plaintiff is successful.

Court of appeals. See *federal court structure*.

Deposition. A part of discovery in which a witness or party to the case is asked questions under oath about the case. Depositions are transcribed and often recorded on video, and the testimony can be used in summary judgment motions and, sometimes, at trial. See *discovery*.

Discovery. The parties' exchange of information relevant to the claims in a lawsuit. Discovery includes depositions; the exchange of documents, computer files, and other information; and the hiring of experts to offer opinions about critical issues in the case. Discovery usually occurs after the complaint and answer and any motion to dismiss have been filed, and before summary judgment and/or trial. See *motion to dismiss*; *summary judgment*.

District court. See *federal court structure*.

Exclusionary rule. A rule that prevents evidence collected in violation of a defendant's constitutional rights from being used in their criminal prosecution. The Supreme Court ruled in *Mapp v. Ohio* (1961) that the exclusionary rule applied to state courts. Before *Mapp*, the exclusionary rule applied only to federal courts.

Federal court structure. In the federal system, there are three levels of courts: The lowest level is comprised of district courts, the trial-level courts. District courts have jurisdiction over cases from the time the complaint is first filed through discovery and trial. There are multiple district court judges in each federal district, and ninety-four federal districts across the country. Courts of appeals hear appeals from the federal district courts in their jurisdiction. Courts of appeals usually hear appeals in three-judge panels; they can also be asked to rehear appeals en banc, before all or many of the judges sitting on that court of appeals. Courts of appeals are organized into twelve regional circuits—all but one of which include multiple states—plus one circuit court that hears appeals from all the districts in specialized cases, like those involving patent law. Finally, there is the nine-justice United States Supreme Court, which can decide to hear appeals from the courts of appeals. Although parties have a right to appeal decisions in their cases to the courts of appeals, they must request review by the Supreme Court. The Court receives thousands of these requests—called petitions for a writ of certiorari—and grants fewer than one hundred each year.

Fee shifting. Although each party usually pays for their own attorneys, some statutes allow for fee shifting, whereby the losers pay the winners' attorneys' fees. Section 1988 is a fee-shifting statute. In Section 1988, the fee shifting typically goes in one direction: defendants pay plaintiffs' attorneys' fees if plaintiffs win, but plaintiffs do not pay defendants' attorneys' fees unless the judge concludes that the case was frivolous. See *Section 1988.*

General warrant. A warrant based on no evidence of wrongdoing that places no limits on places that can be searched and what can be seized. The Fourth Amendment, which requires that warrants "particularly describ[e] the place to be searched, and the persons or things to be seized," was a response to general warrants used by the British Parliament in colonial America. See *warrant.*

Indemnification. If a local government indemnifies their officers, it pays any settlements or judgments entered against them. Local governments' obligations to indemnify their officers are sometimes required by state law, and sometimes as part of a union agreement or a local government practice or policy.

Injunction. A court order commanding a party—usually a defendant—to do something or stop doing something. An injunction can be narrow (to stop strip-searching people arrested for minor crimes) or broad (to develop new policies, trainings, and supervision aimed at reducing excessive force by officers).

"John Doe" defendants. Sometimes, when people file a lawsuit, they do not know the names of the individual officers who allegedly violated their rights. In such a case, when the plaintiffs file a complaint they will typically name the city and "John Doe" defendants, and include allegations against those "John Doe" defendants. Eventually, when plaintiffs figure out the real names of those "John Does," usually during discovery, they can amend the complaint to add in their real names.

"Knock and announce." A rule, part of Fourth Amendment doctrine, that requires law enforcement officers to knock and announce their presence before conducting a search. The obligation to "knock and announce" before a search has been limited in several ways, including by the rise of no-knock warrants and searches. See *no-knock warrants.*

"Knock and talk." The police practice of going to the entrance of a person's home, knocking at the front door, and then speaking with the person inside. Knock and talks generally don't trigger any of the protections of the Fourth Amendment, so officers can knock and talk without a warrant, probable cause, or reasonable suspicion.

Motion to dismiss. A motion made by defendants at the beginning of a lawsuit, asking the court to dismiss the case because the allegations in the plaintiffs' complaint do not state a claim for relief—meaning, the allegations would not be sufficient, if true, to establish the defendants' wrongdoing. Before *Ashcroft v. Iqbal* (2009) and *Bell Atlantic v. Twombly* (2007), the Supreme Court instructed district courts to grant a motion to dismiss only if, assuming all of the allegations in the complaint were true, the plaintiffs could not prevail. After *Iqbal* and *Twombly*, district courts faced with a motion to dismiss must assess which allegations in the complaint are "plausible," and then decide whether those allegations state a claim for relief. A motion to dismiss can also, more generally, refer to any request to the judge by defendants to dismiss part or all of the plaintiffs' case. After discovery, such a motion is referred to as a motion for summary judgment. See *summary judgment; Ashcroft v. Iqbal; Bell Atlantic v. Twombly.*

Municipal liability. A municipal liability claim is a legal claim against a local government—typically a county or a city. Municipal liability claims are also sometimes called *Monell* claims, which is a reference to the Supreme Court case that first ruled that local governments could be sued under Section 1983. To establish municipal liability under Section 1983, plaintiffs must show that the local government had a "policy or custom" that "caused" their constitutional rights to be violated. See *Monell v. Department of Social Services.*

No-knock warrants. A warrant executed without law enforcement first knocking and announcing their presence. Although the notion that officers should knock and announce their presence before executing a warrant is centuries old, judges sometimes issue no-knock warrants if they are convinced that officers knocking and announcing their presence would lead to the destruction of evidence or increased danger. The Supreme Court has also ruled that officers can make a no-knock entry—even if they do not have a no-knock warrant—if they have "reasonable suspicion" that knocking and announcing would be dangerous or prevent effective investigation of the crime.

Pleadings. The first filings in a lawsuit—the complaint and answer. See *answer*; *complaint.*

Probable cause. The Fourth Amendment provides that "no Warrants shall issue, but upon probable cause." Probable cause is, in theory, required before arresting a person or searching a home, although a multitude of exceptions have virtually swallowed up the rule. The Supreme Court has defined probable cause as "not a high bar," requiring "only a probability or substantial chance of criminal activity."

Pro bono. Short for "pro bono publico," a Latin term that means "for the public good." When lawyers represent people pro bono, they do so without charge.

Qualified immunity. A legal defense for police officers and other government officials from damages liability, even if they have violated the Constitution, so long as they have not violated what the Supreme Court calls "clearly established law." There is no qualified immunity for local governments and no qualified immunity for claims seeking injunctive relief.

Reasonable suspicion. The Supreme Court first announced this standard in *Terry v. Ohio* (1968), when it ruled that an officer did not need probable cause before stopping and frisking someone—reasonable suspicion is enough. The Court in *Terry* defined reasonable suspicion as something less than probable cause but more than an "inchoate and unparticularized suspicion or hunch." In practice, reasonable suspicion has been interpreted to be a very low bar, and is not only the standard for stops and frisks but also for other intrusions, like no-knock searches.

Section 1983. The statute, formally 42 U.S.C. § 1983, that allows people to sue local governments and government officers for violating the Constitution and to seek damages or injunctive relief. State officials can also be sued under Section 1983, but states themselves cannot; nor can federal officers and the federal government. In *Bivens v. Six Unknown Federal Narcotics Agents* (1971), the Supreme Court ruled that federal agents can be sued directly under the Constitution, but the Supreme Court has greatly restricted that right in recent years.

Section 1988. The fee-shifting statute, formally 42 U.S.C. § 1988, that allows prevailing plaintiffs in Section 1983 cases to recover their reasonable attorneys' fees. See *fee shifting.*

Summary judgment. When defendants move for summary judgment, they are asking the judge to dismiss some or all of the plaintiffs' claims because, given the evidence unearthed during discovery, no reasonable jury could find for the plaintiffs. Judges are supposed to review the evidence "in the light most favorable" to the plaintiffs—meaning that they should assume that the jury would believe the plaintiffs' witnesses and evidence, and grant summary judgment only if a reasonable jury could not find for the plaintiffs even after giving them every benefit of the doubt. Plaintiffs sometimes (though infrequently) move for summary judgment; when they do, these roles are reversed.

Vicarious liability. A legal doctrine that holds one party responsible for the improper conduct of another. For example, employers are generally vicariously liable for the misconduct of their employees, and so must pay any settlement or judgment arising from their misconduct on the job. In *Monell v. Department of Social Services* (1978), the Supreme Court considered, but rejected, the argument that local governments should be vicariously liable for unconstitutional conduct by their officers, ruling instead that local governments must have a "policy or custom" that "caused" the constitutional violation in order to be held responsible under Section 1983.

Warrant. A document issued by a judge or magistrate that authorizes law enforcement officers to search a place or arrest a person. Warrants can only be issued upon a showing of probable cause. See *probable cause*.

KEY CASES

Ashcroft v. Iqbal, 556 U.S. 662 (2009). Javaid Iqbal was arrested following the September 11 attacks, held in highly restrictive conditions, and repeatedly assaulted. Iqbal sued Attorney General Ashcroft and FBI Director Mueller, alleging that they had instituted a policy to arrest thousands of Arab and Muslim men and hold them in highly restrictive conditions based on their religion and national origin. In a 5–4 decision, the Supreme Court dismissed Iqbal's case against Ashcroft and Mueller because the allegations in the complaint were not "plausible" in the view of the five-Justice majority. *Iqbal* built on the Supreme Court's decision in *Twombly* (2007) and is generally regarded as having made it more difficult for plaintiffs to draft complaints that can withstand a motion to dismiss.

Baxter v. Bracey, 751 Fed. Appx. 869 (6th. Cir. 2018), *cert. denied,* **140 S. Ct. 1862 (2020).** In *Baxter*, the Sixth Circuit granted qualified immunity to officers who released a police dog on a suspect who was sitting down in surrender with his hands in the air, even though a prior Sixth Circuit case had held it was unconstitutional to release a police dog on a person who had surrendered by lying down. *Baxter*, like *Jessop* and *Kelsay*, is an example of just how factually similar a prior court case must be to "clearly establish" the law for qualified immunity purposes.

Bell Atlantic v. Twombly, 550 U.S. 544 (2007). In *Twombly*, the Supreme Court dismissed an antitrust claim because the complaint did not include factual allegations showing an illegal agreement by the companies. The *Twombly* decision rejected the Court's instruction in *Conley v. Gibson* (1957) that "a complaint should not be dismissed for failure to state a claim unless it appears beyond doubt that the plaintiff can prove no set of facts in support of his claim which would entitle him to relief" and ruled, instead, that the allegations in a complaint must be "plausible." The Court's requirement in *Twombly* that a complaint be "plausible" was restrictively interpreted by the Court two years later in *Iqbal* (2009).

Brady v. Maryland, 373 U.S. 83 (1963). In *Brady*, the Supreme Court ruled that prosecutors must turn over all exculpatory evidence—evidence that might be favorable to a criminal defendant—to that defendant.

Brown v. Board of Education, 347 U.S. 483 (1954). This unanimous Supreme Court decision ruled that separating children in public schools on the basis of race was unconstitutional, and overturned the "separate but equal" principle set forth by the Supreme Court's 1896 decision in *Plessy v. Ferguson*.

Brown v. Board of Education, 349 U.S. 294 (1955). In this decision, commonly referred to as *Brown II*, the Supreme Court considered how best to implement its 1954 decision declaring racial discrimination in public education to be unconstitutional. A unanimous court concluded that lower courts should design remedies befitting the circumstances in each local school district, and issue orders "necessary and proper to admit to public schools on a racially nondiscriminatory basis with all deliberate speed the parties to these cases."

City of Canton v. Harris, 489 U.S. 378 (1989). In *City of Canton*, the Supreme Court ruled that a local government could be held liable under Section 1983 for failing to train its officers, if that failure amounts to a deliberate indifference to the constitutional rights of people with whom the police come into contact.

City of Los Angeles v. Lyons, 461 U.S. 95 (1983). In this 5–4 decision, the Court ruled that the plaintiff could not seek injunctive relief after being subjected to a chokehold by a Los Angeles police officer, because the plaintiff could not "establish a real and immediate threat that he would again be stopped for a traffic violation, or for any other offense, by an officer who would illegally choke him into unconsciousness without any provocation."

City of Riverside v. Rivera, 477 U.S. 561 (1986). The Court ruled, 5–4, that the plaintiffs were entitled to more than $245,000 in attorneys' fees following a jury verdict of $33,350 for the plaintiffs. But the Justices were divided, 4–4, about whether attorneys' fees under 42 U.S.C. § 1988 should substantially exceed what the jury awarded the plaintiffs at trial—Justice Powell, the ninth Justice, upheld the attorneys' fee award in the case, deferring to the lower court's detailed findings, but expressed "serious doubts as to the fairness of the fees awarded in the case."

Conley v. Gibson, 355 U.S. 41 (1957). In a case alleging racial discrimination by union leaders, the Supreme Court unanimously ruled that, at the motion-to-dismiss stage, the allegations in a plaintiff's complaint should be assumed true, and the motion should not be granted "unless it appears beyond doubt that the plaintiff can prove no set of facts in support of his claim which would entitle him to relief." *Conley* is generally understood to have been effectively overturned by the Supreme Court's decisions in *Twombly* and *Iqbal*.

Connick v. Thompson, 563 U.S. 51 (2011). In a 5–4 decision, the Supreme Court narrowly interpreted the standard for "failure to train" *Monell* claims first recognized by *City of Canton v. Harris* (1989). As a result, the prosecutor's office could not be held liable for withholding *Brady* material from John Thompson, even though four other criminal convictions had been overturned for withholding *Brady* material in recent years by the same office. See *Monell v. Department of Social Services*; *Brady v. Maryland*.

Evans v. Jeff D., 475 U.S. 717 (1986). The Supreme Court held that settlement agreements in Section 1983 cases could waive plaintiffs' rights to seek attorneys' fees under Section 1988.

Graham v. Connor, 490 U.S. 386 (1989). In *Graham*, the Supreme Court set a hazy standard for Fourth Amendment excessive-force claims. According to *Graham*, courts must consider the totality of the circumstances when deciding whether force was excessive, including "the severity of the crime at issue, whether the suspect poses an immediate threat to the safety of the officers or others, and whether he is actively resisting arrest . . . or attempting to evade arrest by flight."

Hague v. C.I.O., 307 U.S. 496 (1939). In *Hague,* the Supreme Court affirmed the grant of a sweeping injunction to address First Amendment violations by a mayor. It is an example of an early civil rights case by the Court allowing injunctive relief, in contrast to later decisions by the Court limiting entitlement to injunctive relief.

Harlow v. Fitzgerald, 457 U.S. 800 (1982). In *Harlow*, the Supreme Court ruled that an officer is entitled to qualified immunity so long as he did not violate "clearly established law," and that the standard is objective (meaning that it does not turn on evidence of the officer's state of mind). *Harlow* overturned the Supreme Court's decision in *Pierson v. Ray* (1967) that qualified immunity turned on an officer's "good faith." As a result, an officer can enjoy the protections of qualified immunity, even if they violated the Constitution and acted in bad faith, so long as the plaintiff cannot point to a prior court decision with similar facts.

Hope v. Pelzer, 536 U.S. 730 (2002). *Hope* is a rare case in which the Supreme Court ruled that an officer was *not* entitled to qualified immunity. Prison guards had shackled the plaintiff to a hitching post all day beneath the Alabama sun. Although there was no prior court case with similar facts, the Court ruled that the Eighth Amendment violation was "obvious."

Hudson v. Michigan, 547 U.S. 586 (2006). In a 5–4 decision, the Supreme Court ruled that evidence seized when police violate the "knock and announce" rule can still be used in a defendant's criminal prosecution.

Jessop v. City of Fresno, 936 F.3d 937 (9th Cir. 2019), *cert. denied*, **140 S. Ct. 2793 (2020).** In *Jessop*, the court of appeals granted qualified immunity to officers who stole more than $225,000 in cash and rare coins while executing a warrant because prior court decisions "did not put the constitutional question beyond debate."

Katz v. United States, 389 U.S. 347 (1967). In *Katz*, the Supreme Court ruled that the Fourth Amendment applies anywhere a person has a "reasonable expectation of privacy."

Kelsay v. Ernst, 933 F.3d 975 (8th Cir. 2019), *cert. denied*, **140 S. Ct. 2760 (2020).** The court of appeals ruled that an officer who threw a woman to the ground, knocking her unconscious, simply because she walked away from him, was entitled to qualified immunity.

Mapp v. Ohio, 367 U.S. 643 (1961). In *Mapp*, the Supreme Court ruled that evidence unconstitutionally seized by police, in violation of the Fourth Amendment, could be excluded from criminal trials in state court.

McCoy v. Alamu, 141 S. Ct. 1364 (2021). In *McCoy*, the Supreme Court summarily reversed a lower court decision granting qualified immunity to an officer who sprayed a prisoner with a chemical agent. Although the Supreme Court did not issue an opinion, the reversal—which cited *Taylor v. Riojas*—has been interpreted as a signal by the Court that it may be stepping away from its most robust descriptions of the qualified immunity doctrine.

Mincey v. Arizona, 437 U.S 385 (1978). In this opinion, the Supreme Court explained that officers do not need a warrant when "the exigencies of the situation make the needs of law enforcement so compelling that a warrantless search is objectively reasonable under the Fourth Amendment."

Miranda v. Arizona, 384 U.S. 436 (1966). *Miranda* held that officers must notify people of their right to an attorney and their right to remain silent before being questioned. Statements obtained without *Miranda* warnings cannot be used by criminal prosecutors to prove their case-in-chief. The Supreme Court held, in *Vega v. Tekoh* (2022), that the failure to give *Miranda* warnings cannot be the basis for a Section 1983 claim.

Monell v. Department of Social Services, 436 U.S. 658 (1978). In *Monell*, the Supreme Court ruled that municipalities could be held liable under Section 1983 if they had a "policy or custom" that "caused" the constitutional violation.

Monroe v. Pape, 365 U.S. 167 (1961). In *Monroe*, the Supreme Court held that people could sue law enforcement officers and other government officials for constitutional violations under Section 1983. *Monroe* also held that local governments could *not* be sued under Section 1983—this aspect of the *Monroe* decision was overruled by *Monell v. Department of Social Services* (1978).

O'Shea v. Littleton, 414 U.S. 488 (1974). In *O'Shea*, the Supreme Court ruled that the plaintiffs could not seek an injunction to combat widespread criminal justice abuses in Cairo, Illinois. *O'Shea* was among several Supreme Court decisions—including *Younger, Rizzo*, and *Lyons*—limiting the power of plaintiffs to seek injunctions for civil rights violations in the 1970s and 1980s.

Owen v. City of Independence, 445 U.S. 622 (1980). In *Owen*, a 5–4 decision, the Supreme Court ruled that municipalities sued under Section 1983 are not entitled to the protections of qualified immunity.

Pierson v. Ray, 386 U.S. 547 (1967). In *Pierson*, the Supreme Court first ruled that officers were entitled to a qualified immunity from suit if they acted in good faith. The good-faith standard was eliminated by the Supreme Court in 1982, in *Harlow v. Fitzgerald*, and replaced with "clearly established law," an objective standard not dependent on the officer's state of mind.

Plessy v. Ferguson, 163 U.S. 537 (1896). *Plessy* upheld the constitutionality of racial segregation under the "separate but equal" doctrine, and was overturned by the Supreme Court's decision in *Brown v. Board of Education* (1954).

Rizzo v. Goode, 423 U.S. 362 (1976). In *Rizzo*, the Supreme Court ruled that the plaintiffs could not seek an injunction to combat widespread mistreatment of Black people by the Philadelphia Police Department.

Scott v. Harris, 550 U.S. 372 (2007). In *Scott*, the Supreme Court ruled that an officer had used reasonable—and thus constitutional—force when he pushed his bumper into the rear of the plaintiff's car, causing him to run off the road and paralyzing him. The majority's decision relied heavily on video of the event, but a later study found that people viewing that video have different interpretations of what happened that correlate to their race and political views, among other factors.

Screws v. United States, 325 U.S. 91 (1945). The Supreme Court, in *Screws*, ruled that officers are acting "under color of state law" even if they violate the law, so long as they are acting "under 'pretense' of law." Although *Screws* was a criminal case, its interpretation of "color of state law" was applied in Section 1983 cases and, ultimately, in *Monroe v. Pape* (1961).

Swann v. Charlotte-Mecklenburg Board of Education, 402 U.S. 1 (1971). In *Swann*, a unanimous decision, the Supreme Court held that district courts had broad powers to order injunctive relief aimed at desegregating schools following the Court's decision in *Brown v. Board of Education* (1954).

Taylor v. Riojas, 141 S. Ct. 52 (2020) (per curiam). The Supreme Court reversed the lower courts' grant of qualified immunity in *Taylor*, ruling that "any reasonable officer should have realized that Taylor's conditions of confinement [in 'shockingly unsanitary' prison cells] offended the Constitution." *Taylor* is the first Supreme Court case since *Hope v. Pelzer* (2002) to hold that an officer can be denied qualified immunity for obvious constitutional violations.

Tennessee v. Garner, 471 U.S. 1 (1985). In *Garner*, the Supreme Court clarified that the Fourth Amendment—not the Fourteenth—applies when a police officer uses deadly force in the course of an arrest or other seizure, and ruled that an officer violates the Fourth Amendment when using deadly force unless they have probable cause to believe that the suspect has committed a felony and poses a threat to the officer or the community.

Terry v. Ohio, 392 U.S. 1 (1968). In *Terry*, the Supreme Court ruled that the Fourth Amendment does not require an officer to have probable cause before stopping and frisking someone—reasonable suspicion is enough. The Court in *Terry* defined reasonable suspicion as something less than probable cause but something more than an "inchoate and unparticularized suspicion or hunch."

Younger v. Harris, 401 U.S. 37 (1971). In *Younger*, the Supreme Court ruled that plaintiffs could not get an injunction to stop pending or threatened criminal prosecutions. Justice Hugo Black's opinion described in sweeping terms the importance of protecting local governments from undue federal oversight, describing the "ideals and dreams of 'Our Federalism,'" that required state institutions "be allowed to perform their separate functions in their separate ways." *Younger* was relied upon by the Supreme Court in later cases limiting the power of plaintiffs in civil rights cases to seek injunctive relief, including *O'Shea*, *Rizzo*, and *Lyons*.

NOTES

INTRODUCTION

ix **On the afternoon of February 8:** These facts are drawn from the complaint, the summary judgment opposition filed by the plaintiff, and the depositions of the defendants and plaintiff in Norris v. Hicks, No. 1:18-cv-02163-MLB (N.D. Ga. May 15, 2018); an interview and email correspondence with Norris's attorney, Darryl Scott; body camera footage from the incident; and news stories including Billy Binion, "Over 24 Cops Raided the Wrong Address and Wrecked an Elderly Man's Home. They All Got Qualified Immunity," *Reason*, June 9, 2021, reason.com/2021/06/09/qualified-immunity-police-onree-norris-raid-wrong-address-11th-circuit/; Brendan Keefe and Lindsey Basye, "Qualified Immunity: Police Off the Hook for No-Knock Raid on Wrong House," 11Alive, Sept. 11, 2020, www.11alive.com/article/news/investigations/the-reveal/henry-county-no-knock-warrant-wrong-house/85-3af2b307-8a6a-4f8c-8355-3ebe58a8c508; and Nick Sibilla, "Cop Who Wrongly Led No-Knock Raid Against 78-Year-Old-Grandfather Can't Be Sued, Court Rules," *Forbes*, June 8, 2021, www.forbes.com/sites/nicksibilla/2021/06/08/cop-who-led-accidental-no-knock-raid-against-78-year-old-grandfather-cant-be-sued-court-rules/?sh=2537ac3468b3. In my description of Onree Norris's case, and in my descriptions of all of the cases in this book, some of the facts I recount are disputed by the parties. My goal throughout is to present the facts in the light most favorable to the plaintiff, which is the standard that courts are instructed to apply when deciding whether to allow a case to move forward in litigation.

xi **That's what Onree Norris:** See Keefe and Basye, "Police Off the Hook."

xii **If you believe that our prisons:** Kate Levine has sounded "a cautionary note about the use of individual prosecutions to remedy police brutality," because "police prosecutions legitimize the criminal legal system while at the same time displaying the same racism and ineffectiveness that have been shown to pervade our prison-backed criminal machinery." Kate Levine, "Police Prosecutions and Punitive Instincts," *Washington University Law Review* 98 (2021): 997.

xii **police officers are criminally charged:** For data about the frequency with which police are criminally prosecuted, and the decisions by officers, prosecutors, and jurors that lead to low rates of prosecution and conviction, see Kimberly Kindy and Kimbriell Kelly, "Thousands Dead, Few Prosecuted," *Washington Post*, April 11, 2015 (noting the scarcity of charges against police officers despite thousands of deaths at their hands between 2005 and 2015), www.washingtonpost.com/sf/investigative/2015/04/11/thousands-dead-few-prosecuted; German Lopez, "Police Officers Are Prosecuted for Murder in Less Than 2 Percent of Fatal Shootings," *Vox*, April 2, 2021, www.vox.com/21497089/derek-chauvin-george-floyd-trial-police-prosecutions-black-lives-matter. The Henry A. Wallace Police Crime Database, which tracks prosecutions of police officers and is relied upon by Lopez, can be found at policecrime.bgsu.edu/.

xii **conducting shoddy investigations:** For research about the shortcomings of police internal investigations, see Rachel Moran, "Ending the Internal Affairs Farce," *Buffalo Law Review* 64 (2016): 853–68; Joanna C. Schwartz, "What Police Learn from Lawsuits," *Cardozo Law Review* 33 (2012): 862–74. For a sample of news reports about various police departments' lax investigation and disciplinary practices, see Evan Allen, Matt Rocheleau, and Andrew Ryan, "Within the Boston Police Department, Complaints Against Officers Are Rarely Confirmed or Result in Punishment," *Boston Globe*, July 18, 2020, www.bostonglobe.com/2020/07/18/metro/within-boston-police-department-complaints-against-officers-are-rarely-confirmed-or-result-punishment/; Bill Cummings, "CT's Secretive Police Disciplinary System Rarely Leads to Serious Punishment," *Connecticut Post*, June 23, 2021, www.ctpost.com/projects/2021/police-misconduct/; Violet Ikonomova, "'Deeply Broken': How Detroit Lets Bad Cops Off the Hook," *Deadline Detroit*, April 28, 2022, www.deadlinedetroit.com/articles/30418/deeply_broken_how_detroit_lets_bad_cops_off_the_hook; Rio Lacanlale, "Report: Las Vegas Police Misconduct Complaints Rarely Lead to Discipline," *Las Vegas Review-Journal*, June 2, 2021, www.reviewjournal.com/crime/report-las-vegas-police-misconduct-complaints-rarely-lead-to-discipline-2369536/; Robert Salonga, "Exclusive: New San Jose Police Records Show Officers Rarely Disciplined for Serious Use of Force," *San Jose Mercury News*, Oct. 4, 2020, www.mercurynews.com/2020/10/04/exclusive-new-san-jose-police-records-show-officers-rarely-disciplined-for-serious-use-of-force.

xii **elaborate processes they can use:** For a description of these processes and the frequency with which officer discipline and firings are overturned, see Stephen Rushin, "Police Arbitration," *Vanderbilt Law Review* 74 (2021): 1023–64; Stephen Rushin, "Police Union Contracts," *Duke Law Journal* 66 (2017): 1222–39.

xiii **"who may harbor doubts":** Owen v. City of Independence, 445 U.S. 622, 652 (1980).

xiii **lead them to "discharge . . . offending officials":** Newport v. Fact Concerts, 453 U.S. 247, 269 (1981).

xiii **and "institute internal rules and programs":** *Owen*, 445 U.S. at 652.

xiii **violated "clearly established law":** Harlow v. Fitzgerald, 457 U.S. 800, 818 (1982).

xiv **"presumptively unreasonable":** Norris v. Hicks, 855 Fed. Appx. 515, 521 (11th Cir. May 5, 2021) (citation omitted).

xiv **"a reasonable effort to ascertain":** *Norris*, 855 Fed. Appx. at 522 (citation omitted).

xiv **the very same court:** Treat v. Lowe, 668 F. Appx. 870 (11th Cir. 2016).

xiv **But that prior court decision:** *Norris*, 855 Fed. Appx. at 522n9.

xvi **How could lawsuit payouts:** *Owen*, 445 U.S. at 652.

xvi **How could the cases we worked:** *Newport*, 453 U.S. at 269; *Owen*, 445 U.S. at 652.

xviii **outgrowth of slave patrols:** Outside the Southeast, police departments were modeled after the London Metropolitan Police. For a discussion of these dual origin stories of American policing, see Samuel Walker, "Governing the American Police: Wrestling with the Problems of Democracy," *University of Chicago Legal Forum* 2016 (2016): 623–25.

xviii **"as feared on the border":** Doug J. Swanson, *Cult of Glory: The Bold and Brutal History of the Texas Rangers* (New York: Viking, 2020), 4.

xix **Black women:** For relative inattention paid to police killings of Black women, see Kimberlé Williams Crenshaw and Andrea J. Ritchie, "Say Her Name: Resisting Police Brutality Against Black Women," *African American Policy Forum* (2015): 4–7, static1.squarespace.com/static/53f20d90e4b0b80451158d8c/t/55a810d7e4b058f342f55873/1437077719984/AAPF_SM_Brief_full_singles.compressed.pdf.

xix **more likely to be killed by the police:** For research that Black people—particularly Black men—are disproportionately likely to be killed by police, see Jeffrey A. Fagan and Alexis D. Campbell, "Race and Reasonableness in Police Killings," *Boston University Law Review* 100 (2020): 951–1016; Jon Swaine et al., "Young Black Men Killed by U.S. Police at Highest Rate in Year of 1,134 Deaths," *Guardian*, Dec. 31, 2015; Global Burden of Disease 2019 Police Violence U.S. Subnational Collaborators, "Fatal Police Violence by Race and State in the USA, 1980–2019: A Network Meta-regression," *Lancet* 398 (2021): 1239–55.

xix **to be unarmed:** For evidence that Black people killed by police are disproportionately likely to be unarmed, see, for example, Elle Lett et al., "Racial Inequity in Fatal U.S. Police Shootings, 2015–2020," *Journal of Epidemiology and Community Health*, Oct. 27, 2020, 394–97.

xix **more likely to be stopped:** For evidence that Black people are more likely to be stopped, searched, and assaulted by police, see, for example, Erika Harrell and Elizabeth Davis, "Contacts Between Police and the Public, 2018—Statistical Tables," Bureau of Justice Statistics, Dec. 17, 2020; Rory Kramer and Brianna Remster, "Stop, Frisk, and Assault? Racial Disparities in Police Use of Force During Investigations," *Law and Society Review* 52 (2018): 987 (studying stops in New York City) ("In sum, black individuals [in New York City] are not only more likely to be stopped by police, they are also more likely to be subjected to police use of force during that interaction, and more likely to be seen as threatening to officers, resulting in a greater rate of police drawing their weapons.").

xix **Latinx and Indigenous people also suffer:** See, for example, Julissa Arce, "It's Long Past Time We Recognized All the Latinos Killed at the Hands of Police," *Time*, July 21, 2020; Silvia Foster-Frau, "Latinos Are Disproportionately Killed by Police but Often Left Out of the Debate About Brutality, Some Advocates Say," *Washington Post*, June 2, 2021; Elise Hansen, "The Forgotten Minority in Police Shootings," CNN, November 13, 2017 ("Native Americans are killed in police encounters at a higher rate than any other racial or ethnic group.").

xxi **Proposed reforms were voted down:** For the failures of police reform efforts, see, for example, Holly Bailey and Tess Allen, "On 2nd Anniversary of Floyd's Death, Fading Momentum for Police Reform," *Washington Post*, May 25, 2022.

xxi **The Black Lives Matter murals:** Charles M. Blow, "The Great Erasure," *New York Times*, May 20, 2022.

CHAPTER 1. HOW WE GOT HERE

1 **In the early hours:** These facts are drawn from the complaint and briefs in trial court and on appeal in *Monroe v. Pape*, No. 59-C-329 (N.D. Ill. March 2, 1959); email exchanges with Houston Stevens; an interview with James Montgomery; a podcast by Institute for Justice, *Bound by Oath*, "Under Color of Law," March 1, 2021; and an article by Myriam E. Gilles, "Police, Race, and Crime in 1950s Chicago: Monroe v. Pape as Legal Noir," in *Civil Rights Stories*, ed. Myriam E. Gilles and Risa L. Goluboff (New York: Foundation Press, 2008), 41–59.

1 **with reverence, as "Chicago's Toughest Cop":** Jack Clark, "Blood in the Street: 'Chicago's Toughest Cop,'" *Chicago Reader*, March 23, 2000; Stephan Benzkofer, "The City's Toughest Cop," *Chicago Tribune*, Jan. 1, 2012.

2 **"Those were killer cops":** Institute for Justice, *Bound by Oath*, "Under Color of Law."

2 **An attorney at the Illinois branch:** The Monroes were initially referred to a prominent Black female attorney in Chicago, Jewel Lafontant. Lafontant's associate, James Montgomery, then referred the case to his law school classmate, Donald Page Moore, at the ACLU. For further description of how the ACLU ended up representing the Monroes, see Institute for Justice, *Bound by Oath*, "Under Color of Law."

2 **"I suspect that any realistic trial lawyer":** "Constitutional Law: 'Under Color of' Law and the Civil Rights Act," *Duke Law Journal* (1961): 458n43 (quoting Moore, "The Monroe Case," *Durham Morning Herald*, March 9, 1961, 4A).

3 **The Supreme Court agreed:** Monroe v. Pape, 365 U.S. 167 (1961).

4 **One of those statutes:** For a description of these and other legislative efforts undertaken by Congress in 1866–75, see, for example, Harry A. Blackmun, "Section 1983 and Federal Protection of Individual Rights—Will the Statute Remain Alive or Fade Away?," *New York University Law Review* 60 (1985): 1–29; Eugene Gressman, "The Unhappy History of Civil Rights Legislation," *Michigan Law Review* 50 (1952): 1323–58; Marshall S. Shapo, "Constitutional Tort: *Monroe v. Pape*, and the Frontiers Beyond," *Northwestern University Law Review* 60 (1965): 277–329.

4 **tortured and killed:** For one description of this violence, see "Reconstruction in America: Racial Violence After the Civil War, 1865–1876" (Montgomery, Ala.: Equal Justice Initiative, 2020), eji.org/wp-content/uploads/2020/07/reconstruction-in-america -report.pdf.

4 **Congressmen who spoke:** Shapo, "Constitutional Tort," 277.

4 **state courts were hostile places:** For a history of restrictions on state court testimony by Black and Chinese people, see Alfred Avins, "The Right to Be a Witness and the Fourteenth Amendment," *Missouri Law Review* 31 (1966): 471–504.

4 **"able to rise above prejudices":** Monroe v. Pape, 365 U.S. 167, 252n83 (1961) (Harlan, J., concurring) (quoting Representative John Coburn, Cong. Globe, 42nd Cong., 1st Sess., 460).

5 **"covert attempt to transfer":** *Monroe*, 365 U.S. at 179 (quoting Representative Michael Kerr, Cong. Globe, 42nd Cong., 1st Sess., App. 50).

5 **"may be of the slightest":** *Monroe*, 365 U.S. at 180 (quoting Senator Allen G. Thurman, Cong. Globe, 42nd Cong., 1st Sess., App. 216).

5 **In 1873, just two years:** Slaughterhouse Cases, 83 U.S. (16 Wall.) 36 (1873).

5 **combat private actors' violence:** These cases include United States v. Cruikshank, 92 U.S. 542 (1876); United States v. Harris, 106 U.S. 629 (1883); Civil Rights Cases, 109 U.S. 3 (1883). For a description of their impact, see Blackmun, "Section 1983 and Federal Protection of Individual Rights," 9–10 ("With a few quick thrusts, the Court cut

the heart out of the Civil Rights Acts. . . . The uncontrolled private abuses that had so concerned the majority in Congress apparently could not constitutionally be reached by the federal courts, since those private abuses did not constitute 'state action.'").

5 **"separate but equal":** Plessy v. Ferguson, 163 U.S. 537 (1896).

6 **Congress didn't push back:** For a description of this period, see Honorable Paul J. Watford, Hallows Lecture, "*Screws v. United States* and the Birth of Federal Civil Rights Enforcement," *Marquette Law Review* 98 (2014): 474.

6 **With this decisive retreat:** For a description of this period, see Blackmun, "Section 1983 and Federal Protection of Individual Rights," 11–12.

6 **Black people were disenfranchised:** Black women did not have the constitutional right to vote until the Nineteenth Amendment was ratified in 1920; after 1920, Black women and men were kept from the polls with literacy tests, poll taxes, and threats of violence. For further description of this disenfranchisement, see Martha Prescod Norman, "Shining in the Dark: Black Women and the Struggle for the Vote, 1955–1965," in *African American Women and the Vote, 1837–1965*, ed. Ann Dexter Gordon et al. (Amherst: University of Massachusetts Press, 1997), 173–90.

6 **In the early twentieth century:** For a description of this period, see Katherine A. Macfarlane, "Accelerated Civil Rights Settlements in the Shadow of Section 1983," *Utah Law Review* 2018 (2018): 662–65.

6 **sixteen years before:** Houston Stevens tells the story of his family leaving Opelika, Alabama, in Institute for Justice, *Bound by Oath*, "Under Color of Law."

6 **As Houston later described it**: Institute for Justice, *Bound by Oath*, "Under Color of Law."

7 **the Chicago Commission on Race Relations:** The Chicago Commission on Race Relations, *The Negro in Chicago: A Study of Race Relations and a Race Riot* (Chicago: University Chicago Press, 1922): 34.

7 **"the third degree":** National Commission on Law Observance and Enforcement (Wickersham Commission), *Report on Lawlessness in Law Enforcement* (1931): 4.

7 **Following uprisings in Harlem:** See *Report of Subcommittee Which Investigated the Disturbance of March 19th, to the Honorable Fiorello H. LaGuardia*, May 29, 1935, moses .law.umn.edu/racial-justice/img/010/HarlemRiotReport1935.pdf; Baker v. City of Detroit, 483 F. Supp. 930, 940–41 (E.D. Mich. 1979) ("In the June riots of [1943], the Detroit police ran true to form. The trouble reached riot proportions because the police of Detroit once again enforced the law under an unequal hand. They used 'persuasion' rather than firm action with white rioters while against Negroes they used the ultimate in force; night sticks, revolvers, riot guns, sub-machine guns, and deer guns.") (quoting Thurgood Marshall, "Activities of Police During the Riots June 21 and 22, 1943," in Walter White and Thurgood Marshall, *What Caused the Detroit Riot? An Analysis* (New York: National Association for the Advancement of Colored People, 1943)).

7 **Supreme Court came to revisit:** For discussions of the developing law in this period, see Shapo, "Constitutional Tort," 282–87; Comment, "The Civil Rights Act: Emergence of an Adequate Federal Civil Remedy?," *Indiana Law Journal* 26 (1951): 363; "Developments in the Law: Section 1983 and Federalism," *Harvard Law Review* 90 (1977): 1167–75.

7 **A key decision:** Screws v. United States, 325 U.S. 91 (1945).

8 **newly formed Civil Rights Section:** For a description of the early years of the Department of Justice's civil rights division and the decision to pursue the *Screws* case, see Watford, "*Screws v. United States*," 474–77 (citing Tom C. Clark, "A Federal Prosecutor Looks at the Civil Rights Statutes," *Columbia Law Review* 47 (1947): 180).

8 **The federal indictment charged:** *Screws*, 325 U.S. at 93.

8 **In reaching this conclusion:** *Screws*, 325 U.S. at 111.

8 **Although *Screws* was a criminal case:** For a discussion of the expansion of *Screws*'s logic to civil cases, see Shapo, "Constitutional Tort," 290; Thomas J. Klitgaard, "The Civil Rights Acts and Mr. Monroe," *California Law Review* 49 (1961): 160.

9 **But, the ACLU report emphasized:** ACLU, *Secret Detention by the Chicago Police* (Glencoe, Ill.: Free Press, 1959), 7.

9 **Moore and other civil rights attorneys:** Charles R. Epp, *Making Rights Real: Activists, Bureaucrats, and the Creation of the Legalistic State* (Chicago: University of Chicago Press, 2009), 63–64.

10 **Section 1983 was meant to:** *Monroe*, 365 U.S. at 172.

10 **The jury awarded the Monroes:** "Order Pape, 4 Others to Pay $13,000," *Chicago Daily Tribune*, Dec. 5, 1962.

10 **In the years after *Monroe v. Pape* was decided:** Shapo, "Constitutional Tort," 278; Christine Whitman, "Constitutional Torts," *Michigan Law Review* 79 (1980): 6.

10 **Annual civil rights filings:** Theodore Eisenberg, "Section 1983: Doctrinal Foundations and an Empirical Study," *Cornell Law Review* 67 (1982): 523.

10 **Back in 1871 congressmen who supported:** Owen v. City of Independence, 445 U.S. 622, 636 (quoting Representative Samuel Shellabarger, Cong. Globe, 42nd Cong., 1st Sess., App. 68).

10 **To hear the Supreme Court:** For just one example, see City of Monterey v. Del Monte Dunes, 526 U.S. 687, 727 (1999) (Scalia, J., concurring) (writing that Section 1983 "is designed to provide compensation for injuries arising from the violation of legal duties, and thereby, of course, to deter future violations") (citation omitted).

11 **The Supreme Court imagined:** City of Newport v. Fact Concerts, 453 U.S. 247, 269 (1981).

11 **"so that if there is any doubt":** Pembaur v. City of Cincinnati, 475 U.S. 469, 495 (1986) (Powell, J., dissenting) (quoting Owen v. City of Independence, 445 U.S. 622, 652 (1980)).

11 **"a vital component":** *Owen*, 445 U.S. at 651.

11 **Ruggero J. Aldisert:** Ruggero J. Aldisert, "Judicial Expansion of Federal Jurisdiction: A Federal Judge's Thoughts on Section 1983, Comity, and the Federal Caseload," *Law and Social Order* (1973): 558.

11 **Section 1983 "made the federal court":** Aldisert, "Judicial Expansion," 569.

11 **Marvin Aspen, an attorney who defended:** William Kling, "City Attorney Charges Civil Rights Law Is Abused," *Chicago Tribune*, Aug. 2, 1966.

12 **As Aspen told the students:** Kling, "City Attorney."

12 **"the only realistic avenue":** Harlow v. Fitzgerald, 457 U.S. 800, 814 (1982).

12 **As Justice Lewis F. Powell Jr. wrote:** *Harlow*, 457 U.S. at 814 (quoting Gregoire v. Biddle, 177 F.2d 579, 581 (2d Cir. 1949), cert. denied, 339 U.S. 949 (1950).

13 **Four months after the Court:** Mapp v. Ohio, 367 U.S. 643 (1961).

13 **Five years after deciding *Monroe*:** Miranda v. Arizona, 384 U.S. 436 (1966).

13 **But in the decades that followed:** For discussions of the limitations on *Mapp* and *Miranda* and the conservative turn on the Supreme Court, see Erwin Chemerinsky, *Presumed Guilty: How the Supreme Court Empowered the Police and Subverted Civil Rights* (New York: Liveright, 2021), 141–74.

13 **Police unions rose in power:** For one discussion of the rise of police unions, see Adam Serwer, "The Authoritarian Instincts of Police Unions," *Atlantic*, July/Aug. 2021.

13–14 **decreased public transparency and accountability:** Studies of hundreds of police union contracts across the country have found that the contracts limit officer interrogations and the length of internal investigations, require that disciplinary records be destroyed, prevent anonymous civilian complaints, and ban civilian oversight. Stephen Rushin, "Police Union Contracts," *Duke Law Review* (2017): 1222–39; Reade Levinson, "Across the U.S., Police Contracts Shield Officers from Scrutiny and Discipline," Reuters, Jan. 13, 2017.

14 **state and local laws were enacted:** These laws are discussed in depth in chapter 10.
14 **there are approximately eighteen thousand:** Duren Banks, Joshua Hendrix, Matthew Hickman, and Tracey Kyckelhahn, "National Sources of Law Enforcement Employment Data," United States Department of Justice Bureau of Justice Statistics (October 4, 2016), https://bjs.ojp.gov/content/pub/pdf/nsleed.pdf.
15 **Reverend John Porter:** Skip Bossette and Lillian S. Calhoun, "March Against Police Brutality, Cop's Recall," *Chicago Defender*, April 24, 1965.
15 **He remained a hero:** Gilles, "Police, Race, and Crime," 57.
15 **A 1994 article:** Anne Keegan, "Toughest Cop in Town," *Chicago Tribune*, Feb. 9, 1994.
15 **"Pape did no more":** Bossette and Calhoun, "March Against Police Brutality."
16 **widespread patterns of unconstitutional conduct:** U.S. Department of Justice and U.S. Attorney's Office Northern District of Illinois, Investigation of the Chicago Police Department, Jan. 13, 2017, 8–9, www.justice.gov/opa/file/925846/download.

CHAPTER 2. LAWYERS

17 **Alonzo Grant worked:** These facts are drawn from the complaint, briefs, depositions, and trial transcripts in Grant v. City of Syracuse, No. 5:15-cv-00445 (N.D.N.Y. April 14, 2015); interviews and email exchanges with two of the Grants' attorneys, Jesse Ryder and Charles Bonner; and videos by Ryder and Bonner of Stephanie and Alonzo Grant and their family and neighbors soon after the incident.
20 **Winning is hard:** In my study of 1,183 police misconduct cases filed around the country, 273 were filed and litigated by people without lawyers. Of that 273, 16 percent recovered something. More than 40 percent were dismissed by judges at the outset of the case, before the defendant was even served with the complaint. The remainder were dismissed by the court at some point during the litigation. Joanna C. Schwartz, "Qualified Immunity's Selection Effects," *Northwestern University Law Review* 114 (2020): 1130n122.
20–21 **You can count on one hand:** Joanna C. Schwartz, "Civil Rights Ecosystems," *Michigan Law Review* 118 (2020): 1577–79.
21 **Less than 1 percent of people:** Matthew R. Durose et al., "Contacts Between Police and the Public: Findings from the 2002 National Survey," Bureau of Justice Statistics, April 2005, 16–20 (finding that the police had used force against 664,458 people, 87.3 percent of whom believed that the police acted improperly, and just 7,416 (1.3 percent) of whom filed a lawsuit regarding the alleged misconduct). Note that this survey concerns only police uses of force. Each year, millions of people believe they are wrongfully stopped by the police while driving or walking. Elizabeth Davis et al., "Contacts Between Police and the Public, 2015," Bureau of Justice Statistics, Oct. 2018, 4, 11, 14. We do not know how often people sue who believe they have been mistreated by the police in ways that do not involve the use of force but one assumes they even less frequently sue because they suffer less in the way of compensable damages.
21 **campaigns against police brutality:** For a discussion of these efforts, see Charles R. Epp, *Making Rights Real: Activists, Bureaucrats, and the Creation of the Legalistic State* (Chicago: University of Chicago Press, 2009), 43–45. For a broader discussion of the growth of the civil rights and public interest legal bar, see Stephen C. Yeazell, "*Brown,*

the Civil Rights Movement, and the Silent Litigation Revolution," *Vanderbilt Law Review* 57 (2004): 1975–2003.

21 **civil rights organizations recruited lawyers:** For stories of lawyers' experiences during this time, see Epp, *Making Rights Real*, 65–66; Kent Spriggs, ed., *Voices of Civil Rights Lawyers: Reflections from the Deep South, 1964–1980* (Gainesville: University Press of Florida, 2017), 178, 182.

21 **During that same period:** Epp, *Making Rights Real*, 66–67.

22 **"'private attorney general'":** Newman v. Piggie Park Enterprises Inc., 390 U.S. 400, 402 (1968).

22 **Judges began using:** Mary Frances Derfner, "One Giant Step: The Civil Rights Awards Act of 1976," *Saint Louis University Law Journal* 21 (1977): 443–44.

23 **Judges reasoned that:** For example, see Incarcerated Men of Allen County Jail v. Fair, 507 F.2d 281, 285 (6th Cir. 1974).

23 **the Supreme Court stepped in:** Alyeska Pipeline Service Co. v. Wilderness Society, 421 U.S. 240 (1975).

23 **As the legislative statement read:** S. Rep. 94-1011 (1976).

23 **Alabama senator James Allen:** Civil Rights Attorney's Fees Awards Act of 1976 (Public Law 94-559, S. 2278) at 27 (1976).

23 **Senator Allen was no friend:** William Robbins, "Senate Cuts Off Filibuster; Voids House Busing Curb," *New York Times*, Dec. 15, 1974; Armand Derfner, "Background and Origin of the Civil Rights Attorney's Fees Awards Act of 1976," *Urban Law* 37 (2005): 653.

23 **"massive, nationwide giveaway":** George C. Smith, "Lawyers Split the Fee and Taxpayers Foot the Bill," *Wall Street Journal*, Feb. 25, 1986.

23 **the first, *City of Riverside v. Rivera*:** These facts are set out in the Supreme Court's decision, City of Riverside v. Rivera, 477 U.S. 561, 564 (1986).

24 **The city sought review:** *Rivera*, 477 U.S. at 573–74.

24 **The trial judge in *Rivera* had found:** *Rivera*, 477 U.S. at 574.

24 **To limit the attorneys' fee award:** *Rivera*, 477 U.S. at 576.

25 **As Justice Rehnquist:** *Rivera*, 477 U.S. at 595 (Rehnquist, J., dissenting).

25 **Justice Powell expressed "serious doubts":** 477 U.S. at 586n3 (Powell, J., concurring in the judgment).

25 ***Evans v. Jeff D.:*** Evans v. Jeff D., 475 U.S. 717 (1986).

26 **waved away that possibility:** *Evans*, 475 U.S. at 741n34.

26 **in the dissenting justices' view:** *Evans*, 475 U.S. at 755 (Brennan, J., dissenting).

26 **When plaintiffs recover money:** In my study of 1,183 police misconduct cases, plaintiffs recovered money—through settlements or judgments—in approximately 57.7 percent of cases. Of the 682 cases in which plaintiffs succeeded, 12 were plaintiffs' verdicts after trial—1.8 percent of the cases in which plaintiffs were victorious, and 1 percent of all cases filed. In 2 of those 12 cases, the parties settled after a plaintiffs' verdict at trial. Joanna C. Schwartz, "How Qualified Immunity Fails," *Yale Law Journal* 127 (2017): 46–47.

26 **the contingency-fee system:** For further elaboration of the effects of *Evans* on civil rights plaintiffs' attorneys' decisions, see Paul D. Reingold, "Requiem for Section 1983," *Duke Journal of Constitutional Law and Public Policy* (2008): 1–47.

27 **"cases may be overstaffed":** Hensley v. Eckerhart, 461 U.S. 424, 433–34 (1983).

27 **satellite litigation:** James K. Green and Barbara Kritchevsky, "Litigating Attorney's Fees: Running the Gauntlet," *Urban Lawyer* (Fall 2005): 713 ("Fee litigation can be as time-consuming and complex as that on the merits. It can be a second gauntlet through which plaintiffs must pass to vindicate their constitutional rights.").

27 **particularly colorful language:** Schwartz, "Qualified Immunity's Selection Effects," 1136.

27 **"likable," "credible," and "articulate":** Schwartz, "Qualified Immunity's Selection Effects," 1134.

28 **disproportionately the victims:** Davis et al., "Contacts Between Police and the Public, 2015," 4, 8, 16 (finding that Black residents were more likely to be stopped by police than white or Hispanic residents; that Black and Hispanic residents were more likely than white residents to have multiple contacts with police; and that police were twice as likely to threaten or use force against Black and Hispanic residents as white residents); Doris A. Fuller et al., *Overlooked in the Undercounted: The Role of Mental Illness in Fatal Law Enforcement Encounters*, Treatment Advocacy Center, Dec. 2015, 1 (reporting evidence that the mentally ill make up a disproportionate number of people killed by police); Christy Mallory et al., *Discrimination and Harassment by Law Enforcement Officers in the LGBT Community*, Williams Institute, March 2015, 4–11 (describing studies showing discrimination and harassment of LGBTQ+ communities by law enforcement).

29 **if he sold candy bars:** Schwartz, "Qualified Immunity's Selection Effects," 1143n175.

29 **Some lawyers who have spent years:** Schwartz, "Qualified Immunity's Selection Effects," 1149.

29 **he called Charles Bonner:** Information about Bonner, Ryder, and their representation of the Grants is taken from interviews with Bonner and Ryder and from Bonner's book, *Tip of the Arrow: The Selma Student Nonviolent Movement: A Study in Leadership* (Conneaut Lake, Pa.: Page Publishing, 2020).

31 **The judge also ruled:** *Memorandum, Decision, and Order,* Grant v. City of Syracuse, No. 5:15-cv-00445 (N.D.N.Y. Feb. 8, 2019).

31 **court of appeals affirmed the jury verdict:** Grant v. Lockett, Nos. 19-469, 19-738, 19-1558, 2021 WL 5816245 (2d Cir. Dec. 8, 2021).

31 **As a local criminal defense:** Declaration of William Sullivan in Support of Plaintiff Alonzo Grant's Motion for Attorneys Fees and Costs, Grant v. City of Syracuse, No. 5:15-cv-00445 (N.D.N.Y. Nov. 20, 2018).

CHAPTER 3. THE COMPLAINT

33 **unimaginable news:** Details of Vicki Timpa's efforts to find out what happened to her son, Tony, are taken from interviews and emails with Geoff Henley and Susan Hutchison, the Timpas' attorneys; email correspondence with reporter Cary Aspinwall; and news reports, including Cary Aspinwall, "Police Responded to His 911 Call for Help. He Died. What Happened to Tony Timpa?," *Dallas Morning News,* Aug. 2, 2019, www .dallasnews.com/news/investigations/2019/08/02/police-responded-to-his-911-call -for-help-he-died-what-happened-to-tony-timpa/; Ken Kalthoff, "Tony Timpa's Mother Anxious for Trial of Officers Blamed in Lawsuit for His Death," NBC Dallas Fort Worth, Dec. 16, 2021, www.nbcdfw.com/news/local/tony-timpas-mother-anxious-for -trial-of-officers-blamed-in-lawsuit-for-his-death/2840597/.

34 **"I want to know what happened":** Aspinwall, "Police Responded."

34 **"Sudden Death":** Aspinwall, "Police Responded."

35 **Texas law allows:** Tex. Gov't Code Section 552.

35 **its own brand of confusion:** Jack B. Weinstein and Daniel H. Distler, "Comments on Procedural Reform: Drafting Pleading Rules," *Columbia Law Review* 57 (1957): 520–21.

36 **"short and plain statement":** Fed. R. Civ. P 8(a)(2).

36 **the Federal Rules expanded:** For a description of how discovery powers came to expand during the drafting of the Federal Rules, see Stephen N. Subrin, "Fishing Expeditions Allowed: The Historical Background of the 1938 Federal Discovery Rules," *Boston College Law Review* 39 (1998): 713–30.

36 **a case called *Conley v. Gibson*:** Conley v. Gibson, 355 U.S. 41 (1957).

36 **The union moved to dismiss:** *Conley*, 355 U.S. at 47.

37 **The Supreme Court rejected the union's argument:** *Conley*, 355 U.S. at 45–46.

37 **This easily met standard:** *Conley*, 355 U.S. at 47–48.

37 **T. Emmet Clarie:** Valley v. Maule, 297 F. Supp. 958 (D. Conn. 1968).

37 **"In recent years there has been":** *Maule*, 297 F. Supp. at 960–61.

38 **court of appeals judge John Gibbons:** Rotolo v. Borough of Charleroi, 532 F.2d 920, 927 (3rd Cir. 1976) (Gibbons, J., concurring and dissenting).

38 **When two Cornell law professors:** For a detailed description of this research and findings, see Theodore Eisenberg and Stewart Schwab, "The Reality of Constitutional Tort Litigation," *Cornell Law Review* 72 (1987): 641–95.

38 **"result[ed] in the transfer":** Eisenberg and Schwab, "Reality of Constitutional Tort Litigation," 693n212.

38 **"decision makers demand evidence":** Eisenberg and Schwab, "Reality of Constitutional Tort Litigation," 695.

38 **many judges around the country:** For a partial list of decisions requiring extra detail in civil rights plaintiffs' complaints during this period, see Downs v. Department of Public Welfare, 368 F. Supp. 454 (E.D. Pa. 1973); Hahn v. Sargent, 388 F. Supp. 445 (D. Mass. 1975); Hall v. Pennsylvania State Police, 570 F.2d 86 (3d Cir. 1978); Kauffman v. Moss, 420 F.2d 1270 (3d Cir. 1970); Light v. Blackwell, 472 F. Supp. 333 (E.D. Ark. 1979); Patton v. Dumpson, 425 F. Supp. 621 (S.D.N.Y. 1977); Pettman v. U.S. Chess Federation, 675 F. Supp. 175 (S.D.N.Y. 1987); Rotolo v. Borough of Charleroi, 532 F.2d 920 (3d Cir. 1976); Sixth Camden Corp. v. Evesham Tp., Burlington County, 420 F. Supp. 709 (D.N.J. 1976); Weise v. Reisner, 318 F. Supp. 580 (E.D. Wisc. 1970); Whelehan v. Monroe County, 558 F. Supp. 1093 (W.D.N.Y. 1983).

38 **twice reject:** Leatherman v. Tarrant County Narcotics Intelligence and Coordination Unit, 507 U.S. 163 (1993); Swierkiewicz v. Sorema NA, 534 U.S. 506 (2002).

39 **Javaid Iqbal, a Pakistani citizen:** Details about Javaid Iqbal, his experience in federal custody, and his lawsuit are drawn from trial and appellate court filings in Elmaghraby v. Ashcroft, No. 4-cv-01809 (E.D.N.Y. May 3, 2004), and from Shirin Sinnar, "The Lost Story of *Iqbal*," *Georgetown Law Journal* 105 (2017): 379–439.

40 **"best forgotten":** Bell Atlantic Corp. v. Twombly, 550 U.S. 544, 563 (2007).

40 **"a largely groundless claim":** *Twombly*, 550 U.S. at 558–59 (citation omitted).

40 **"the common lament":** *Twombly*, 550 U.S. at 559. In support of this assertion Justice Souter cited Frank H. Easterbrook, "Discovery as Abuse," *Boston University Law Review* 69 (1989): 638, but Easterbrook's article did not offer empirical support for this claim.

40 **In 2009, the Supreme Court dismissed:** Ashcroft v. Iqbal, 556 U.S. 662 (2009).

40 **"plausible" claims:** *Twombly*, 550 U.S. at 570.

40 **"judicial experience and common sense":** *Iqbal*, 556 U.S. at 679.

41 **"given more likely explanations":** *Iqbal*, 556 U.S. at 681.

41 **The most likely explanation:** *Iqbal*, 556 U.S. at 682.

41 **"Litigation, though necessary":** *Iqbal*, 556 U.S. at 685.

42 **circulated for decades:** For discussions of these claims about discovery and their lack of empirical support, see Alexander A. Reinert, "The Narrative of Costs, the Costs of Narrative," *Cardozo Law Review* 40 (2018): 121–44.

42 **Judge Paul Niemeyer repeated one:** Paul V. Niemeyer, "Here We Go Again: Are the Federal Discovery Rules Really in Need of Amendment?," *Boston College Law Review* 39 (1998): 518.

42 **Multiple studies have found:** For descriptions of some of these studies, see Judith A. McKenna and Elizabeth C. Wiggins, "Empirical Research on Civil Discovery," *Boston College Law Review* 39 (1998): 800; Danya Shocair Reda, "The Cost-and-Delay Narrative in Civil Justice Reform: Its Fallacies and Functions," *Oregon Law Review* 90 (2012): 1111–16; Thomas E. Willging et al., "An Empirical Study of Discovery and Disclosure Practice Under the 1993 Federal Rule Amendments," *Boston College Law Review* 39 (1998): 531.

42 **a survey of twenty-three hundred attorneys:** Emery G. Lee III and Thomas E. Willging, *National, Case-Based Civil Rules Survey: Preliminary Report to the Judicial Conference Advisory Committee on Civil Rules* (Washington, D.C.: Federal Judicial Center, 2009), 27–28, 33.

43 **"seem to contradict":** Alexander A. Reinert, "The Costs of Heightened Pleading," *Indiana Law Journal* 86 (2011): 166.

43 **particularly difficult:** Although several studies have attempted to measure the effect of the plausibility pleading standard, with varying results, Alex Reinert has offered compelling evidence that civil rights and discrimination cases are particularly vulnerable to dismissal on *Twombly/Iqbal* grounds. Alexander A. Reinert, "Measuring the Impact of Plausibility Pleading," *Virginia Law Review* 101 (2015): 2151–52.

43 **judge David Hamilton:** McCauley v. City of Chicago, 671 F.3d 611, 627 (7th Cir. 2011) (Hamilton, J., dissenting in part).

44 **The city argued that the complaint:** Defendant City of Dallas's Motion Pursuant to Rule 12(b)(6) to Dismiss Plaintiffs' Federal Claims Alleged Against It in Plaintiffs' First Amended Complaint, and Brief in Support, Timpa v. City of Dallas, No. 3:16-cv-03089 (N.D. Tex. Jan. 17, 2017) (citations omitted).

45 **The evidence reluctantly turned over:** Information about what happened the night Tony Timpa died is drawn from the body camera recordings produced by the City of Dallas. Cary Aspinwall and Dave Boucher, "'You're Gonna Kill Me!': Dallas Police Body Cam Footage Reveals the Final Minutes of Tony Timpa's Life," *Dallas Morning News*, July 30, 2019, www.dallasnews.com/news/investigations/2019/07/31/you-re -gonna-kill-me-dallas-police-body-cam-footage-reveals-the-final-minutes-of-tony -timpa-s-life/. Although the judge in Timpa's case originally disclosed the video only to the Timpas, he ultimately ordered that these recordings be publicly disclosed—an effort that took *Dallas Morning News* reporter Cary Aspinwall three years. For a description of those efforts, see Cassandra Jaramillo, "How the Dallas Police's Open Portal Led to the True, Untold Story of Tony Timpa's Death," *Dallas Morning News*, Nov. 17, 2021, www.dallasnews.com/news/investigations/2021/11/17/how-the-dallas-polices -open-portal-led-to-the-true-untold-story-of-tony-timpas-death/.

45 **what is called a prone position:** Brief of Professor Seth Stoughton as Amicus Curiae in Support of Plaintiffs-Appellants in the U.S. Court of Appeals for the Fifth Circuit, Timpa v. City of Dallas, 20-10876 (Jan. 15, 2021).

45 **Dallas police policy manual:** Plaintiffs' Response to Defendants' Motion for Summary Judgment, Timpa v. City of Dallas, No. 3:16-cv-03089 (N.D. Tex. March 9, 2020).

47 **A grand jury indicted:** Ryan Mills, "Tony Timpa Suffered the Same Fate as George Floyd—but Received None of the Attention," *National Review*, May 6, 2021, www .nationalreview.com/news/tony-timpa-suffered-the-same-fate-as-george-floyd-but -received-none-of-the-attention/.

47 **disciplinary hearing:** Cary Aspinwall and Dave Boucher, "Dallas Police Officers: Mocking Tony Timpa Was 'Strategy,'" *Dallas Morning News*, Aug. 2, 2019, www.dallasnews .com/news/investigations/2019/08/02/dallas-police-officers-mocking-tony-timpa -was-strategy/.

47 **Dillard and Vasquez remain:** Kelli Smith, "SCOTUS Declines Dallas' Request to Halt Case Against Police Involved in Tony Timpa's Death," *Dallas Morning News*, May 31, 2022, www.dallasnews.com/news/courts/2022/05/31/scotus-declines-dallas-request -to-halt-case-against-police-involved-in-tony-timpas-death/.

48 **"end-run around":** Ambellu v. Re'ese Adbarat Debre Selam Kidist Mariam, 406 F. Supp. 3d 72, 83 (D.D.C. 2019).

CHAPTER 4. THE CONSTITUTION

49 **On July 15, 2012:** These facts are drawn from the complaint, briefs, affidavits, and depositions in Young v. Borders, No. 5:13-cv-00113 (M.D. Fla. March 6, 2013); video interviews of Miranda Mauck and Andrew Scott's parents, included in the 2018 Illuminating Injustice Award Recipients—the Family of Andrew Scott, www.youtube.com /watch?v=nHJfFZaPpGo; interviews with Mark NeJame and Jason Recksiedler, the lawyers for Scott's parents and Mauck; and news stories including Ludmilla Lelis, "Leesburg Man Fatally Shot by Deputies Was Defending Himself, NeJame Says," *Orlando Sentinel*, Aug. 7, 2012; Lawrence Hurley, Andrew Chung, and Andrea Januta, "When Cops and America's Cherished Gun Rights Clash, Cops Win," Reuters, Nov. 20, 2020.

49 **Jonathan Brown:** After Andrew Scott was killed by Deputy Sylvester, Jonathan Brown was arrested for attempted murder. In November 2012, all charges against Brown were dropped. Brown's attorney told a reporter, "Jonathan was made to be a scapegoat—that's the gist of it—law enforcement overreacted, and killed an innocent man, they needed to find somebody to blame, other than themselves." "Charges Dropped Against Man Deputies Sought in Attempted Murder," *Click Orlando*, Nov. 21, 2012, www.clickorlando.com/news/2012/11/22/charges-dropped-against-man-deputies -sought-in-attempted-murder/.

51 **no disciplinary charges:** Hurley, Chung, and Januta, "When Cops and America's Cherished Gun Rights Clash."

51 **No criminal charges were brought:** Hurley, Chung, and Januta, "When Cops and America's Cherished Gun Rights Clash."

53 **watershed case, *Mapp v. Ohio*:** Mapp v. Ohio, 367 U.S. 643 (1961).

54 **regularly stopped and searched:** Brief of American Civil Liberties Union, American Civil Liberties Union of Ohio, and New York Civil Liberties Union, Amici Curiae, Terry v. Ohio, 1967 WL 113689, at *8 (Sept. 29, 1967) ("It cannot be doubted that for many years, state police officers have been stopping and frisking suspects, without their consent, without a search warrant or probable cause, and using the yield of such searches to convict them of crimes.").

54 **"not a high bar":** District of Columbia v. Wesby, 138 S. Ct. 577, 586 (2018) (citing cases).

54 **"the ability of the police":** Brief of Americans for Effective Law Enforcement, as Amicus Curiae, Terry v. State of Ohio, 1967 WL 93602, at *4 (Nov. 17, 1967).

54 **"proponents of stop and frisk"**: Brief for the NAACP Legal Defense and Educational Fund Inc. as Amicus Curiae, 1967 WL 113672, at *59 (Aug. 31, 1967).

55 **"The policeman today"**: Brief for the NAACP Legal Defense and Educational Fund Inc. as Amicus Curiae, 1967 WL 113672, at *60–62 (Aug. 31, 1967).

55 **"difficult and troublesome"**: Terry v. Ohio 392 U.S. 1, 9 (1968). For a description of the evolution of the Supreme Court's decision in *Terry*, see John Q. Barrett, "Deciding the Stop and Frisk Cases: A Look Inside the Supreme Court's Conference," *St. John's Law Review* 72 (1998): 749–844.

55 **rejected the notion that stops and frisks:** *Terry*, 392 U.S. at 16.

55 **"the Fourth Amendment's general proscription"**: *Terry*, 392 U.S. at 20.

55 **"inchoate and unparticularized"**: *Terry*, 392 U.S. at 27.

55 **"individual cases"**: *Terry*, 392 U.S. at 29.

55 **"the most doctrinaire"**: "The Law: The Court's Uncompromising Libertarian," *Time*, Nov. 24, 1975.

56 **Terry was decided:** See Erwin Chemerinsky, *Presumed Guilty* (New York: Liveright, 2021), 115-16. For detailed investigation and analysis of Black rebellions during this period, see Elizabeth Hinton, *America on Fire: The Untold Story of Police Violence and Black Rebellion Since the 1960s* (New York: Liveright, 2021).

56 **run-of-the-mill behavior:** For examples of the types of nonserious behaviors and activities that have been criminalized, see Devon W. Carbado, "Blue-on-Black Violence: A Provisional Model of Some of the Causes," *Georgetown Law Journal* 104 (2016): 1487–88; Devon W. Carbado, "From Stopping Black People to Killing Black People: The Fourth Amendment Pathways to Police Violence," *California Law Review* 105 (2016): 154.

56 **a police officer's reasonable suspicion:** Utah v. Strieff, 579 U.S. 232, 252 (2016) (Sotomayor, J., dissenting).

56 **So long as the officer:** Whren v. United States, 517 U.S. 806, 813 (1996).

57 **As Chief Justice Warren recognized:** *Terry*, 392 U.S. at 17n13 (citation omitted).

57 **"annoying, frightening, and perhaps humiliating"**: *Terry*, 392 U.S. at 25.

57 **Studies of police stops:** See, for example, Mike Carter, "Report: Seattle Police Stop Black People, Native Americans at Far Higher Rate Than White People," *Seattle Times*, July 26, 2021; Paul Duggan, "A Disproportionate Number of D.C. Police Stops Involved African Americans," *Washington Post*, Sept. 9, 2019; Alan Feuer, "Black New Yorkers Are Twice as Likely to Be Stopped by the Police, Data Shows," *New York Times*, Sept. 23, 2020; Carlos Granda and Grace Manthey, "Data Analysis Shows Racial Disparity in Police Stops in Recent Years by Los Angeles Law Enforcement," ABC7, Sept. 8, 2020, abc7.com/lapd-lasd-racial-disparities-police-stops/6414103/.

57 **"The police killings of Michael Brown"**: Carbado, "From Stopping Black People," 163.

58 **"all invasions on the part"**: Boyd v. United States, 116 U.S. 616, 630 (1886).

58 **"at the very core"**: Silverman v. United States, 365 U.S. 505, 511 (1961).

58 **"when it comes to the Fourth Amendment"**: Florida v. Jardines, 569 U.S. 1, 6 (2013).

58 **if police fly a plane:** California v. Ciraolo, 476 U.S. 207 (1986).

58 **a person's garbage:** California v. Greenwood, 486 U.S. 35 (1988).

59 **an "implicit license":** *Jardines*, 569 U.S. at 8.

59 **police needed a warrant:** Katz v. United States, 389 U.S. 347, 357 (1967).

59 **"the deliberate, impartial judgment"**: *Katz*, 389 U.S. at 357 (citation omitted).

59 **"the exigencies of the situation make the needs"**: Mincey v. Arizona, 437 U.S. 385, 394 (1978) (citation omitted).

59 **consider the "totality of the circumstances":** Missouri v. McNeely, 569 U.S. 141, 142 (2013).

59 **warrantless searches are justified:** Brigham City v. Stuart, 547 U.S. 398, 403–5 (2006) (collecting cases).

59 **"become so riddled with exceptions":** California v. Acevedo, 500 U.S. 565, 582 (1991) (Scalia, J., concurring).

60 **"flexible requirement":** Wilson v. Arkansas, 514 U.S. 927, 934 (1995).

60 **"leave to the lower courts":** *Wilson*, 514 U.S. at 936.

60 **Two years later, in another unanimous decision:** Richards v. Wisconsin, 520 U.S. 385, 394 (1997).

60 **"the appropriate balance":** *Richards*, 520 U.S. at 394.

60 **In a 2006 decision:** Hudson v. Michigan, 547 U.S. 586, 594 (2006) (citations omitted).

61 **property destruction, injury, and death:** For a description of the history and harms of no-knock raids, see Radley Balko, "Breonna Taylor's Death Sparked Remarkable Changes to No-Knock Raids Across America," *Washington Post*, Oct. 15, 2021.

61 **Deputy Sylvester contended:** Motion for Summary Judgment of Defendants Sheriff and Sylvester and Memorandum of Law, Young v. Borders, No. 5:13-cv-00113 (M.D. Fla. May 1, 2014).

61 **Florida courts had found:** Young v. Borders, No. 5:13-cv-00113, 2014 WL 11444072 at *10 (M.D. Fla. Sept. 18, 2014) (citing Florida law).

61 **"constructive entry":** Plaintiffs' Response to Defendants' Motion for Summary Judgment, Young v. Borders, No. 5:13-cv-00113 (M.D. Fla. May 15, 2014).

62 **The judge sided:** Young v. Borders, No. 5:13-cv-00113, 2014 WL 11444072 (M.D. Fla. Sept. 18, 2014).

63 **In 1985, in a case:** Tennessee v. Garner, 471 U.S. 1 (1985).

63 **the Supreme Court ruled that the Tennessee statute:** *Garner*, 471 U.S. at 6 (citations omitted).

63 **Justice Rehnquist, writing for the Court:** Graham v. Connor, 490 U.S. 386, 396 (1989).

63 **"tense, uncertain, and rapidly evolving" circumstances:** *Graham*, 490 U.S. at 397.

64 *Graham* **instructs courts to assess:** *Graham*, 490 U.S. at 396.

64 **"Not every push or shove":** *Graham*, 490 U.S. at 396 (citation omitted).

64 **vast majority of police training manuals:** For studies of the prevalence with which police department policies rely on *Graham*, see sources cited in Ingrid V. Eagly and Joanna C. Schwartz, "Lexipol's Fight Against Police Reform," *Indiana Law Journal* 97 (2022): 10–11.

64 **But** *Graham* **has been criticized:** Rachel Harmon, "When Is Police Violence Justified?," *Northwestern University Law Review* 102 (2008): 1127; Brandon Garrett and Seth Stoughton, "A Tactical Fourth Amendment," *Virginia Law Review* 103 (2017): 217–18.

64 **police experts believe:** For long-standing calls for limits on officer discretion, see sources cited in Eagly and Schwartz, "Lexipol's Fight," 11–13.

64 **Some large police departments:** For studies from departments across the country showing that limits on police power can reduce force incidents, see sources cited in Eagly and Schwartz, "Lexipol's Fight," 17.

65 **Since June 2020:** For descriptions of limits on force enacted after Floyd's death, see Farnoush Amiri, Colleen Slevin, and Camille Fassett, "Floyd Killing Prompts Some States to Limit or Ban Chokeholds," AP News, May 23, 2021; Grace Hauck, "Chicago Revises Foot Chase Policy After Fatal Police Shootings of Adam Toledo, Anthony Alvarez," *USA Today*, May 27, 2021.

65 **"tragic," "sad," and "unfortunate":** Young v. Borders, No. 5:13-cv-00113, 2014 WL 11444072, at *2 (M.D. Fla. Sept. 18, 2014).

66 **"In light of the information":** *Young*, 2014 WL 11444072, at *18.

66 **The court of appeals affirmed, "echo[ing] the district court's expression":** Young v. Borders, 620 Fed. Appx. 889, 890 (11th Cir. 2015).

66 **sought a rehearing by all eleven:** Young v. Borders, 850 F.3d 1274 (11th Cir. 2017).

66 **"sorry for your loss":** Theresa Campbell, "'I Demand Justice for My Son,'" NeJame Law, Aug. 14, 2012, www.nejamelaw.com/news/2012/august/i-demand-justice-for -my-son/index.html.

67 **Consider, for example, David Collie:** These facts are drawn from summary judg- ment briefs submitted by the parties and the district court's opinion in Collie v. Barron, No. 4:17-cv-00211, 2017 WL 3129797 (N.D. Tex. July 21, 2017); an interview with Nate Washington, Collie's attorney; and from newspaper stories, including Andrew Chung et al., "Shot by Cops, Thwarted by Judges and Geography," Reuters, Aug. 25, 2020, www.reuters.com/investigates/special-report/usa-police-immunity-variations/; Caleb Downs, "Newly Released Dashcam Video Shows Off-Duty Fort Worth Police Officer Shoot Man in Back as He Walked Away," *Dallas Morning News*, Dec. 28, 2016, www.dallasnews.com/news/crime/2016/12/28/newly-released-dashcam-video -shows-off-duty-fort-worth-officer-shoot-man-in-back-as-he-walked-away/; Mazin Sidahmed, "Texas Officer Shot Black Man as He Walked Away, Dashcam Video Sug- gests," *Guardian*, Dec. 28, 2016; Cleve R. Wootson Jr., "Police Say a Black Man Was Shot After Pulling a Blade on Officers. A New Video Raises Doubts," *Washington Post*, Dec. 28, 2016.

68 **The court of appeals called:** Collie v. Barron, 747 Fed. Appx. 950, 950 (2018).

68 **"The Fourth Amendment does not insist":** Georgia v. Randolph, 547 U.S. 103, 125 (2006).

69 **"You shoot me":** Chung et al., "Shot by Cops."

CHAPTER 5. QUALIFIED IMMUNITY

71 **In the late evening:** These facts are drawn from the complaint, discovery, briefs, and court opinions in *Mattos v. Agarano*, No. 1:07-cv-00220 (D. Hawaii April 26, 2007); an interview with Eric Seitz, Mattos's attorney; and "Isle Case Sets Standard on Taser Use, Attorney Says of Settlement," *Maui News*, Jan. 2013.

72 **The district court denied:** Mattos v. Agarano, No. 1:07-cv-00220, 2008 WL 465595 (D. Hawaii Feb. 21, 2008).

72 **When Aikala appealed:** Mattos v. Agarano, 590 F.3d 1082 (9th Cir. 2010).

73 **the appeals court recognized:** Mattos v. Agarano, 661 F.3d 433, 451 (9th Cir. 2011) (en banc). Note that ten (not eleven) appeals judges ultimately decided the case; one of the judges selected to be on the panel passed away and was not replaced.

74 **In the late summer:** The facts of the case are set out in *Pierson* v. Ray, 386 U.S. 547 (1967) and the briefs submitted by the parties to the Supreme Court.

74 **"A policeman's lot":** *Pierson*, 386 U.S. at 555.

75 **arguably most seismic:** Harlow v. Fitzgerald, 457 U.S. 800 (1982).

75 **but also "society as a whole":** *Harlow*, 457 U.S. at 814 (quoting Gregoire v. Biddle, 177 F.2d 579, 581 (2d Cir. 1949)).

75 **the Court called "clearly established law":** *Harlow*, 457 U.S. at 818.

76 **repeatedly reversed lower courts:** White v. Pauly, 137 S. Ct. 548, 551–52 (2017) (per curiam).

76 **"at a high level of generality":** Ashcroft v. al-Kidd, 563 U.S. 731, 742 (2011).

76 *Baxter v. Bracey:* Baxter v. Bracey, 751 Fed. Appx. 869 (6th Cir. 2018).

76 *Kelsay v. Ernst:* Kelsay v. Ernst, 933 F.3d 975 (8th Cir. 2019).

76 **"where a nonviolent misdemeanant":** *Kelsay,* 933 F.3d at 980.

77 **"a deputy was forbidden":** *Kelsay,* 933 F.3d at 980.

77 **"ought to have recognized":** Jessop v. City of Fresno, 936 F.3d 937, 942 (9th Cir. 2019) (citations omitted).

77 **Officers have killed people:** Written Testimony of S. Lee Merritt, Esquire to the Senate Judiciary Committee (June 16, 2020), www.judiciary.senate.gov/imo/media/doc/Merritt%20Testimony.pdf.

77 **Eight years earlier:** Saucier v. Katz, 533 U.S. 194, 201 (2001).

78 **But in 2009:** Pearson v. Callahan, 555 U.S. 223 (2009).

78 **Next, that prior lawsuit:** That opinion may have to be published in the books of federal court decisions issued each year—decisions that are available online but "unpublished" cannot clearly establish the law in some parts of the country. See Joanna C. Schwartz, "Qualified Immunity's Boldest Lie," *Chicago Law Review* 88 (2021): 623. As it turns out, the federal circuit where Jayzel Mattos's case was heard relies on both published and unpublished cases to clearly establish the law. In contrast, the circuit where Onree Norris's case (described in the Introduction) was heard only considers published cases when deciding if the law is clearly established. The judge in Norris's case granted the officers qualified immunity, even though there was a prior factually similar case, because that prior case was unpublished.

79 **can immediately appeal that decision:** Mitchell v. Forsyth, 472 U.S. 511 (1985). Grants and denials of preliminary injunctions, described in chapter 9, can also be immediately appealed.

80 **October 25, 2010:** These facts are drawn from the complaint, briefs, discovery materials, and trial and appellate court opinions in Cole v. Hunter, No. 3:13-cv-02719 (N.D. Tex. July 15, 2013), and from interviews and emails with Amir Ali, one of Cole's attorneys.

81 **denied both requests:** Cole v. Hunter, No. 3:13-cv-02719, 2014 WL 266501 (N.D. Tex. Jan. 24, 2014); Cole v. Hunter, 68 F. Supp. 3d 628 (N.D. Tex. 2014).

81 **First, the defendants appealed:** Cole v. Carson, 802 F.3d 752 (5th Cir. 2015).

81 **The Supreme Court did not issue:** Hunter v. Cole, 137 S. Ct. 497 (2016).

81 **It took the court of appeals:** Cole v. Carson, 905 F.3d 334 (5th Cir. 2018).

81 **This time their motion:** Cole v. Carson, 935 F.3d 444 (5th Cir. 2019) (en banc).

83 **I studied police misconduct settlements:** Joanna C. Schwartz, "Police Indemnification," *New York University Law Review* 89 (2014): 885–1005.

83 **Officers in only two:** Schwartz, "Police Indemnification," 939. As I describe in "Police Indemnification," representatives from two other jurisdiction—the Illinois State Police and the Jacksonville Sheriff's Office—could each recall a case where an officer contributed to a settlement but could not recall whether those obligations arose during my study period. An officer from the Los Angeles Police Department was not indemnified for a $300 punitive damages judgment but was never required to pay that sum.

83 **"gives government officials breathing room":** *al-Kidd,* 563 U.S. at 743.

83 **"allows police officers to respond":** International Association of Chiefs of Police, *IACP Statement on Qualified Immunity,* www.theiacp.org/sites/default/files/IACP%20Statement%20on%20Qualified%20Immunity.pdf.

84 **for every case dismissed:** Joanna C. Schwartz, "After Qualified Immunity," *Columbia Law Review* 120 (2020): 329.

84 **officers and "society as a whole":** *Harlow,* 457 U.S. at 814.

84 **"the driving force" behind qualified immunity:** *Pearson v. Callahan*, 555 U.S. 223, at 231 (2009) (quoting Anderson v. Creighton, 483 U.S. 635, 640n2 (1987)).

84 **in more than 37 percent:** Joanna C. Schwartz, "How Qualified Immunity Fails," *Yale Law Journal* 127 (2017): 60.

84 **"a mare's nest of complexity":** John C. Jeffries, "What's Wrong with Qualified Immunity?," *Florida Law Review* 62 (2010): 852.

84 **One court of appeals judge:** Charles R. Wilson, "'Location, Location, Location': Recent Developments in the Qualified Immunity Defense," *New York University Annual Survey of American Law* 57 (2000): 447.

84 **just 8.6 percent:** Schwartz, "How Qualified Immunity Fails."

85 **factually similar cases are necessary:** Kisela v. Hughes, 138 S. Ct. 1148, 1152–53 (2018) (citations omitted).

85 **But upon studying:** For a discussion of these findings, see Joanna C. Schwartz, "Qualified Immunity's Boldest Lie," *University of Chicago Law Review* 88 (2021): 605–84.

85 **Instead, officers are taught:** Graham v. Connor, 490 U.S. 386, 397 (1989).

85 **"It strains credulity":** Manzares v. Roosevelt Cnty. Adult Det. Ctr., 331 F. Supp. 3d 1260, 1293n10 (D.N.M. 2018).

85 **Less than 4 percent:** Schwartz, "How Qualified Immunity Fails."

86 **"We do [these cases]":** "Isle Case Sets Standard on Taser Use."

86 **If one had to pick:** Ziglar v. Abbasi, 137 S. Ct. 1843, 1872 (2017) (Thomas, J., concurring in part and concurring in the judgment).

87 **"'shoot first, think later' approach to policing":** Mullenix v. Luna, 577 U.S. 7, 26 (2015) (per curiam) (Sotomayor, J., dissenting).

87 **"precisely the sort of 'freewheeling policy choice[s]'":** *Ziglar*, 137 S. Ct. at 1871 (Thomas, J., concurring in part and concurring in the judgment) (citations omitted).

87 **Lower court judges appointed:** For a sampling of criticisms from judges appointed since President Carter, see Stephen R. Reinhardt, "The Demise of Habeas Corpus and the Rise of Qualified Immunity: The Court's Ever Increasing Limitations on the Development and Enforcement of Constitutional Rights and Some Particularly Unfortunate Consequences," *Michigan Law Review* 113 (2015): 1219–54 (written by President Jimmy Carter's appointee Judge Stephen Reinhardt); Calixto v. City of New York, No. 1:15-cv-6676, 2018 WL 10128043 (E.D.N.Y. April 12, 2018) (written by President Ronald Reagan's appointee Judge Raymond J. Dearie); Ziglar v. Abbasi, 137 S. Ct. 1843 (2017) (concurrence written by George H. W. Bush's appointee Justice Clarence Thomas); United States v. Weaver, 975 F.3d 94 (2d Cir. 2020) (concurrence written by President William J. Clinton's appointee Judge Guido Calabresi); Jordan v. Howard, 440 F. Supp. 3d 843 (S.D. Ohio 2020) (written by President George W. Bush's appointee Judge Thomas M. Rose); Jamison v. McClendon, 476 F. Supp. 3d 386 (S.D. Miss. 2020) (written by President Barack Obama's appointee Judge Carlton Reeves); Zadeh v. Robinson, 928 F.3d 457 (5th Cir. 2019) (partial concurrence and dissent written by President Donald J. Trump's appointee Judge Don R. Willett).

87 **"qualified immunity smacks of":** *Zadeh*, 928 F.3d at 479 (Willet, J., concurring in part and dissenting in part).

87 **"an Escherian Stairwell":** *Zadeh*, 928 F.3d at 480.

87 **In its 2019–20 term:** For stories about these cases and the Supreme Court's decisions not to grant certiorari, see, for example, Nina Totenberg, "Supreme Court Will Not Reexamine Doctrine That Shields Police in Misconduct Suits," NPR, June 15, 2020; Richard Wolf, "Legal Immunity for Police Misconduct, Under Attack from Left and Right, May Get Supreme Court Review," *USA Today*, May 29, 2020. Three of those petitions for

certiorari were filed in cases described earlier in chapter 5: *Baxter v. Bracey* (where a burglary suspect who had surrendered was attacked by a police dog); *Kelsay v. Ernst* (where an officer threw a woman to the ground, knocking her unconscious, simply because she walked away from him); and *Jessop v. Fresno* (where officers stole more than $225,000 in money and coins seized during a search).

88 **"shockingly unsanitary cells":** Taylor v. Riojas, 141 S. Ct. 52, 53 (2020) (per curiam).

88 **"any reasonable officer should have realized":** *Taylor*, 141 S. Ct. at 54.

88 *Hope v. Pelzer:* Hope v. Pelzer, 536 U.S. 730 (2002).

88 *McCoy v. Alamu:* McCoy v. Alamu, 950 F.3d 226, 229 (5th Cir. 2020).

88 **When the court of appeals granted:** *McCoy*, 950 F.3d at 232–33 (citation omitted).

88 **the Supreme Court vacated:** McCoy v. Alamu, 141 S. Ct. 1364 (2021) (memorandum opinion).

89 **the trial court dismissed:** Timpa v. Dillard, No. 3:16-cv-03089, 2020 WL 3798875 (N.D. Tex. July 6, 2020).

89 **In December 2021, more than five years:** Timpa v. Dillard, 20 F.4th 1020 (5th Cir. 2021).

90 **a "shocker":** Cassandra Jaramillo, "Federal Court Overturns Decision in Case of Tony Timpa, Who Died in Dallas Police Custody," *Dallas Morning News*, Dec. 15, 2021 (quoting Dallas civil rights attorney David Henderson), www.dallasnews.com/news/investigations/2021/12/15/federal-court-overturns-decision-in-death-of-tony-timpa-who-died-in-dallas-police-custody/.

90 **Perhaps the judges were compelled:** Lombardo v. City of St. Louis, 141 S. Ct. 2239 (2021) (per curiam).

90 **As Vicki told reporters:** Ken Kalthoff, "Tony Timpa's Mother Anxious for Trial of Officers Blamed in Lawsuit for His Death," NBC Dallas Fort Worth, Dec. 16, 2021, www.nbcdfw.com/news/local/tony-timpas-mother-anxious-for-trial-of-officers-blamed-in-lawsuit-for-his-death/2840597/.

CHAPTER 6. SUING THE CITY

94 **"can seem like a respite":** John Eligon, "Does Race Matter in America's Most Diverse ZIP Codes?," *New York Times*, Nov. 24, 2017.

94 **its mostly white police force:** Shane Bauer, "How a Deadly Police Force Ruled a City," *New Yorker*, Nov. 16, 2020.

94 **nineteen people:** Sam Levin, "19 Dead in a Decade: The Small American City Where Violent Police Thrive," *Guardian*, June 13, 2020.

94 **More people are shot:** Stephen Stock et al., "Vallejo Police Have Highest Rate of Residents Shot Per Capita in Northern California; NBC Bay Area Probes Causes," NBC Bay Area, May 18, 2019, www.nbcbayarea.com/news/local/vallejo-police-highest-rate-of-residents-shot-per-capita-in-northern-california-nbc-bay-area-probes-causes/190344/. Between 2011 and 2019, when the NBC report was published, 16 people had been killed by Vallejo police, which amounted to 13.8 people killed per 100,000 residents.

94 **More people are killed:** Bauer, "How a Deadly Police Force." Among the 100 largest police departments, the only city with a higher rate of killings than Vallejo during the study period was St. Louis, Missouri.

94 **A Pew Research Center survey:** Rich Morin and Andrew Mercer, "A Closer Look at Police Officers Who Have Fired Their Weapon on Duty," Pew Research Center, Feb. 8, 2017, www.pewresearch.org/fact-tank/2017/02/08/a-closer-look-at-police-officers-who-have-fired-their-weapon-on-duty/.

94 **nearly 40 percent:** Geoffrey King, "Vallejo Police Bend Badges to Mark Fatal Shootings," *Open Vallejo*, July 28, 2020, openvallejo.org/2020/07/28/vallejo-police-bend -badge-tips-to-mark-fatal-shootings/.

94 **eighty-five Section 1983 lawsuits:** In my count of eighty-five lawsuits filed against the Vallejo Police Department and its officers, I am not including four cases that appear to be duplicate filings by pro se plaintiffs. For further discussion of these cases, see Joanna C. Schwartz, "Civil Rights Without Representation," *William and Mary Law Review* 64 (2023), https://papers.ssrn.com/sol3/papers.cfm?abstract_id=4046203.

95 **On February 27, 2012:** Complaint, Deleon v. Vallejo Police Dep't, No. 2:12-cv-0510 (E.D. Cal. Feb. 27, 2012).

95 **On February 29, 2012:** Complaint, Wilson v. City of Vallejo, No. 2:12-cv-0547 (E.D. Cal. Feb. 29, 2012).

95 **On March 6, 2012:** Complaint, Cooley v. City of Vallejo, No. 2:12-cv-0591 (E.D. Cal. March 6, 2012).

95 **On May 14, 2012:** Complaint, Muhammad v. City of Vallejo, No. 2:12-cv-1304 (E.D. Cal. May 14, 2012).

95 **On May 29, 2012:** Complaint, Black v. City of Vallejo, No. 2:12-cv-1439 (E.D. Cal. May 29, 2012).

95 **On June 18, 2012:** Complaint, White v. Nichelini, No. 2:12-cv-1629 (E.D. Cal. June 18, 2012).

96 **On July 30, 2012, Roosevelt:** Complaint, Robinson v. Jaksch, No. 2:12-cv-1992 (E.D. Cal. July 30, 2012).

96 **On July 30, 2012, Dennis:** Amended Complaint, Gardner v. Vallejo Police Department, No. 2:12-cv-1981 (E.D. Cal. July 30, 2012).

96 **On September 24, 2012:** Complaint, Tayag v. Mazer, No. 2:12-cv-2423 (E.D. Cal. Sept. 24, 2012).

96 **On October 12, 2012:** Complaint, Nichols v. City of Vallejo, No. 2:12-cv-2564 (E.D. Cal. Oct. 12, 2012).

96 **killed six people:** Alex Emslie, "Questions Surround Surge in Vallejo Police Shootings," KQED, May 20, 2014, www.kqed.org/news/135682/amid-a-series-of-vallejo -police-shootings-one-officers-name-stands-out.

96 **"If you were to ask me":** Emslie, "Questions Surround Surge."

97 **In the early morning hours:** These facts are drawn from the briefs and court decisions in Johnson v. Vallejo, 2:13-cv-01072 (E.D. Cal. May 30, 2013); interviews with Kris Kelley, Mario Romero's sister, and Michael Verna, one of the lawyers for the plaintiffs; and news reports including Laurence Du Sault and Open Vallejo, "The City Where Investigations of Police Take So Long, Officers Kill Again Before Reviews Are Done," ProPublica, July 7, 2022.

98 **Three months before killing Romero:** Scott Morris, "Ten Years Since Vallejo's Deadliest Year, $12.7 Million Has Been Paid to Settle Civil Rights Lawsuits," *Vallejo Sun*, Jan. 4, 2022, www.vallejosun.com/ten-years-since-vallejo-polices-deadliest-year -12-6-million-has-been-paid-to-settle-civil-rights-lawsuits/.

98 **Seven weeks after killing Romero:** Alex Emslie, "The Killing of Jeremiah Moore: Parents Want Answers in 2012 Vallejo Police Shooting," KQED, April 9, 2014, www .kqed.org/news/131648/police-involved-killing-of-vallejo-man-remains-unresolved -18-months-later.

98 **Officer Kenney left the Vallejo:** John Glidden and Nate Gartrell, "Ex–Vallejo Officer Involved with Multiple Officer-Involved Shootings Starts Consulting Firm," *Vallejo Times-Herald*, March 28, 2019, www.timesheraldonline.com/2019/03/28/ex-vallejo

-officer-involved-with-multiple-officer-involved-shootings-starts-consulting-firm/. My analysis of federal lawsuits filed against Vallejo and its officers revealed eight lawsuits filed against Kenney between 2010–2018. For a tally of the shootings by Officer Kenney, see King, "Vallejo Police Bend Badges."

98 **Vallejo paid more than $2.5 million:** Scott Morris, "For Vallejo Officers Who Use Force, a Pattern of Promotions and Awards," *Vallejo Sun*, July 27, 2020, www.vallejosun .com/for-vallejo-officers-who-use-force-a-pattern-of-promotions-and-awards/.

98 **But the district attorney:** Albert Samaha, "Three Shootings in Vallejo," *BuzzFeed*, March 9, 2015, www.buzzfeed.com/albertsamaha/three-shootings-in-vallejo. For a detailed description of the Vallejo Police Department's investigation of the Romero shooting, and its internal investigations more generally, see Du Sault and Open Vallejo, "The City Where Investigations of Police Take So Long."

98 **Kenney was promoted:** Samaha, "Three Shootings in Vallejo."

98 **the Fatal 14:** For descriptions of the Fatal 14, see Ericka Cruz Guevarra and Julie Chang, "Vallejo Police Chief Launches 'Official Inquiry' into Alleged Badge Bending Tradition to Mark Fatal Shootings," KQED, July 29, 2020, www.kqed.org/news /11830960/ousted-vallejo-officer-alleges-tradition-of-bending-badges-to-mark -police-killings; Levin, "19 Dead in a Decade."

98 **these fourteen officers:** Stephen Stock et al., "NBC Bay Area Investigation Links Group of Vallejo Officers to Majority of Use of Force Incidents," NBC Bay Area, Dec. 29, 2019, www.nbcbayarea.com/news/local/nbc-bay-area-investigation-links-group -of-vallejo-police-officers-to-majority-of-use-of-force-incidents/2201307/.

98 **Yet, during that decade:** For reports that no Vallejo police officers were disciplined for using force between 2010 and 2020, see Darwin BondGram, "In One California City, Police Kill with Near Impunity," *Appeal*, Dec. 18, 2019 ("The investigative files for the 27 officer-involved shootings made public by the police department this year show that no officer has been disciplined in the past decade for using deadly force."), theappeal .org/vallejo-california-police-shootings/; Levin, "19 Dead in a Decade"; Morris, "For Vallejo Officers." One of the Fatal 14 was disciplined but not for use of force. See Ericka Cruz Guevarra, "'It's Not Real Justice': Vallejo Officer Fired, but Not for Deadly Force," KQED, Oct. 1, 2020, www.kqed.org/news/11840604/its-not-real-justice -vallejo-officer-fired-but-not-for-deadly-force. In 2022, another officer was disciplined for putting his foot on the head of a restrained suspect for a minute and a half; this appears to be the only documented discipline for a Vallejo officer for a use of force since 2010. See Thomas Gase, "Vallejo Police Officer Colin Eaton Disciplined for Excessive Force in 2020 According to Investigation," *Vallejo Times-Herald*, Feb. 16, 2022, www .timesheraldonline.com/2022/02/16/vallejo-police-officer-colin-eaton-disciplined -for-excessive-force-in-2020-according-to-investigation/.

98 **"Badge of Honor":** The "Badge of Honor" ritual was first uncovered by journalist Geoffrey King in 2020. King, "Vallejo Police Bend Badges." For further discussion of the ritual, see Guevarra and Chang, "Vallejo Police Chief."

98 **Vallejo officers have now confirmed:** Brian Krans, "How Badge Bending Became a Ritual Among Vallejo Police," *Vallejo Sun*, March 31, 2022, www.vallejosun.com/how -badge-bending-became-a-ritual-among-vallejo-police/.

99 **The blunted edges:** King, "Vallejo Police Bend Badges."

99 **Captain Whitney was fired:** See Melanie Woodrow, "I-Team Exclusive: Former Vallejo PD Captain Speaks Out, Claims He Was Fired for Whistleblowing," ABC7, Dec. 24, 2020, abc7news.com/vallejo-police-department-john-whitney-pd-badge-bending -whistleblower/9038302/.

99 **"Some days I feel":** King, "Vallejo Police Bend Badges."

99 **Moore's research revealed:** For the complete findings, see ACLU, *Secret Detention by the Chicago Police* (Glencoe, Ill.: Free Press, 1959), 5–6.

100 **"the community receives the benefits":** Brief of Petitioners, On Writ of Certiorari to the U.S. Court of Appeals for the Seventh Circuit, Monroe v. Pape, 1960 WL 98617, at *40 (Aug. 25, 1960).

100 **"appl[y] deterrent pressures":** Brief of Petitioners, *Monroe*, 1960 WL 98617, at *42.

100 **In the Court's view:** Monroe v. Pape, 365 U.S. 167 (1961).

101 **Seventeen years later:** Monell v. Department of Social Services, 436 U.S. 658 (1978). *Monell* still did not allow states to be sued under Section 1983. The Eleventh Amendment has been read to prevent states from being sued for constitutional violations. As a result, *Monell* claims cannot be brought against state police agencies. They also cannot be brought against task forces, like the task force that broke down the doors to Onree Norris's home in the introduction.

101 **"policy or custom":** *Monell*, 436 U.S. at 690–91.

101 **"expressly leav[ing] further development":** *Monell*, 436 U.S. at 695.

101 **"deeply divided":** City of Canton v. Harris, 489 U.S. 378, 385 (1989).

101 ***Owen v. City of Independence:*** Owen v. City of Independence, 445 U.S. 622 (1980).

101 **"The threat that damages":** *Owen*, 445 U.S. at 652.

102 **"excessive judicial intrusion":** *Owen*, 445 U.S. at 668 (Powell, J., dissenting).

102 **"many local governments lack":** *Owen*, 445 U.S. at 670 (Powell, J., dissenting).

103 **"final policymaking authority":** Pembaur v. City of Cincinnati, 475 U.S. 469 (1986).

103 **informal custom or policy:** Connick v. Thompson, 563 U.S. 51, 61 (2011). In the view of some courts and scholars there are four theories of municipal liability, with failure to train and supervise officers—a theory outlined in City of Canton v. Harris, 489 U.S. 378, 385 (1989)—as separate from the unwritten custom and policy theory. Others view these "failure to" claims under the umbrella of the unwritten custom and policy theory. For the sake of simplicity, I am following the latter approach.

103 **Instead, it is usually:** *Monell* liability can also be established if a police chief knows of a constitutional violation by a subordinate and approves of it. This is referred to as the "ratification" theory of *Monell* liability. St. Louis v. Praprotnik, 485 U.S. 112 (1988).

103 **"deliberate indifference":** *City of Canton*, 489 U.S. at 389.

104 **"lesser standard":** *City of Canton*, 489 U.S. at 391–92.

104 **In a footnote:** *City of Canton*, 489 U.S. at 390n10.

104 **Twenty-two years later:** *Connick*, 563 U.S. 51.

104 **In 1985, twenty-six years:** These facts are drawn from the majority and dissenting opinions in *Connick*, 563 U.S. 51.

105 **Prosecutors have a constitutional obligation:** Brady v. Maryland, 373 U.S. 83 (1963).

106 **A jury ruled in Thompson's favor:** Sam Roberts, "John Thompson, Cleared After 14 Years on Death Row, Dies at 55," *New York Times*, Oct. 4, 2017.

107 **"additional training would have been":** *Connick*, 563 U.S. at 68.

107 **"None of those cases involved":** *Connick*, 563 U.S. at 62–63.

108 **Before getting to discovery:** Ashcroft v. Iqbal, 566 U.S. 662 (2009).

108 **Some people have gotten past:** For an example of a *Monell* claim against the Vallejo Police Department that survived a motion to dismiss with evidence of past lawsuit filings, see Bagos v. City of Vallejo, No. 2:20-cv-00185, 2020 WL 6043949, at *5 (E.D. Cal. Oct. 13, 2020). The judge in *Bagos* makes clear, though, that prior lawsuits would not be sufficient at the summary judgment stage. *Bagos*, 2020 WL 6043949, at *5.

109 **In only one:** Memorandum and Order, Ledesma v. City of Vallejo, No. 2:17-cv-0106 (E.D. Cal. Feb. 26, 2019).

110 **"The volume of killings":** Plaintiffs' Joint Memorandum of Points and Authorities in Opposition to Defendants' Partial Motion for Summary Judgment of Plaintiffs' *Monell* Claims, Johnson v. Vallejo, No. 2:13-cv-1072, at 19 (E.D. Cal. Jan. 14, 2015) (quoting Zimring Declaration).

110 **"didn't see a pattern":** Plaintiffs' Joint Memorandum, Johnson v. Vallejo, No. 2:13-cv-1072, at 20 (quoting Zimring Declaration).

111 **Judge Mendez acknowledged:** Johnson v. Vallejo, 99 F. Supp. 3d 1212, 1222 (E.D. Cal. 2015).

111 **Judge Mendez recognized:** *Johnson*, 99 F. Supp. 3d at 1222.

112 **Jared Huey:** Notice of Settlement, Huey v. City of Vallejo, No. 2:13-cv-00916 (E.D. Cal. April 29, 2015); Settlement Agreement and Mutual Release, Huey v. City of Vallejo, No. 2:13-cv-00916 (undated).

112 **When he granted the City:** Judge Mendez ruled that Jeremiah Moore's family adequately stated a claim against Officer Kenney and the City of Vallejo on October 17, 2014. Moore v. City of Vallejo, 73 F. Supp. 3d 1253 (E.D. Cal. Oct. 17, 2014). Judge Mendez denied Officer Kenney's summary judgment motion in the case brought by Anton Barrett's family on April 30, 2015. Order After Hearing on Motion for Summary Judgment/Partial Summary Judgment of Issues, Estate of Anton Barrett v. City of Vallejo, No. 2:13-CV-00846 (E.D. Cal. April 30, 2015).

112 **The case brought:** Settlement Agreement and Release, Estate of Anton Pat Barrett v. City of Vallejo (July 9, 2015); Full and Final Settlement Agreement and Release, Moore v. City of Vallejo (May 13, 2016).

113 **$2 million:** Morris, "Ten Years Since"; Stipulation for Settlement, Joseph v. City of Vallejo (July 1, 2015).

113 **no way to recover:** Some circuits have taken things one step further, ruling that a grant of qualified immunity forecloses a *Monell* claim for failure to train, because local governments cannot be deliberately indifferent to the need for better training about a right that is not clearly established. I describe this phenomenon, what I call "backdoor municipal immunity," and why circuit courts should eschew it, in Joanna C. Schwartz, "Backdoor Municipal Immunity," *Yale Law Review Forum* (2022), https://papers.ssrn.com/sol3/papers.cfm?abstract_id=4090879.

113 **four Latina women sued:** Details about the civil and criminal cases come from the court filings, discovery materials, and summary judgment decision in Alfaro v. City of Houston, No. 4:11-cv-1541 (S.D. Tex. April 21, 2011); an interview with Benjamin Hall, one of Edith Alfaro's attorneys; and Jayme Fraser, "Ex–HPD Officer Sentenced to Life in Rape," *Houston Chronicle*, Oct. 8, 2012, www.chron.com/news/houston-texas/article/Ex-HPD-officer-sentenced-to-life-in-rape-3928437.php.

114 **the judge who heard the case:** Alfaro v. City of Houston, No. 4:11-cv-1541, 2013 WL 3457060, at *14 (S.D. Tex. July 9, 2013).

114 **"Without her, who would know":** Fraser, "Ex–HPD Officer."

115 **an estimated $16 million:** Bauer, "How a Deadly Police Force." Note that the City of Vallejo has had some form of municipal liability insurance during this period, so these costs have been borne, in part, by its insurers. Scott Morris, "Expensive and Dangerous: Vallejo Police May Pay More per Officer in Civil Rights Cases Than Any Other Agency," *Vallejo Sun*, June 9, 2019, www.vallejosun.com/expensive-and-dangerous-vallejo-police-may-pay-more-per-officer-in-civil-rights-cases-than-any-other-agency/.

115 **Officer Tonn had been sitting:** Details of Sean Monterrosa's killing are described in Laurence Du Sault and Geoffrey King, "Detective on Leave over Sean Monterrosa Shooting," *Open Vallejo*, July 11, 2021; KTVU Staff, "Monterrosa Violated Policy, Investigation Concludes," FOX KTVU, Dec. 2, 2021.

115 **"Fucking stupid":** Bauer, "How a Deadly Police Force."

115 **"You're going to be all right":** Bauer, "How a Deadly Police Force."

115 **In December 2021:** Ericka Cruz Guevarra et al., "Vallejo Plans to Fire the Cop Who Killed Sean Monterrosa," KQED, Dec. 13, 2021, www.kqed.org/news/11898785/vallejo -plans-to-fire-the-cop-who-killed-sean-monterrosa.

115 **In May 2022:** Scott Morris, "Vallejo Officer Who Killed Sean Monterrosa's Termination Overturned," *Vallejo Sun*, May 27, 2022, www.vallejosun.com/vallejo-officer-who -killed-sean-monterrosas-termination-overturned/.

116 **Several civil rights attorneys:** See, for example, Dorsey v. City of Vallejo, No. 2:21-cv-00255 (E.D. Cal. Feb. 9, 2021).

CHAPTER 7. JUDGES

117 **Its pages told a story:** These facts are drawn from the briefs, discovery, and trial and appellate court decisions in Tolan v. The City of Bellaire, No. 4:09-cv-01324 (S.D. Tex. May 1, 2009); an interview with Marian Tolan; Robbie Tolan's book, *No Justice: One White Police Officer, One Black Family, and How One Bullet Ripped Us Apart* (New York: Center Street, 2018); and news reports including Barry Svrluga, "The Black Baseball Prospect, the Police Shooting, and the Club He Never Wanted to Join," *Washington Post*, Dec. 31, 2020; Mike Tolson, "Bellaire Police Shooting Unearths Racial Unease," *Houston Chronicle*, July 25, 2011, www.chron.com/news/houston-texas/article/Bellaire -police-shooting-unearths-racial-unease-1585181.php.

119 **270 or so:** According to the 2010 Census, there were 16,855 residents of Bellaire, Texas: 72.6 percent were non-Hispanic white; 9.5 percent were Latinx; 14.1 percent were Asian; and 1.6 percent were Black.

119 **"Bellaire police officers have a pattern":** Complaint, Tolan v. Cotton, No. 4:09-cv-1324 (S.D. Tex. May 1, 2009).

120 **As Robbie Tolan recounts:** Tolan, *No Justice*, 188.

120 **According to the Tolans' lawyers:** Tolan, *No Justice*, 188.

120 **Judges are charged with:** For discussion of judges' active role in multiple aspects of modern civil litigation, see Judith Resnik, "Managerial Judges," *Harvard Law Review* 96 (1982): 374–448.

121 **cannot be appealed:** Another category of decisions that can be immediately appealed are grants or denials of preliminary injunctions, as described in chapter 9.

121 **the standard for reversal:** The standard of review for appellate courts depends on the type of question they are reviewing. Legal questions are reviewed de novo; questions of fact can be reversed only if the lower court's decision was clearly erroneous; and courts of appeals can reverse judges' discretionary decisions only if they have abused their discretion.

121 **what the trial court says:** For discussion of how the Federal Rules of Civil Procedure's expansion of pretrial procedures, combined with deferential standards of appelate review, give trial courts additional power, see Stephen C. Yeazell, "The Misunderstood Consequences of Modern Civil Process," *Wisconsin Law Review* (1994): 631–78.

122 **"If you get a certain judge":** Joanna C. Schwartz, "Qualified Immunity's Selection Effects," *Northwestern University Law Review* 114 (2020): 1141.

122 **Analysis of thousands:** For the complete studies, see Aaron L. Nielson and Christopher J. Walker, "Strategic Immunity," *Emory Law Journal* 66 (2016): 55–122; Aaron L. Nielson and Christopher J. Walker, "The New Qualified Immunity," *Southern California Law Review* 89 (2015): 1–65.

122 **white judges grant:** Jill D. Weinberg and Laura Beth Nielson, "Examining Empathy: Discrimination, Experience, and Judicial Decisionmaking," *Southern California Law Review* 85 (2012): 313–52.

122 **appeals judges with daughters:** Adam N. Glynn and Maya Sen, "Identifying Judicial Empathy: Does Having Daughters Cause Judges to Rule for Women's Issues?," *American Journal of Political Science* 59 (2014): 43, 47.

122 **Chief Justice John Roberts mused:** Transcript of oral argument at 9, Lange v. California, 141 S. Ct. 2011 (2021).

122 **Five years earlier, in 2016:** Commonwealth v. Warren, 475 Mass. 530, 539 (2016).

123 **Remember Marvin Aspen:** William Kling, "City Attorney Charges Civil Rights Law Is Abused," *Chicago Tribune*, Aug. 2, 1966.

123 **Remember Judge Ruggero Aldisert:** Ruggero J. Aldisert, "Judicial Expansion of Federal Jurisdiction: A Federal Judge's Thoughts on Section 1983, Comity, and the Federal Caseload," *Law and Social Order* (1973): 569.

123 **Remember Judge Paul Niemeyer:** Paul V. Niemeyer, "Here We Go Again: Are the Federal Discovery Rules Really in Need of Amendment?," *Boston College Law Review* 39 (1998): 518.

125 **According to Judge Harmon:** Order on Discovery Motions, Tolan v. Cotton, 4:09-cv-01324 (S.D. Tex. March 25, 2010).

126 **Magistrate Judge Stacy agreed:** Memorandum and Order Granting in Part and Denying in Part Defendants' Opposed Motion for Protection and to Stay Discovery, Tolan v. Cotton, 4:09-cv-01324 (S.D. Tex. Oct. 23, 2009).

126 **On May 11, 2010:** ABC7, "Protest Planned After Bellaire Shooting Verdict," May 12, 2010, https://abc7news.com/archive/7435154/.

126 **On January 1, 2011:** The version of the facts alleged by defendants at summary judgment is set out in Defendants', Edwards and Cotton, Motion for Summary Judgment, Tolan v. Cotton, 4:09-cv-01324 (S.D. Tex. Jan. 1, 2011).

127 **In their opposition:** The plaintiffs' version of the facts at summary judgment are set out in Plaintiffs' Opposition to Defendants Edwards's and Cotton's Motion for Summary Judgment, Tolan v. Cotton, 4:09-cv-01324 (S.D. Tex. Jan. 24, 2011).

127 **Judges are instructed:** Scott v. Harris, 550 U.S. 372, 378 (2007) (citation omitted); Fed. R. Civ. P. 56.

127–128 **"Forcefully and intentionally":** Tolan v. Cotton, 854 F. Supp. 2d 444, 469 (2012).

128 **"because Sergeant Cotton feared":** *Tolan*, 854 F. Supp. 2d at 477.

128 **appeals court affirmed:** Tolan v. Cotton, 713 F.3d 299, 303 (5th Cir. 2013).

128 **It was clearly established:** *Tolan*, 713 F.3d at 306 (citation omitted).

128 **Robbie could not overcome:** *Tolan*, 713 F.3d at 306–7 (citations omitted).

128 **request for a rehearing:** Tolan v. Cotton, 538 Fed. Appx. 374 (5th Cir. 2013).

129 **But the Court granted:** Tolan v. Cotton, 572 U.S. 650 (2014) (per curiam).

129 **"The witnesses on both sides":** *Tolan*, 572 U.S. at 660.

129 **the court of appeals reversed:** Tolan v. Cotton, 573 Fed. Appx. 330 (5th Cir. 2014).

130 **"The Plaintiffs argue":** Opinion and Order, Tolan v. Cotton, No. 4:09-cv-01324 (S.D. Tex. Aug. 14, 2015).

131 **"I'm very tempted":** Transcript of hearing at 3–4, Tolan v. Cotton, No. 4:09-cv-01324 (S.D. Tex. Sept. 11, 2015).

131 **recuse herself:** Plaintiffs' Emergency Motion for Recusal and Request for Leave to File Motion to Transfer, Tolan v. Cotton, No. 4:09-cv-01324 (S.D. Tex. Sept. 13, 2015).

131 **Judge Harmon denied the request:** Order on Emergency Motion for Recusal and Request for Leave to File Motion to Transfer, Tolan v. Cotton, No. 4:09-cv-01324 (S.D. Tex. Sept. 14, 2015).

132 **As Robbie explained in his book:** Tolan, *No Justice*, 215, 218–19.

CHAPTER 8. JURIES

135 **August 12, 2014:** These facts are drawn from the complaint, discovery documents, briefs, and trial transcripts in Liese v. Delio, No. 6:14-cv-01788 (M.D. Fla. Nov. 3, 2014); interviews and email exchanges with Rob Liese and his attorney, William Ruffier; video of the assault; and news reports, including Jeff Deal, "Man Battered by Former Orlando Police Officer Hopes for Restitution," WFTV, Sept. 28, 2017, www.wftv.com/news/local/man-battered-by-former-orlando-police-officer-hopes-for-restitution/616347379/; Michelle Meredith, "Former Orlando Officer Sentenced to Jail for On-Duty Beating," WESH 2 News, Nov. 9, 2016, www.wesh.com/article/former-orlando-officer-sentenced-to-jail-for-on-duty-beating/8263671; "Victim of Orlando Police Battery Wants Judge to Reduce Jail Time for Former Officer," WFTV, Feb. 10, 2017, www.wftv.com/news/local/victim-of-orlando-police-battery-wants-judge-to-reduce-jail-time-for-former-officer-/493045588/; "Former Orlando Police Officer Guilty of Battery Sentenced to 51 Weeks in Jail," WFTV, Nov. 9, 2016, www.wftv.com/news/local/former-orlando-police-officer-guilty-of-battery-sentenced-to-51-weeks-in-jail/465668022/.

137 **This was enough:** Order, Liese v. Delio, No. 6:14-cv-01788, 2016 WL 7325648 (M.D. Fla. March 21, 2016).

137 **When I reviewed 1,183:** In my study of 1,183 police misconduct cases, only 10 cases ended with a plaintiffs' verdict, although 2 additional cases settled following a plaintiffs' verdict. For the distribution of case outcomes, see Joanna C. Schwartz, "How Qualified Immunity Fails," *Yale Law Journal* 127 (2017): 46, table 12.

137 **Other studies have similarly found:** For other studies of plaintiffs' win rates and the amounts plaintiffs recover, see, for example, Theodore Eisenberg, "Litigation Models and Trial Outcomes in Civil Rights and Prisoner Cases," *Georgetown Law Journal* 77 (1998): 1567–602; Theodore Eisenberg and Stewart Schwab, "The Reality of Constitutional Tort Litigation," *Cornell Law Review* 72 (1987): 641–95; Margo Schlanger, "Inmate Litigation," *Harvard Law Review* 116 (2003): 1598.

138 **Gallup has polled:** Justin McCarthy, "U.S. Confidence in Organized Religion Remains Low," Gallup, July 8, 2019.

138 **In June 2020:** Aimee Ortiz, "Confidence in Police Is at Record Low, Gallup Survey Finds," *New York Times*, Aug. 12, 2020.

139 ***Scott v. Harris:*** Scott v. Harris, 550 U.S. 372 (2007).

139 **Fourth Amendment excessive-force standard:** Graham v. Connor, 490 U.S. 386, 397 (1989) (citation omitted).

139 **The officers appealed:** Harris v. Coweta County, 406 F.3d 1307 (11th Cir. 2005).

140 **During oral argument:** Oral argument at 27 (Justice Alito), 28 (Justice Scalia), 31 (Justice Breyer), Scott v. Harris, 550 U.S. 372 (Feb. 26, 2007).

140 **He wrote in his dissent:** Harris, 550 U.S. at 390 (Stevens, J., dissenting).

140 **Law professors Dan Kahan:** Dan M. Kahan, David A. Hoffman, and Donald Braman, "Whose Eyes Are You Going to Believe? *Scott v. Harris* and the Perils of Cognitive Illiberalism," *Harvard Law Review* 122 (2009): 837–906.

140 **Congress and the Supreme Court:** The Jury Selection and Service Act of 1968, 28 U.S.C. §§ 1861–74 (2006); Thiel v. Southern Pac. Co., 328 U.S. 217 (1946); J.E.B. v. Alabama ex rel. T.B., 511 U.S. 127 (1994).

141 **"as assurance of a diffused impartiality":** Taylor v. Louisiana, 419 U.S. 522, 530–31 (1975) (quoting Thiel v. Southern Pacific Co., 328 U.S. 217 (1946) (Frankfurter, J., dissenting)).

141 **diverse juries make better decisions:** Samuel R. Sommers, "On Racial Diversity and Group Decision Making: Identifying Multiple Effects of Racial Composition on Jury Deliberations," *Journal of Personality and Social Psychology* 90 (2006): 597–612.

141 **"key-man" method:** For descriptions of the key-man method, see Laura G. Dooley, "The Dilution Effect: Federalization, Fair Cross-Sections, and the Concept of Community," *DePaul Law Review* 54 (2004): 84; Alexander E. Preller, "Jury Duty Is a Poll Tax: The Case for Severing the Link Between Voter Registration and Jury Service," *Columbia Journal of Law and Social Problems* 46 (2012): 4.

141 **"fair cross section":** 28 U.S.C. § 1861.

141 **not exclude people:** 28 U.S.C. § 1862.

141 **People who have felony charges:** 28 U.S.C. § 1865.

141 **Best estimates are:** Sarah K. S. Shannon et al., "The Growth, Scope, and Spatial Distribution of People with Felony Records in the United States, 1948–2010," *Demography* 54 (2017): 1795–1818.

142 **Two-thirds of federal districts:** Jeffrey Abramson, "Jury Selection in the Weeds: Whither the Democratic Shore?," *University of Michigan Journal of Law Reform* 52 (2018): 2n4.

142 **Latinx and Black people are underrepresented:** The Florida Division of Elections has statistics on registered voter racial/ethnic demographics at dos.myflorida.com /elections/data-statistics/voter-registration-statistics/. Census.gov has quick facts on Florida at www.census.gov/quickfacts/FL, including racial/ethnic demographics. The most recent Census.gov estimate is from July 2019, www.census.gov/quickfacts/FL, and the most recent Florida Division of Elections voter registration report is from October 2020, files.floridados.gov/media/703594/2-by-county-by-race.pdf, but I relied on the data for the February 2020 report, files.floridados.gov/media/702730/2-by -county-by-race.pdf, because that is the closest available date to July 2019.

142 **Federal law allows district courts:** 28 U.S.C. § 1863(b)(2). For a survey of the sources states rely upon when building their jury lists, see Preller, "Jury Duty Is a Poll Tax," 42.

142 **federal courts have rejected:** United States v. Pritt, 6:09-cr-110, 2010 WL 2342440 at *6 (M.D. Fla. June 8, 2020). For examples of other courts reaching this same conclusion, see Abramson, "Jury Selection in the Weeds," 32–33.

142 **when Section 1983 became law:** Cong. Globe, 42nd Cong., 1st Sess., 459–60 (1871) ("The United States courts are further above mere local influence than the county courts; their judges can act with more independence; their sympathies are not so nearly identified with those of the vicinage; the jurors are taken from the State, and not the neighborhood; they will be able to rise above prejudices or bad passions or terror more easily. We believe that we can trust our United States courts, and we propose to do so.").

142 **less diverse and less sympathetic:** Joanna C. Schwartz, "Civil Rights Ecosystems," *Michigan Law Review* 118 (2020): 1573, 1587 (describing Philadelphia and Orlando civil rights attorneys' preference for state court juries). See also Dooley, "Dilution Effect," 105–9.

142 **almost one-quarter Black:** For the demographics of Orlando, Florida, see U.S. Census, www.census.gov/quickfacts/orlandocityflorida (reporting that, in 2021, Black

people made up 24.2 percent of the population of Orlando); Florida Department of Health, Population Dashboard, www.flhealthcharts.gov/ChartsReports/rdPage.aspx ?rdReport=PopAtlas.PopulationAtlasDASHBOARD&rdLinkDataLayers=PopAtlas .PopulationAtlasDASHBOARD (reporting that, in 2009, Black people made up 21.7 percent of the population of Orange County, where Orlando is located). For the demographics of the Middle District of Florida, see Abramson, "Jury Selection in the Weeds," 29–30 (reporting that Black people made up 12.5 percent of the Middle District of Florida's population over age eighteen in 2009). See also telephone interview with Middle District of Florida attorney F (on file with author) ("[T]he jurors here are pretty damn conservative in the federal court because you cover—I mean, it's the red part of the state. So, even the City of Jacksonville is—City of Jacksonville, you got a much more diverse community. But you start going to Clay County, Nassau County, Baker County. Baker County, you got mostly prison workers. They work for the Department of Corrections, that's the big industry out west of Jacksonville.").

143 **Washington State task force:** Ashish S. Joshi and Christina T. Kline, "Lack of Jury Diversity: A National Problem with Individual Consequences," American Bar Association, Sept. 1, 2015.

143 **Even when a questionnaire:** See Tresa Baldas, "No-Shows for Jury Duty Hurt Diversity of Michigan Pools," *Detroit Free Press*, April 13, 2012; Hong Tran, "Jury Diversity: Policy, Legislative, and Legal Arguments to Address the Lack of Diversity in Juries," *Defense*, May 2013.

143 **likely to be culled:** Abramson, "Jury Selection in the Weeds," 8–32; Baldas, "No-Shows"; Tran, "Jury Diversity."

143 **One such study:** Abramson, "Jury Selection in the Weeds," 29–32.

144 **"It is rather":** United States v. Pritt, No. 6:09-cr-110, 2010 WL 2342440, at *6 (M.D. Fla. June 8, 2010).

145 **"Very few of them":** Caleb Foote, "Tort Remedies for Police Violations of Individual Rights," *Minnesota Law Review* 39 (1955): 500 (citations omitted).

146 **"to the extent":** Foote, "Tort Remedies," 512–13.

153 **"Mr. Liese has a very humble background":** "Jury: Former Orlando Police Officer Violated Inmate's Rights in Excessive Force Case," WFTV, April 22, 2016, www.wftv .com/news/local/jury-former-orlando-police-officer-violated-inmates-rights -in-excessive-force-case/236145416/.

153 **Delio did not escape consequences:** "Jury: Former Orlando Police Officer"; Meredith, "Former Orlando Officer."

153 **letter to the judge:** "Victim of Orlando Police Battery."

154 **spotty employment history:** Jeff Deal, "Man Beaten by Former OPD Officer Will Not Get Restitution by City," WFTV, Feb. 15, 2018.

154 **"When any large and identifiable segment":** Peters v. Kiff, 407 U.S. 493, 503–4 (1972).

CHAPTER 9. COURT-ORDERED REFORMS

157 **James Campbell:** These facts are drawn from the pleadings, briefs, and preliminary injunction hearing, trial testimony, and appellate decisions in Campbell v. Miller, No. 1:03-00180 (S.D. Ind. Feb. 7, 2003), and from interviews with James Campbell and his lawyer, Michael Sutherlin.

161 **"real and immediate threat":** Campbell v. Miller, No. 1:03-cv-0180, 2003 WL 21544257, at *1 (S.D. Ind. June 25, 2003) (citation omitted).

161 **"The very purpose of § 1983":** Mitchum v. Foster, 407 U.S. 225, 242 (1972).

162 **In 1939, the Supreme Court's decision:** Hague v. Committee for Industrial Organization, 307 U.S. 496 (1939).

162 **In 1954:** Brown v. Board of Education, 347 U.S. 483 (1954).

162 **in 1955:** Brown v. Board of Education, 349 U.S. 294, 301 (1955).

162 **In the decade after:** See, for example, Baker v. Carr, 369 U.S. 186, 208–37 (1962); Gray v. Sanders, 372 U.S. 368, 376–81 (1963); Griffin v. County School Board, 377 U.S. 218, 230–34 (1964); Reynolds v. Sims, 377 U.S. 533, 583–87 (1964); Swann v. Charlotte-Mecklenburg Board of Education, 402 U.S. 1, 15–18 (1971); Wesberry v. Sanders, 376 U.S. 1, 7–18 (1964).

162 **"Once a right":** *Swann*, 402 U.S. at 15.

163 **"the grave character":** Lankford v. Gelston, 364 F.2d 197, 203 (4th Cir. 1966).

163 **"A court should not bind":** Long v. D.C., 469 F.2d 927, 932 (D.C. Cir. 1972).

164 **beat this retreat:** Younger v. Harris, 401 U.S. 37 (1971).

164 **"imaginary or speculative":** *Younger*, 401 U.S. at 42.

164 **"ideals and dreams of 'Our Federalism'":** *Younger*, 401 U.S. at 44.

164 **"Whatever the balance":** *Younger*, 401 U.S. at 61 (Douglas, J., dissenting).

165 **"In times of repression":** *Younger*, 401 U.S. at 58 (Douglas, J., dissenting).

165 **Three years later:** O'Shea v. Littleton, 414 U.S. 488 (1974).

165 **"racial powder keg":** Michael P. Seng, "The Cairo Experience: Civil Rights Litigation in a Racial Powder Keg," *Oregon Law Review* 61 (1982): 285. Conditions in Cairo, Illinois, in the late 1960s are powerfully described in Elizabeth Hinton, *America on Fire: The Untold History of Police Violence and Black Rebellion Since the 1960s* (New York: Liveright, 2021), 46–53.

165 **Robert Hunt Jr.:** Seng, "Cairo Experience," 285.

165 **Days of protest:** Paul Good, *Cairo, Illinois: Racism at Floodtide* (U.S. Commission on Civil Rights, 1973).

165 **The situation in Cairo:** Seng, "Cairo Experience," 294.

166 **residents of Cairo sued:** Seng, "Cairo Experience," 296.

166 **According to Justice White:** *O'Shea*, 414 U.S. at 498.

166 **"recognition of the need":** *O'Shea*, 414 U.S. at 499.

166 **"What has been alleged":** *O'Shea*, 414 U.S. at 509 (Douglas, J., dissenting).

167 **"difficult, if not impossible":** *O'Shea*, 414 U.S. at 510 (Douglas, J., dissenting).

167 **Then came *Rizzo v. Goode*:** Rizzo v. Goode, 423 U.S. 362 (1976).

167 **meticulous opinion:** Council of Organizations on Philadelphia Police Accountability and Responsibility v. Rizzo, 357 F. Supp. 1289, 1318–19 (E.D. Pa. 1973).

167 **"more nearly in accord":** *Rizzo*, 423 U.S. at 381 (Blackmun, J., dissenting) (quoting a December 18, 1973, memorandum by the district court in *Council of Organizations on Philadelphia Police Accountability and Responsibility v. Rizzo*).

167 **The court of appeals affirmed:** Goode v. Rizzo, 506 F.2d 542 (3rd Cir. 1974).

168 **"carefully and conscientiously":** *Rizzo*, 423 U.S. at 367.

168 **according to Justice Rehnquist:** *Rizzo*, 423 U.S. at 372.

168 **"a sharp limitation":** *Rizzo*, 423 U.S. at 378–79 (quoting Cafeteria Workers v. McElroy, 367 U.S. 886 (1961)).

168 **"by reason of . . . neglect":** *Rizzo*, 423 U.S. at 384–85 (Blackmun, J., dissenting) (quoting Monroe v. Pape, 365 U.S. 167, 180 (1961)).

168 **"one of those rightly rare":** *Rizzo*, 423 U.S. at 387 (Blackmun, J., dissenting).

169 **The Supreme Court completed:** City of Los Angeles v. Lyons, 461 U.S. 95 (1983).

169 **"subdue *any* resistance":** *Lyons*, 461 U.S. at 118–19 (Marshall, J., dissenting).

169 **at least 975 times:** *Lyons*, 461 U.S. at 116 (Marshall, J., dissenting).

169 **75 percent of the people:** *Lyons*, 461 U.S. at 116n3 (Marshall, J., dissenting).

170 **"unconscionable in a civilized society":** *Lyons*, 461 U.S. at 100 (quoting the district court).

170 **court of appeals:** Lyons v. City of Los Angeles, 656 F.2d 417 (9th Cir. 1981).

170 **"the need for a proper balance":** *Lyons*, 461 U.S. at 112.

170 **"great and immediate":** *Lyons*, 461 U.S. at 105–06 (emphasis in original).

170 **"it may be that among the countless encounters":** *Lyons*, 461 U.S. at 108.

171 **"no more entitled":** *Lyons*, 461 U.S. at 111.

171 **"The Court today holds":** *Lyons*, 461 U.S. at 113 (Marshall, J., dissenting).

171 **"removes an entire class":** *Lyons*, 461 U.S. at 137 (Marshall, J., dissenting).

172 **Following a veto threat:** For further description of the legislative history of the bill, see Marshall Miller, "Police Brutality," *Yale Law and Policy Review* 17 (1998): 161–73; Matthew J. Silveira, "An Unexpected Application of 42 U.S.C. § 14141: Using Investigative Findings for § 1983 Litigation," *UCLA Law Review* 52 (2004): 606–11.

173 **Since 1994, the Department of Justice:** For further discussion of the Department of Justice's investigations and consent decrees, and the impact of their work, see Civil Rights Division, U.S. Department of Justice, "The Civil Rights Division's Pattern and Practice Police Reform Work: 1994–Present" (Jan. 2017), www.justice.gov/crt/file /922421/download.

173 **has not adequately:** For further thoughts about the strengths and limitations of Department of Justice investigations, see Joanna C. Schwartz, "Who Can Police the Police?," *Chicago Legal Forum* (2016): 446–48.

174 **Channeling the concerns of opponents:** Campbell v. Miller, 373 F.3d 834, 835–36 (7th Cir. 2004).

174 **crediting Campbell's description:** Campbell v. City of Indianapolis, No. 1:03-cv-00180, 2005 WL 2396925, at *6 (S.D. Ind. Sept. 28, 2005).

175 **a terse opinion:** Campbell v. City of Indianapolis, No. 1:03-cv-00180, 2006 WL 753135, at *1 (S.D. Ind. March 21, 2006).

175 **court of appeals reversed:** Campbell v. Miller, 499 F.3d 711, 718 (7th Cir. 2007).

175 **"real and immediate" threat:** The facts of this case are taken from an interview with James Campbell and the complaint and other filings in Campbell v. The City of Indianapolis, No. 1:10-cv-1079 (S.D. Ind. Aug 26, 2010).

CHAPTER 10. OFFICERS' BANK ACCOUNTS

180 **basketball legend:** Phil Reisman, "Clay Tiffany: A Coda from Readers and Reisman," *Journal News*, April 4, 2016, www.lohud.com/story/opinion/columnists/phil-reisman /2015/04/06/phil-reisman-rip-clay-tiffany/25381131/.

180 **"He seemed to have become agitated":** Reisman, "Clay Tiffany."

180 **he took his case to trial:** Judgment, Tiffany v. Village of Briarcliff, No. 1:95-cv-08335 (S.D.N.Y. Oct. 8, 1999).

180 **Tiffany was pulled over:** These facts come from the complaints, discovery, briefs, and other papers in Tiffany v. Tartaglione, No. 7:00-cv-02283 (S.D.N.Y. March 24, 2000).

183 **One month after:** Marcela Rojas, "Activist, Officer Reach Settlement," *Journal News*, Sept. 11, 2003.

183 **Tartaglione was criminally prosecuted but acquitted:** Tartaglione v. Pugliese, No. 01-cv-9874, 2002 WL 31387255, at *4 (S.D.N.Y. Oct. 23, 2002).

183 **alleged that village officials violated:** *Tartaglione*, 2002 WL 31387255, at *4.

183 **affirmed on appeal:** Tartaglione v. Pugliese, 89 Fed. Appx. 304 (2d Cir. 2004).

183 **$300,000 in back pay:** Rojas, "Activist, Officer Reach Settlement."

184 **The findings were as stark:** These findings are described in additional detail in Joanna C. Schwartz, "Police Indemnification," *New York University Law Review* 89 (2014): 885–1005.

184 **In just two of the forty-four:** As I describe in "Police Indemnification," representatives from two other jurisdictions—the Illinois State Police and the Jacksonville Sheriff's Office—could each recall a case where an officer contributed to a settlement but could not recall whether those obligations arose during my study period. An officer from the Los Angeles Police Department was not indemnified for a $300 punitive damages judgment but was never required to pay that sum.

186 **published a story describing:** Jay McMullen, "Tells How City Wiggles Out of Paying Damages for Cops," *Chicago Daily News*, March 6, 1959.

186 **Charles Pressman:** Joan Giangrasse Kates, "Charles Pressman, Chicago Defense Attorney, Dies at 92," *Chicago Tribune*, Oct. 25, 2015, www.chicagotribune.com/news/ct-charles-pressman-obituary-met-20151025-story.html.

187 **Descriptions of legislative intent:** Joanna C. Schwartz, "Qualified Immunity and Federalism All the Way Down," *Georgetown Law Journal* 109 (2020): 323 (citing cases that describe the legislative intent behind indemnification statutes in California, Connecticut, Alabama, and Alaska).

188 **Nassau County:** Schwartz, "Qualified Immunity and Federalism," 324–25 (citing a case that describes the limits of Nassau County's indemnification law).

188 **"neither certain nor universal":** Peter H. Schuck, *Suing Government: Citizen Remedies for Official Wrongs* (New Haven, Conn.: Yale University Press, 1983), 85.

188 **the Greenwood Village city council:** John Aguilar, "Denver Suburb Passes Resolution Shielding Officers from Key Portion of Colorado's New Police Reform Law," *Denver Post*, July 8, 2020.

189 **"got it wrong":** Daniel Connolly, "To Say That Officers Are Not Disciplined Is False," *New York Law Journal*, March 15, 2019.

189 **In Minneapolis:** City of Minneapolis v. Lehner, No. A16-0608, 2017 WL 24682, at *1–2 (Minn. Ct. App. Jan. 3, 2017) (describing this process).

190 **discouraging plaintiffs:** Defense counsel's tactical use of indemnification in El Paso, San Bernardino, New York City, and elsewhere is described in detail in Schwartz, "Police Indemnification," 931–36.

191 **Steven Grassilli:** The details of this case are set out in Grassilli v. Barr, 142 Cal. App. 4th 1260 (2006). The details of the indemnification dispute can be found in Schwartz, "Police Indemnification," 935–36.

192 **As one juror said:** Erin Ailworth and Sara Lin, "Man Was Harassed by CHP, Jury Rules," *Los Angeles Times*, April 29, 2012.

192 **The court of appeals reduced:** *Grassilli*, 142 Cal. App. 4th at 1291–92.

193 **unlikely to sue a driver:** Tom Baker, "Blood Money, New Money, and the Moral Economy of Tort Law in Action," *Law and Society Review* 35 (2001): 279–319 (describing this phenomenon).

193 **deeper pockets:** I describe these dynamics in greater detail in Schwartz, "Qualified Immunity and Federalism," 333–36.

193 **Tucker Carlson:** Billy Binion, "Tucker Carlson Might Want to End Qualified Immunity if He Actually Knew What It Was," *Reason*, June 26, 2020.

194 **Nick Tartaglione was arrested:** Jonathan Bandler, "Still No Trial Date for Tartaglione Five Years After Orange County Quadruple Homicide," *Journal News*, April 9, 2021.

194 **cut Epstein down:** Jonathan Bandler, "Prosecutors: Missing Video of Jeffrey Epstein's Suicide Found; Why Tartaglione's Lawyer Wants It," *Journal News*, Dec. 19, 2019.

CHAPTER 11. LOCAL GOVERNMENT BUDGETS

195 **"Sunday Morning Coming Down":** Cady Drell et al., "40 Saddest Country Songs of All Time," *Rolling Stone*, Sept. 17, 2019, www.rollingstone.com/music/music-lists/40-saddest-country-songs-of-all-time-158907/johnny-cash-sunday-morning-coming-down-42023/.

195 **One was not:** These facts are drawn from the complaint, briefs, discovery, and trial testimony in *Obrycka v. City of Chicago*, No. 1:07-cv-02372 (N.D. Ill. April 30, 2007); an interview and emails with Terry Ekl, Obrycka's attorney; video of the assault; and news stories including "Judge: Police 'Code of Silence' in Bar Beating," ABC7, Feb. 23, 2012, abc7chicago.com/archive/8555746/; Anne Sweeney, "Bartender Testified: Cop Tossed Me 'Like a Rag Doll,'" *Chicago Tribune*, Oct. 30, 2012; Annie Sweeney, Jeremy Gorner, and Jason Meisner, "Video Release of Police Shootings, Incidents Marks Seismic Shift in Chicago's Secrecy," *Chicago Tribune*, June 3, 2016.

197 **The jury awarded:** Order in a Civil Action, Obrycka v. City of Chicago, No. 1:07-cv-2372 (Feb. 6, 2013) (describing $1.8 million awarded to the Ekl, Williams & Provenzale firm, and its April 23, 2013, order awarding $148,955 to another attorney who worked on the case).

197 **far from the largest:** Stacy St. Clair, Jeff Coen, and Jason Meisner, "Chicago Cop Shot Friend, Jury Finds, Ordering City to Pay $44.7 Million: 'I Feel Whole Again,'" *Chicago Tribune*, Oct. 27, 2017.

198 **half a billion dollars:** Amelia Thomson-DeVeaux, Laura Bronner, and Damini Sharma, "Cities Spend Millions on Police Misconduct Every Year. Here's Why It's So Difficult to Hold Departments Accountable," *FiveThirtyEight*, Feb. 22, 2021.

198 **city's legal department:** City of Chicago, 2020 Budget Overview, www.chicago.gov/content/dam/city/depts/obm/supp_info/2020Budget/2020BudgetOverview.pdf.

198 **decides to hire private lawyers:** See Dan Hinkel, "A Hidden Cost of Chicago Police Misconduct: $213 Million to Private Lawyers Since 2004," *Chicago Tribune*, Sept. 12, 2019.

199 **"If the City must pay":** Brief for Petitioners, Monroe v. Pape, 1960 WL 98617 at **42–43 (Aug. 25, 1960) (citation omitted).

200 **"borne out by statistics":** Brief for Petitioners, Monroe v. Pape, 1960 WL 98617 at *63.

200 **"The decision in *Monroe*":** Monell v. Department of Social Services, 436 U.S. 658, 724 (1978) (Rehnquist, J., dissenting).

201 *Owen v. City of Independence:* Owen v. City of Independence, 445 U.S. 622 (1980).

201 **"converts municipal governance":** *Owen*, 445 U.S. at 665 (Powell, J., dissenting).

201 **"inject constant consideration":** *Owen*, 445 U.S. at 668 (Powell, J., dissenting).

201 **"many local governments lack":** *Owen*, 445 U.S. at 670 (Powell, J., dissenting).

201 **"The fact is that suing":** George C. Smith, "Lawyers Split the Fee and Taxpayers Foot the Bill," *Wall Street Journal*, Feb. 25, 1986.

202 **"In the past decade":** Renée Graham, "Unless Qualified Immunity Ends, There's No Police Accountability," *Boston Globe*, May 12, 2021.

202 **a series of reports:** "More Lawyers, Less Public Services: The Cost of Litigation to California's Cities and Counties," California Citizens Against Lawsuit Abuse, californiacala.org/reports-1/more-lawyers-less-public-services-the-cost-of-litigation-to-californias-cities-and-counties.

202 **only a modest share:** Joanna C. Schwartz, "How Governments Pay: Lawsuits, Budgets, and Police Reform," *UCLA Law Review* 63 (2016): 1164–65 (reporting that the executive director of two hundred risk pools that insure small municipalities estimates that "contributions to risk pools . . . are minimal in a local government's overall budget," amounting to, at most, "just a percent or two of a city's budget" (first alteration in original)), 1224–34 (reporting that expenses related to police misconduct lawsuits are usually far less than 1 percent of general budgets in one hundred jurisdictions across the country).

203 **$468 million:** *City of Chicago 2022 Budget Overview*, Office of Mayor Lori E. Lightfoot, 111, chicityclerk.s3.amazonaws.com/s3fs-public/O2021-4239.pdf.

203 **$275 million retroactive pay increase:** Heather Cherone, "City Council Approves Lightfoot's $16.7 Billion Budget with Support from Progressives," WTTW News, Oct. 27, 2021, news.wttw.com/2021/10/27/city-council-approves-lightfoot-s-167-billion-budget-support-progressives.

203 **annual police spending:** Joanna C. Schwartz, "Qualified Immunity and Federalism All the Way Down," *Georgetown Law Journal* 109 (2020): 337–38.

203 **settlements and judgments:** Schwartz, "Qualified Immunity and Federalism," 338.

203 **But, in these places:** Schwartz, "Qualified Immunity and Federalism," 337.

204 **contribute as a formal matter:** Schwartz, "How Governments Pay," 1173–84.

204 **Take Chicago, for example:** These details about Chicago's budgeting and payments are drawn from Schwartz, "How Governments Pay," 1176–79.

205 **"lead poisoning screening":** Schwartz, "How Governments Pay," 1178 (quoting a former attorney for the City of Chicago).

205 **A spokesperson for the Chicago Police Department:** Schwartz, "How Governments Pay," 1179 (quoting the police department's spokesperson).

205 **California Highway Patrol:** Schwartz, "How Governments Pay," 1200 (quoting the California Highway Patrol's risk manager).

206 **Karolina Obrycka offered to settle:** "Don't Appeal Abbate Verdict; Time for City Hall to Eradicate the 'Code of Silence,'" *Chicago Tribune*, Nov. 15, 2012.

206 **upward of $5 million:** "Don't Appeal Abbate Verdict." Anthony Abbate had a separate team of four private lawyers representing him in the lawsuit. Docket, Obrycka v. City of Chicago, No. 1:07-cv-2372 (N.D. Ill. Apr. 30, 2007).

207 **denied the motion:** Obrycka v. City of Chicago, No. 1:07-cv-02372, 2012 WL 601810 (Feb. 23, 2012). The city also moved for summary judgment on plaintiff's claim that the city was required to indemnify Abbate, and that request was granted.

207 **"one last time":** Obrycka v. City of Chicago, 913 F. Supp. 2d 598, 602 (N.D. Ill. 2012).

207 **fifty-three hundred hours:** City of Chicago's Motion for an Extension of Time to Provide Objections to Plaintiff's Proposed Attorneys' Fees, Obrycka v. City of Chicago, No. 1:07-cv-2372 (N.D. Ill. Dec. 19, 2012).

207 **more than $2 million:** Hinkel, "Hidden Cost."

CHAPTER 12. LEARNING FROM LAWSUITS

209 **Shawn Schenck:** These facts are taken from the second amended complaint in Schenck v. City of New York, No. 1:11-cv-0728 (S.D.N.Y. July 18, 2011), and from Rocco Parascandola, "Cops Conducted Illegal and Humiliating Body Cavity Search on Me, Bronx Man Claims in Suit," *New York Daily News*, Feb. 2, 2011, www.nydailynews.com/new

-york/cops-conducted-illegal-humiliating-body-cavity-search-bronx-man-claims -suit-article-1.134534.

210 **Paul Perry:** These facts are taken from the complaint in Perry v. City of New York, No. 1:13-cv-5973 (S.D.N.Y. Aug. 23, 2013).

210 **London Barajona:** These facts are taken from the complaint in Barajona v. Simpson, No. 1:15-cv-9413 (S.D.N.Y. Dec. 1, 2015).

210 **these nightmarish stories:** For descriptions of some of those stories, see Jennifer Kelley et al., "Lawsuits Show the High Cost of NYPD Abuse in the Bronx," *Intercept*, Aug. 19, 2020, theintercept.com/2020/08/19/nypd-bronx-police-settlements/.

211 **four or five figures:** The settlements in *Schenck, Perry, Barajona*, and other suits naming Abdiel Anderson are collected and can be reviewed at www.50-a.org/officer/54784.

211 **more than $30 million:** Kelley et al., "Lawsuits Show."

211 **ProPublica report:** Mike Hayes, "New York City Paid an NBA Star Millions After an NYPD Officer Broke His Leg. The Officer Paid Little Price," ProPublica, Jan. 12, 2021.

211 **Bronx Narcotic Unit:** Jake Offenhartz, "Here Are NYC's Most Sued Cops Who Are Still on the Job, According to New Public Database," *Gothamist*, March 7, 2019.

211 **Abdiel Anderson:** Jake Offenhartz, "NYC's Most Sued Cop Is Really on a Roll," *Gothamist*, Nov. 21, 2019.

211 **"discharge . . . offending officials":** Newport v. Fact Concerts, 453 U.S. 247, 269 (1981).

211 **"institute internal rules":** Owen v. City of Independence, 445 U.S. 622, 652 (1980).

212 **In a 2016 deposition:** Deposition of Abdiel Anderson, Ramos v. City of New York, No. 1:15-cv-6085 (S.D.N.Y. Oct. 20, 2016).

212 **deposition, under oath:** Richard Emery and Ilann Margalit Maazel, "Why Civil Rights Lawsuits Do Not Deter Police Misconduct: The Conundrum of Indemnification and a Proposed Solution," *Fordham Urban Law Journal* 28 (2000): 590.

212 **Peter Valentin:** Barry Paddock et al., "Exclusive: Detective Is NYPD's Most-Sued Cop, with 28 Lawsuits Filed Against Him Since 2006," *New York Daily News*, Feb. 16, 2014.

213 **Rikers Island:** Ingles v. Toro, No. 1:01-cv-8279 (S.D.N.Y. Sept. 5, 2001).

214 **I was able to track down:** For a detailed description of this methodology and my findings, see Joanna C. Schwartz, "Myths and Mechanics of Deterrence: The Role of Lawsuits in Law Enforcement Decisionmaking," *UCLA Law Review* 57 (2010): 1023–94.

215 **the city's comptroller:** This description of the back-and-forth between the New York Police Department and the New York City comptroller is drawn from Schwartz, "Myths and Mechanics," 1047–48.

216 **"just part of the way":** Schwartz, "Myths and Mechanics," 1049.

216 **handful of jurisdictions:** Detailed findings about these litigation-attentive departments can be found at Joanna C. Schwartz, "What Police Learn from Lawsuits," *Cardozo Law Review* 33 (2012): 841–94.

216 **Chicago's police auditor:** Libby Sander, "Chicago Revamps Investigation of Police Abuse, but Privacy Fight Continues," *New York Times*, July 20, 2007.

217 **As an independent auditor:** Schwartz, "What Police Learn," 872–73 (quoting Los Angeles Sheriff's Department Special Counsel Merrick Bobb).

217 **Portland, Oregon:** For discussions of these findings, see Schwartz, "What Police Learn," 854, 873–74.

218 **"Plaintiff's attorney was the driving force":** Schwartz, "What Police Learn," 874 (quoting Michael Gennaco et al., *Report to the City of Portland Concerning the In-Custody Death of James Chasse*, OIR Group, [2010], 28).

218 **"the mere fact of a settlement":** William Heinzen, Deputy Counselor to the Mayor, "Statement Before the N.Y.C. Council Committee on Governmental Operations," Dec. 11, 2009.

219 **"ClaimStat":** New York City Comptroller Scott M. Stringer, *ClaimStat 2.0: Reducing Claims and Protecting New Yorkers* (New York: Bureau of Policy and Research, 2017), comptroller.nyc.gov/reports/claimstat/reports/claimstat-2-0-reducing-claims-and -protecting-new-yorkers/.

220 **"conduct independent reviews":** David W. Chen, "An Independent Monitor for the Police Is Proposed," *New York Times*, June 12, 2012.

220 **When Phil Eure published his report:** Mark G. Peters and Philip K. Eure, New York City Department of Investigation, Office of the Inspector General for the NYPD, *Using Data from Lawsuits and Legal Claims Involving NYPD to Improve Policing* (April 2015), www1.nyc.gov/assets/doi/reports/pdf/2015/2015-04-20-Litigation-Data-Report.pdf.

221 **The OIG was careful to caution:** Margaret Garnett and Philip K. Eure, New York City Department of Investigation's Inspector General for the NYPD, *Ongoing Examination of Litigation Data Involving NYPD* (April 2018), www1.nyc.gov/assets/doi/reports /pdf/2018/April/21NYPDLitData_Report_43018.pdf.

222 **twenty-five-page response:** New York City Police Department Response to the April 30, 2018, Report from the Office of the Inspector General for the NYPD, Aug. 7, 2018, www1.nyc.gov/assets/doi/oignypd/response/LitigationDataResponse_FINAL _80718.pdf.

222 **both the OIG and the NYPD:** See Margaret Garnett and Philip K. Eure, New York City Department of Investigation, Office of the Inspector General for the NYPD, *2019 Assessment of Litigation Data Involving NYPD* (April 2019); New York City Police Department Response, July 29, 2019.

223 **Phil Eure resigned:** Christopher Dunn and Donna Lieberman, "Mayor Adams Must Hold Law Enforcement Accountable," *New York Daily News*, January 21, 2022.

223 **OIG's May 2022 report:** Jocelyn Strauber and Jeanene Barrett, Office of the Inspector General for the NYPD, *Eighth Annual Report* (March 2022), www1.nyc.gov/assets/doi /press-releases/2022/March/08OIGNYPDAnnualRpt_Release_3312022.pdf.

CHAPTER 13. A BETTER WAY

227 **Indiana congressman Jim Banks:** "Rep. Banks Introduces Qualified Immunity Act," press release of the Office of U.S. Congressman Jim Banks, Aug. 7, 2020.

228 **"Do we really want":** Editorial Board, "Qualified Immunity Provides Reasonable Protection for Police Officers," *Albuquerque Journal*, Aug. 9, 2020.

228 **Virginia State Police Association:** Editorial Board, "Banning Qualified Immunity Is Complicated," *Free Lance-Star*, Sept. 15, 2020.

228 **predictions about civil rights litigation:** These predictions are explored in depth in Joanna C. Schwartz, "After Qualified Immunity," *Columbia Law Review* 120 (2020): 309–88.

228 **"shoot first, think later":** Mullenix v. Luna, 577 U.S. 7, 26 (2015) (Sotomayor, J., dissenting).

231 **police department investigations and discipline:** For one set of possible reforms, see Rachel Moran, "Ending the Internal Affairs Farce," *Buffalo Law Review* 64 (2016): 882–905.

231 **we need a plan B:** Many of these proposals (and some model statutory language) are described in more depth in Alexander Reinert, Joanna C. Schwartz, and James E.

Pfander, "New Federalism and Civil Rights Enforcement," *Northwestern University Law Review* 116 (2021): 737–816.

234 **More than half of the states:** Tami Abdollah, "California Bill Would Strip Bad Cops of Badges, but Doesn't End Immunity from Lawsuits," *USA Today*, Sept. 29, 2021, www.usatoday.com/story/news/2021/09/29/california-law-would-strip-bad-cops -badges-but-immunity-remains/5834132001/?gnt-cfr=1.

236 **Marshall-Motley Scholars Program:** "Single Anonymous Donor Gives $40 Million to Fund 50 Civil Rights Lawyers," CBS News, Jan. 18, 2021.

237 **some districts draw juror names:** Jeffrey Abramson, "Jury Selection in the Weeds: Whither the Democratic Shore?," *University of Michigan Journal of Legal Reform* 52 (2018): 2n4.

237 **expansive approach to juror qualification:** For some proposals in this vein, see Abramson, "Jury Selection in the Weeds," 42–46.

237 **Local government politics:** Will Wright, "Breonna Taylor's Legacy Is Felt in a Year of Surging Activism," *New York Times*, March 14, 2021.

237 **one-third of judges:** "March 2020 Snapshot: Diversity of the Federal Bench (2020)," American Constitution Society, www.acslaw.org/judicial-nominations/diversity-of -the-federal-bench-march-2020/.

237 **the Cato Institute found:** Clark Neily, "Are a Disproportionate Number of Federal Judges Former Government Advocates?," Cato Institute, May 27, 2021, www.cato.org /study/are-disproportionate-number-federal-judges-former-government-advocates.

237 **President Joe Biden has prioritized:** Colleen Long, "Biden Seeking Professional Diversity in His Judicial Picks," *U.S. News*, Feb. 10, 2022.

237 **"experience and common sense":** Ashcroft v. Iqbal, 556 U.S. 665 (2009).

239 **two weeks of intense negotiations:** Leslie Herod and Mari Newman, "Colorado Took a Revolutionary Step to Reform Policing. Here's How We Did It," *USA Today*, Oct. 28, 2021.

INDEX